SAGE was founded in 1965 by Sara Miller McCune to support the dissemination of usable knowledge by publishing innovative and high-quality research and teaching content. Today, we publish over 900 journals, including those of more than 400 learned societies, more than 800 new books per year, and a growing range of library products including archives, data, case studies, reports, and video. SAGE remains majority-owned by our founder, and after Sara's lifetime will become owned by a charitable trust that secures our continued independence.

Los Angeles | London | New Delhi | Singapore | Washington DC | Melbourne

Muslim Women Speak

Thank you for choosing a SAGE product!
If you have any comment, observation or feedback,
I would like to personally hear from you.

Please write to me at **contactceo@sagepub.in**

Vivek Mehra, Managing Director and CEO, SAGE India.

Bulk Sales

SAGE India offers special discounts
for purchase of books in bulk.
We also make available special imprints
and excerpts from our books on demand.

For orders and enquiries, write to us at

Marketing Department
SAGE Publications India Pvt Ltd
B1/I-1, Mohan Cooperative Industrial Area
Mathura Road, Post Bag 7
New Delhi 110044, India

E-mail us at **marketing@sagepub.in**

Get to know more about SAGE

Be invited to SAGE events, get on our mailing list.
Write today to **marketing@sagepub.in**

This book is also available as an e-book.

Muslim Women Speak
Of Dreams and Shackles

Ghazala Jamil

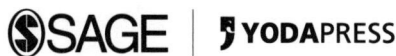

Los Angeles | London | New Delhi
Singapore | Washington DC | Melbourne

Copyright © Ghazala Jamil, 2018

All rights reserved. No part of this book may be reproduced or utilized in any form or by any means, electronic or mechanical, including photocopying, recording, or by any information storage or retrieval system, without permission in writing from the publisher.

First published in 2018 by

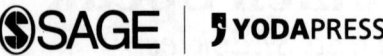

SAGE Publications India Pvt Ltd
B1/I-1 Mohan Cooperative Industrial Area
Mathura Road, New Delhi 110 044, India
www.sagepub.in

YODA Press
79 Gulmohar Enclave
New Delhi 110049
www.yodapress.co.in

SAGE Publications Inc
2455 Teller Road
Thousand Oaks, California 91320, USA

SAGE Publications Ltd
1 Oliver's Yard, 55 City Road
London EC1Y 1SP, United Kingdom

SAGE Publications Asia-Pacific Pte Ltd
3 Church Street
#10-04 Samsung Hub
Singapore 049483

Published by Vivek Mehra for SAGE Publications India Pvt Ltd, typeset in 10/12 pts Berkeley by Zaza Eunice, Hosur, Tamil Nadu, India and printed at Chaman Enterprises, New Delhi.

Library of Congress Cataloging-in-Publication Data Available

ISBN: 978-93-528-0500-6 (HB)

SAGE Yoda Team: Sonjuhi Negi, Alekha Chandra Jena and Ishita Gupta

Contents

Acknowledgements	ix
Introduction	xi
1. Discursive Colonisation	1
2. Representation and 'Listening'	22
3. Portrait of a Researcher as a Muslim Woman	41
4. The Everyday of Inhabiting Margins	52
5. Dreaming in Shackles	69
6. Memory and Experience of Violence	88
7. I Speak, Therefore I Am: Articulation as Shaping of 'Self'	105
8. I Did Not Know Myself	122
9. Select Narratives from States	137
10. A Call for Change	167
Bibliography	176
Index	188
About the Author	190

Chashm-e-nam, jaan-e-shoreeda kafi nahin
Tohmat-e-ishq-e-posheeda kafi nahin
aaj bazaar main pa-bajolan chalo
Faiz Ahmed Faiz

Teary eyes and stormy life are not enough
Even the accusation of a hidden passion is not enough
Come, walk today in public, wearing your shackles
Translated by Ghazala Jamil

Acknowledgements

Let me begin by expressing my gratitude to the Bhartiya Muslim Mahila Aandolan (BMMA) for giving me the opportunity to create this work with the help of all its activists. Special thanks are due to Zakia Soman, one of the founders of BMMA, who trusted my ideas right from the word go and provided me with all possible support and space. Each member on the research team at the field level completely owned this study right after I conceived it in its present shape. Without their collective experience and skills it would not have been possible to realise the theoretical ideas.

This work continued to be a passion for me long after I had submitted the project report to BMMA. I kept chiselling the manuscript though the years, and growing and learning with it. Needless to say all its shortcomings are my own although I do hope that all the participants of the study will own the work in its present form too.

My acquaintance with many of the ideas and approaches presented in this report began as a student of Professor Manoj K. Jha at Jamia Millia Islamia. His faith in my ability to rise up to the demands of any occasion and do the necessary work has seen me successfully finish many assignments including this one. He offered painstaking comments on my ideas and writings, always giving critical suggestions that improved my work while still respecting my voice.

Thank you Arpita Das, my editor at Yoda Press for seeing the potential in the manuscript. Her faith in this work gave me the confidence to put it out in the public domain at a time when the reactions of many others made me anxious.

Thanks are due to my partner and friend Nasir for his love, humour, and indulgence; our daughters Miftah and Mael for accepting *and* challenging their *Ulti-Sulti Amma**. No amount of gratitude can ever capture the love and limitless generosity of my family—Zafar, Salma, Faiz, Paromita, Sidra and Andleeb I can only ever thank inadequately.

The memory of my parents Azmat Ullah and Anwari Begum narrating their own experiences to me, is my most empowering resource. I dedicate this work to you Amma and Abba–for never discouraging me (their

---

* Title of Kamla Bhasin's book. (Trans.) 'Topsy-turvy mom'.

most talkative child) from spinning a yarn and for enabling the daughter to find her voice.

Thanks are due to Baaraan Ijlaal and Sadbhavana Trust for their kind permission to use the artwork on the cover, and to Dipta Bhog and Purwa Bharadwaj for their introduction to the artist and facilitating the permissions.

Research Team Members

A. Siddique, Abhishweta Jha, Aparna, Azra, Balkeis Begum, Farhat Amin, Father Anil, Ghazala, Ghazala Jamil, Hashmi Bano, Isabella, Jamsheena KP, Jasla K, Jeibunisha R, Kamila, Majida CV, Mali Sawariya, Mubeena NP, Muskaan Shaikh, Naaz Raza, Naghma Nadaf, Naish Hasan, Namita Jainer, Nazia Perveen, Nazneen Falaq, Nishat Hussain, Noorjahan Diwan, Noorjahan Safia Niaz, Nusrat Yakub Pathan, Pallavi Patnaik, Parveen Kokianwala, Preety Rani, Rafat Jahan, Rajiya Begum, Riyaz Babu, Rozalin Sahoo, Rubeena Bano, Sabiha Rehman, Salima Akhtar, Samira Shah, Sarwar Raza, Shafeena TNK, Shah Alam, Shahda Bari, Shameem Khan, Shehzadi Parveen, Subair CK, Subhashree Sanyal, Suraiya Shaikh, Tasleem Banoo, Zakia Soman, Zuleikha Jabin.

Introduction

I

Allah ta'ala ne aurat ko bhi insaan banaaya hai

(Allah has created woman too, in the human form)

On the first reading, these words, spoken by a young Muslim woman from Mumbai, are simply a statement of a person of faith about her own creation. On a closer second reading, the statement seems to be accessing and commenting upon various realities. It is a comment on the inequality that women are subjected to, how they are made to feel subhuman, a commodity to be consumed. The statement is an assertion that a woman too is a human being, a human being just like a man. On another and deeper reading the statement seems to include a firm belief of the speaker that there is inherent justice in this narrative of creation of a woman in human form and a complaint that this justice has been subverted. This reading includes a cognisance of her conviction that her emancipation as an equal human being is thus possible within the arena of her own faith.

How do we begin looking at the possibility of a just and humane world that treats Muslim women as equal human beings? In this work I have attempted to engage in a critical exercise of recounting a complex web of problems which get into the very way of imagining such a world. Although critical, it is not meant to be an exercise in cynicism. It is conceived in a way, however inadequate, to regard the experiences of Muslim women in India and the philosophical problems of our times embedded in these experiences. In terms of research, the attempt is to respond to the problem posed by Horkheimer (1931, p. 14), as 'symbolic of the peculiar difficulty of social philosophy—the difficulty concerning the interpenetration of general and particular, of theoretical design and individual experience'. Towards this attempt I navigated the boundaries of disciplines such as Sociology, Politics, Psychology, etc., and used hybrid methodological and epistemological resources. This allowed me to recast the problems of Indian Muslim Woman and Indian Muslims in newer concepts and frames of inquiry.

The philosophical and religious debates about the role and status of women have traversed a wide territory of questions and explanations. Biological essentialism as the explanation of inequality between men and women has had the longest currency. It contained within it the arguments that 'naturalised' the difference between sexes but also the boundaries between private and public, personal and political. In the West, feminism as we know it today actually arose out of the movement for abolishing slavery. The experience of the women participants in the movement raised their consciousness regarding their own subjugation. The second wave of feminism famously proclaimed that 'personal is political' and that a person is 'not born a woman but becomes one'. It also complicated the questions of origin of difference between the sexes. Radical feminists criticised the liberal feminist for underplaying the differences. They asserted that this would automatically lead to undervaluation of women's labour, reproductive function and reflexivity. For them the difference was valuable (Griffin 1996; Dworkin 2006; Gilligan 1982). The much delayed but inevitable questions of difference among women also raised their head. Haraway (1991) discusses this tendency among the feminists to totalise experiences of some women as those of all women. Race, class and colonial history as markers of difference among women's experience of patriarchy received recognition, even as it meant that the unitary image of 'the feminist movement' stood exposed with its deep chasms. While western feminism is debating deeply the allegations of racism, it is only beginning to take cognisance of charges of orientalism.[1]

---

[1] Mainstream white liberal feminists remained oblivious to the questions of race until they were forced by black feminists to confront that their colour blindness was in fact an instance of racism. Their contention was that the movement's representation of women's oppression was actually only white women's oppression. Women of colour in the west have asserted that white women, cosy in their white privilege, have ignored or resisted recognising differentiated experiences of race. Audrey Lorde pointed to 'a pretense to homogeneity of experience covered by the word *sisterhood* that does not in fact exist' (Lorde 1894, p. 116). The issue of differentiated concerns of women have also been raised in the west in the context of colonialism and the concerns of 'Third World women' (Talpade 1988). On the other hand, the orientalism debate has yet to be mainstreamed in the feminist discussion, even though it is now well-recognised that one of the fantasmic images most fundamental to orientalism debates is that of Muslim 'oriental' woman, veiled, oppressed and sexually controlled. Western liberal feminism involves an essentially orientalist position in which white women not only pose as saviours of the 'oriental' Muslim/Arab women but also

Closer home, it would not be an exaggeration to state that the current discourse on the situation, issues and problems of 'Indian Muslims' is grossly lopsided. Over one stream of literature, the image of 'Islamic' terrorism and fundamentalism looms large, and the other stream is keenly interested in the 'under-represented' Indian Muslims, highlighting their poor record on various socio-economic developmental indices. Note that the centring of Muslim men is common to both kinds of discourses. Indeed, social exclusion, school dropout rates, unemployment, and communal violence are the problems faced by both men and women in the community. In the dominant discourses, Muslim men are portrayed as stock characters. These discourses abet and shape an environment that casts them out as easy targets for criticism for their behaviour and choices which are largely caricaturised and stereotyped. But the most important effect of this unhappy situation is that the contemporary crisis of Muslim social life in India is routinely presented as a crisis of and/or crisis caused by Muslim masculinity.

Further, just as gender has been a much misused construct in studies of Muslims in India, I contend that it has also generally not been a concern of researchers interested in Muslim communities in India to use the research situation as an arena for articulation of points of view of Muslims. Muslims remain 'voiceless' despite the awakening of immense interest in studying them across the globe in the aftermath of 11 September 2001 attacks. It is not within the purview of this research to delve into the causes and significance of this interest but I have focused my attention on the twin realities of researching Muslims in India. First, inquiries that focus on how Indian Muslims (especially women) come to know and understand their world, and how they live within its contradictions, are rare, if not completely absent. And second, Muslim women are often relegated to a victim position which is essentialised such that what they think and do never constitutes 'agency'.

In the wake of the events of 11 September 2001, the debate on gender equality in Islam has assumed an important space in media and the public sphere. Muslim communities world over find themselves staring at their own monochromatic pictures drawn by the media, devoid of any diversity and often portraying them in a suspicious light, if not

---

define their needs and rights (Abu-Lughod 2002). In contrast to the race debate, the mainstream feminist movement has found it difficult to deal with latent orientalism because this debate often gets embroiled in the politics of western military interventions in the name of the 'war against terror' and (western liberal) democracy.

in a downright sinister manner. The quantity of research undertaken on various aspects of Muslim societies has grown manifold but the narratives they produce are not always edifying. The media has consistently produced reductive images of Muslim people, spaces and practices that are now deeply pervasive in popular culture. Some of these images are quite straightforward, like those related to terrorism, but some are deeper, for example, Muslims as inherently 'backward' and frequently irrational about their 'hurt sentiments'. These accounts have gained legitimacy in the popular consciousness and are in persistent everyday usage. The image of 'Muslim Women' as the ahistoric victim 'other' is most deeply held and most frequently deployed to breed prejudice against Muslims. Apart from the devastating outcomes of Islamophobia on the global geo-political terrain it also has had a deep impact on the solidarity of Muslim women with the avowed aims of the feminist movement. Muslim women's agency to set the norms and standards of the debates has been seriously compromised by the insistence of the mainstream women's movement that their faith Islam has no potential for their emancipation.

After the unfortunate, gruesome assault and rape of Nirbhaya[2] on 16 December 2012 and the subsequent protests, the mainstream feminist movement in India is increasingly finding itself poised at a juncture where its core concerns have managed to capture space in the public imagination. Their demands can no longer be easily scoffed at and ignored. While posturing against the State and its agencies for their ineffectual response to the incident, the movement was able to metaphorically bring together the entire 'Indian people' to align with their demands

---

[2] On 16 December 2012, a 23-year-old woman was gang-raped by five men and a juvenile. This case received a lot of media attention and caught the imagination of the urban public in India. The case was clearly portrayed, and understood, as a case of sexual violence against women for daring to claim freedom of mobility and the right to access public space. It also put forward a strong demand to the legislature and law enforcement institutions to respond effectively to sexual violence against women. The most noteworthy phenomenon in the case was that the victim was seen by the public as an 'average' young woman and the unfortunate incident as something that could happen to 'anyone'. Thousands joined the protests to demand justice in the case. One of the six accused has since died in custody, allegedly having committed suicide. The lower courts convicted the other five of rape and murder charges, and awarded the death penalty to the four adults, while the juvenile was awarded the maximum possible penalty of three years in a reform facility for delinquents. Subsequently, there have been spirited discussions on capital punishment. The public anger also sparked off demands to suitably amend the juvenile justice act such that the death penalty may be awarded to the juvenile accused as well.

and objectives. This incredible development has infused the movement with great confidence but also strengthened the hegemonic tendencies in what is essentially a movement of upper class, upper caste Hindu women, posturing as 'secular feminism'. Flavia Agnes (1996) cites her experience of participating in feminist forums where she was frequently labelled a Christian feminist and expected to speak from that position while the feminists who came from Hindu families were not burdened similarly, not obliged to comment on their experiences as Hindu women and the oppressive aspects of Hindu personal laws. Feminists from minorities in India have to give up the practices that identify them as Muslims or Christian to prove their secular credentials, while Hindu feminists are by default considered secular notwithstanding the religious symbolism of *bindi* and invocation of Kali, the deity of power.

I have often heard this popular complaint among Muslims that Muslims who become educated and better off, forsake their community. It is perhaps an exaggeration but I have heard numerous anecdotes of educated Indian Muslims finding themselves in positions where they had to explicitly distance themselves from their collective identity saying, 'We are not that kind of Muslim'. What kind of Muslim is this that a Muslim does not wish to be? The answer to this lies as much in the lived realities of Muslims, as in the discursive practices that seek to represent them. Their representation in different arenas is beset with expectations that seek to nullify the very act of representation. This is the mark of an oppressive social process that tries to maintain status quo. Agreeing with Agnes, I contend that the dictum of Muslims being 'communal until proven otherwise' and its corollary of 'Hindus as secular and tolerant by default' is a wider phenomenon deeply entrenched in the feminist movement too. Paulo Friere is speaking of this very phenomenon when he says that these representatives or leaders,

> ...use these resources to control the submerged and dominated consciousness of their comrades, or they become strangers in their own communities and their former leadership position is thus threatened. In order not to lose their leadership status, they will probably tend to continue manipulating the community, but in a more efficient manner (p. 142).

He talks of an oppressed community as the one which is not promoted as a whole but it is only its leaders that are promoted as parts of the whole. He emphasises that this process hinders the promotion of both critical consciousness and critical intervention among the members of the community. It is an irony for the Muslim community that those who are 'representatives' of Muslims in various arenas of public life including collective movements and political parties are able to retain their membership and position only by forcefully proclaiming that they do not represent Muslims.

This hindrance to the development of critical consciousness is slowly on the wane with Indian Muslim or Dalit women learning from the phenomenon of Black feminists questioning white feminists in USA about sidestepping race oppression, and from Palestinian feminists challenging the silence of the Israeli feminists over the atrocities of the State. Nevertheless, it is too early for the feminist movement in India to be honestly able to confront the fracturing of the category of 'Indian Women'. Part of the reason lies in the fact that the movement in independent India has been directed, for the most part, by constitutionalism and has often ended up aiding the State in legitimising itself and its continued marginalisation of several groups such as OBCs and Muslims (Menon 2001). Any concession it makes for the notion of difference does not go beyond the school children's textbook essays on diversity in dresses, cuisines and festivals. The other part lies in the increasing preoccupation of the contemporary feminist movement in India with 'politics of lifestyles' (Giddens 1991) mimicking western societies experiencing late modernity rather than emancipatory politics. The core concerns of the movement are played out in this politics that is focused more and more towards fashioning and expressing a self-identity and self-actualisation, and is based on individual-personal ethics. While there is nothing wrong in this per se, it does bear pointing out that this intense focus sadly leaves out the experiences of Muslim and Dalit women. The loud articulation of politics of lifestyle neither offers any solace to the victims of caste and communal violence nor does it provide a welcoming ground for the much touted broad-based sisterhood.

I remember attending a public meeting after the Nirbhaya rape protests at the Delhi School of Social Work where I taught at the time. The meeting was part of a series of similar meetings in the city aimed at discussing and preparing a charter of demands of women on containing violence against women to be put in front of the state government. The speakers at the meeting were women who were at the forefront of the protests. The fiery speeches were made by protest participants who confessed to not having identified themselves as feminists and never having participated in any collective protest on any issue ever before. Most of their demands were related to concerns of safety in public spaces arising out of the right to a certain lifestyle. In an attempt to broaden the scope of demands and also for the benefit of my students who formed the large part of the audience, I spoke up in the meeting about the violence faced by women solely due to their membership of marginalised and minority identity groups. I pointed out that sexualised violence is directed at them just by virtue of being a member of a minority, that their first priorities are those of emancipation from collective oppression before the individual rights to freedom of movement and choice in lifestyles. The speaker retorted that I was confused and misleading my students by mixing issues. When I tried to argue my stand further she snapped at me disgustedly, saying, 'I don't even know what you are talking about!' and then refused to look at me signalling an end to the discussion. I agree. She did not even know what I was talking about. Over tea after the meeting, another speaker who was a prominent activist from a Left party came to me and told me that she understood my point but implored me to consider that the support the movement was getting from women who had never associated with it was 'unprecedented'. The incident was educative to me as to where the real priorities and actual solidarities of the movement lay as it staked a bigger claim to popular politics and space in public imagination.

In another incident that took place in a seminar on governance in the Tata Institute of Social Sciences, Mumbai, a woman faculty member in the audience began grilling a speaker about the absence of a gendered view of labour questions in his presentation on migrant labour. She alleged that women's issues had been relegated to the backburner in Marxist literature to something that would be addressed later when the larger, more important issues would be solved by a class revolution. I pointed out to her the similar treatment women from minorities get in the women's movement, where they are told that they should forget their specific issues for the 'sisterhood'. No sooner had the words left my lips, I was treated to outraged allegations of dividing and weakening the feminist movement and to patronising declarations that I had failed to understand the issue at hand.

It cannot be stressed enough that Muslim feminists (or Dalit feminists, for that matter) questioning the mainstream feminist movement do not aim to weaken the women's movement. By questioning well-accepted arguments/discourses, they are not challenging the demand for equality per se, they are rather strengthening the demand by furthering the discourse, by complicating the discussions to include differences in women's experiences along class, religion and caste lines.

II

I began this work in 2008 with the premise that strategies that ensure that women take charge of their lives and those under their care, need to be in tune with their realities. If our aim is to understand what kind of action will ameliorate young Muslim women's lives and situation, their own voices need to become the centre of our inquiry. The life stories of young Muslim women—their aspirations, their fears, and their points of view need critical exploration. It is clear that this needs more effort. The 'more' in this case is not merely a mathematical entity. It is the need to alter our approach to understanding the problem, the socio-cultural and politico-economic conditions and uncertainties that impact everyday lives of young Muslim women in India and disrupt the realisation of their full potential.

This work was initiated as a research study commissioned by the *Bhartiya Muslim Mahila Andolan*[3] (BMMA—Indian Muslim Women's Movement) and supported by ActionAid India. BMMA had originally conceived it as a study of Muslim girls' aspirations. It was to begin with a hypothesis that Muslim girls too have similar aspirations as girls from other communities in India. In the initial proposal the study aimed to 'capture and document the aspirations of the girls' and also to 'compile and analyse the socio-economic and educational status of these girls'. With such a definitive hypothesis, the study was poised to set out and compile data with the help of a long questionnaire to determine and measure aspirations. One of the BMMA founder leaders, Zakia Soman, gave me the detailed questionnaire already designed for this purpose and asked me if I would be interested to co-ordinate the massive data collection drive across India and the consequent statistical analysis of the data,

---

[3] BMMA is a national-level membership-based network of organisations and individuals that came together in reaction to the assumption of homogeneity of women's identities by the larger women's movement in India. It articulates a criticism of and dissatisfaction with the mainstream movement's ineffectiveness at addressing the concerns of excluded groups like Dalits and Muslims. BMMA was formed after the 2002 pogrom in Gujarat.

and finally write up the report. I studied the questionnaire and instinctively began by questioning the merit of measuring what percentage of our sample aspired to be teachers, doctors, engineers, etc., in which part of the country. While the discussions were on for taking up the commission of this study as a lead researcher, I voiced reservations regarding the very methods and perspectives with which we approach a group of marginalised people. I argued that the main thrust of the study should be to facilitate the articulation of, the listening to, and the recording of autobiographical narratives of young Muslim women.

To convince BMMA was tough. Civil society organisations in India are most familiar and comfortable with quantitative research. Even when some qualitative data is sought to be collected, any study with even modest ambitions begins by compiling a list of questions that the subject of its enquiry can be subjected to. In my subsequent discussions with Zakia, I advocated the need for an alternative approach to research which would make an attempt to let Muslim women register their 'voice'. I argued that even if we succeeded in showing that young Muslim women had wishes and aspirations like other young women, it would not matter because it was firmly established in dominant discourses that they were victims of Islam and Muslim men, and had no agency. Zakia saw some merit in the argument and supported this alternative vision for the study. All the BMMA constituents—other founder members and the state conveners—were not very familiar with the idea of qualitative research. They feared that if they could not present a situation in terms of aggregates and percentages how would they advocate change in policies, welfare services, etc. Some thought that these were 'new-fangled' ideas and were reluctant to partner.

At the field researchers' training in Delhi, BMMA activists and I thrashed out the issues. Feminist ideas of research were discussed and argued. Field researchers were themselves given an experience of the proposed methods by getting them to participate in the exercises. Most of them were not very proficient in English and not familiar with the academic rhetoric of feminism, but the methods—in-depth interviews, participatory and projective techniques, focus group discussions, and observational narratives by researchers—appealed to them. At the end of the field researchers' training, BMMA activists agreed to use the proposed methods and exercises.

After much deliberation the study in its present form emerged to respond to a set of research assumptions, concerns and questions:

1. Muslim communities in India are as diverse as the country itself. How can we make a meaningful, credible comment on this reality? Are there are any common threads binding lives of Young Muslim women in India?
2. Muslim women will find a 'voice' provided a ready and sympathetic ear is lent to them. What methods can be suited to facilitate them to 'raise their voice' and provide a safe, sympathetic space for them to articulate themselves?
3. Muslim women are always portrayed as 'victims'. How can we highlight that like other human beings they too have agency, however limited it might be perceived as?
4. What happens after an instance of overt communal violence has happened? It is often a well-meaning wish on the part of social commentators that somehow the victims pick up the pieces of their lives and go on. But surely, some things must have changed? What changes cast their shadows in young Muslim women's day-to-day lives?
5. What are the dreams and aspirations of young Indian Muslim women? What are their thoughts on how to reach out and realise the same? What is their perspective on the socio-political situatedness of Indian Muslims—men and women?

With these questions in mind, I set out to design a research study that aimed at presenting a detailed descriptive record of various aspects of everyday lives of young Muslim women in India by bringing forth their autobiographical narratives. The interactions therein would allow young Muslim women to extrapolate on their situation vis-à-vis not only the patriarchal elements within Muslim communities in India, but also the tattered fabric of communal relations enmeshed with barbs of patriarchy in the larger context. Attempt would also be made to delineate agency among young Muslim women in India from their perspective by examining instances of defiance, contestations and negotiation with their everyday realities. And, finally formulate a set of proposals for action aimed at the Muslim community, the civil society, and the State, emanating out of the aspirations articulated by the young Muslim women.

Considering that not much has been said on the matter of young Muslim women before, the study positioned itself at an exploratory level. This not only made it possible for me to make the initial comment on the issues at hand but also left me a lot of flexibility regarding the choice of methods available for use for this enquiry. The choice of methods was influenced by my intention to gain useful insights and present challenging, stimulating ideas and not to collect statistics. The methods enabled the participants and researchers alike to choose or even coin our own language, grammar, and syntax for making statements of our understanding of young Muslim women's everyday lives. These choices also allowed the team to invest and express a faith in young Muslim women as those who are most knowledgeable about their own situation rather than to go to some 'experts' in the field. The methods also allowed us to look at and listen to the diverse facets of the everyday lives of young Muslim women integrated into a unified self-interpretation rather than ask for disjointed pieces of information. The field researchers went into the field *seeking* explanations, *not testing* explanations that we had already 'hypothesised' about.

We listened to young Muslim women in 23 urban and semi-urban centres located in 12 states of India, Kerala, Tamil Nadu, Karnataka, Odisha, Maharashtra, Delhi, Uttar Pradesh, Rajasthan, Bihar, Gujarat, Madhya Pradesh and Chhattisgarh. It is my deepest regret that we could not include many other places from within these states and other states where a sizeable Muslim population resides, especially, West Bengal and Andhra Pradesh.

The field researchers, BMMA activists including BMMA's founders, state convenors and members, have a longstanding history of both, extensive and intensive engagement with Muslim communities, especially poor Muslim women in their respective areas of work across India. Every young Muslim woman who participated in this study was not met with a stranger knocking at the door to ask a list of questions. The interviewer and the animator-facilitator at the workshop for most part was another woman known well to the interviewee as somebody dedicated to the cause of ameliorating the plight of Muslim women. It was the nature of this engagement that afforded us the luxury of choosing the deep narrative and participatory methods.

The workshops held in different urban and semi-urban localities across India became spaces where young Muslim women were able to give expression and thus examine what was routine in their lives but had never been spoken of before. This interplay of expression and examination with many other women became the source of insight into their own selves. Research, thus, became a small but steady wave of Muslim women meeting each other, sharing experiences, listening to each other, sympathising and empathising with each other, crying together, laughing together and gaining strength from each other in the process. And while narrative methods are therapeutic, it has to be underlined that the workshops were not meant to be group-therapy sessions facilitated by a counsellor or a social worker. The workshops were spaces for the comprehension of lived realities, of collaborative acts of 'knowing', and of praxis of oral history as a method (Sarkar 2008).

III

I have attempted in the following chapters to weave a coherent narrative of the research interest in Indian Muslim women from the point of view of an Indian Muslim woman scholar. I would be discussing further the issue of discursive limits placed on the Gramscian and Spivakian 'Subaltern'. Suffice it here to say that the moment of problematising a prevailing discursive content of a stigmatised and subjugated identity is defined not by some altruistic or divine intervention but is indicated by a combination of events or social, political, economic processes occurring together to throw light upon the system of subjugation and enabling people to see it as unjust. This is not to say that some kind of final unveiling and toppling of injustice would take place as a consequence but that in the Foucauldian sense freedom is something that is exercised, rather than achieved, in a process that must run in tandem with careful and creative exercise of power. This narrative study may also help us imagine methods using which we can effectively hope for the emergence of a capacity of people positioned adversely within a system of domination to seize the moment and draw the power to re-imagine themselves.

Chapters 1–3 discuss the research process and how this book came into being. Chapter 1, titled Discursive Colonisation, includes a discussion in which I have reviewed the multiple sites and manner in which the representation of Indian Muslim women has taken place. In Chapter 2, titled Representation and 'Listening', I have discussed the dynamics operating at the sites within which all the participants—the young women, the field researchers and I—produced our own representations with an awareness of representations produced elsewhere. In Chapter 3, Portrait of a Researcher as a Muslim Woman, I lay explicit the considerations operating at the sites of reading, making sense, arranging, and analysing the content and process of representation. The autoethnographic experiences of all the researchers in the study form the fulcrum of this chapter.

The second section extends from Chapters 4 to 7 and includes what we may call meta-narratives. It is my reading of the narratives of the young Muslim women produced in this study—a narrative about these narratives. Chapter 4 is titled The Everyday of Inhabiting Margins. Chapter 7, titled I Speak, Therefore, I Am includes an account of emerging possibility of fashioning a new self. Chapter 5, Dreaming in Shackle includes an account of the aspirations of young Muslim women and the forces that impact the formulation and fruition of these aspirations. The history of the mother-daughter relationship, the dreams of married life and the communitarian nature of the very capacity to aspire are discussed here. Chapter 6, Memory and Experience of Violence grapples with the issues of the disciplining impact of patriarchal and communal violence and the role of collective memory in the same.

For a study professing a narrative approach, it goes without saying, that it is not only the process of production and analysis of the narratives of the participants that must receive our attention but the narratives themselves too. In Chapters 8, 9 and 11, I attempt to present some more narratives produced in the study with brief comments. These have been made available to the readers in the third section, separated from my readings in the earlier sections, in order to enable, or at least leave room for, alternative readings. The narratives woven and presented in the study are sought to be poised as 'counternarratives', counter to the various mainstream narratives. The 'against-the-grain' approach of these counternarratives is especially suited to an attempted process of deliberate disruption by exposing the complexity and inherent contradiction of the 'official' and accepted discourses (Richardson & St. Pierre 2005). The aim is to represent Muslim young women in India in a manner which may not be an exact replica of the actual communities, since some kind of distortions are bound to occur, but rather like an Impressionist painting. Brushing small dabs of paint rather than broad strokes to catch a fleeting yet all-embracing glimpse of the details, the final picture that emerges ends up emphasising the researcher's (artist's) perception of the subject as much as the depiction of the subject per se. I have done the work of extracting and organising the narratives so, undeniably, some residue of what I wish for the reader to read is bound to have slipped through in the process. I hope it does not make alternative readings difficult. There are always these remnants or residual feelings that we inevitably find 'unspeakable' because they lie beyond the limits of vocabularies available to us. While what cannot be said cannot be written, I make a gesture towards Roland Barthes' (1968) assertion of death of the author[4] and rest my case.

---

[4] This conception signals the denial of the role of an originator or source of meaning implicit in a text to its author. In fact, the reader becomes the central figure and eliminates the need for a singular authoritative meaning intended by the author. 'We now know that a text is not a line of words releasing a Single "theological" meaning (the "message" of an Author-God) but a multi-dimensional space in which a variety of writings, none of them original, blend and clash' (Barthes 1968, p. 146).

1
Discursive Colonisation

While the first phase of workshops and interactions for the study was underway, a meeting of BMMA activists was scheduled in Bhopal, Madhya Pradesh. This was also an opportunity to get the first bit of feedback on the experiences of the field researchers. They discussed their experiences of talking to young Muslim women during the workshop. Many of them had been working in urban slums and Muslim localities for years, yet the experiences they had during the interactions using the study methodologies were reported as being powerful and novel. They shared that during the workshops and interviews Muslim girls expressed themselves in a way they had never heard before. The field researchers discussed the workshop settings, methods and questions with much excitement. During various phases of the research, I could not help wondering how the histories and narratives of Muslims in these places seemed to have completely ignored the voice of Muslim women. How was it that over the preceding years, academic, journalistic and activist writing had been commenting on and discussing the marginalisation of Muslim women in India without taking their voices into consideration? It sounds incredibly impossible that this question was being raised for the first time but quite obviously the answers depend upon positioning and the perspective of one who poses the question. When I undertook a review of the literature for this study, it was this question that provided a framework for my readings. I positioned myself as 'a Muslim woman' and found that I was the one who had *already been spoken for* in academic literature. I read the existing literature, and found these to be 'speech-acts' that precluded Muslim women's own articulation.

In the literature on Muslims in India the part that has arguably seen most contestations and controversy is their place in India's history. The historical narratives about Indian Muslims are important because of their increased and strategic use in the contemporary public sphere to define who is, and who is not a citizen of post-independence/post-partition India. Boundaries thus defined are then used to unleash violence on the Muslim minority (Metcalf 1995). This is the legacy of British rule over India which utilised the narratives of Muslims as invaders and oppressors of the 'original' Hindu people native to India. The British positioned themselves as 'better colonial masters than the Muslims' by commissioning history-writing which portrayed Muslims as intolerant, sensual and violent (Chatterjee 1993; Pandey 1990). Metcalf asserts that conventional historiography is still steeped in British idiom and discourse to a large extent but also points out that there is now an increased reflexivity and consciousness among the historians of British India to the colonisation of discourse about Indian Muslims. Despite the ensuing disagreements, it is the strength of Marxist traditions in History as a discipline in India which has allowed them to come up with alternative histories of Muslims that challenge the colonial accounts, for example in the works of historians such as Romila Thapar and Bipan Chandra. Numerous contemporary historians of recorded histories have taken a look at the experiences of Muslims within Histories of Colonial India and Partition (Pandey 2001, 2006; Hasan 1995, 1998, 1997, 2001) with a perspective which is mindful of, but largely unencumbered by, colonial baggage. Mushirul Hasan (1990, 2004, 2008), for instance, has been at the forefront of recording the contemporary history of Muslims in India.

It must be flagged here that the genre of academic literature which is the foremost in talking about Muslims in India is the one that relates to communal relations and violence (Pandey 1992; Van der Veer 1994; Talbot 1995; Varshney 2002; Anand 2005). Some scholars have contended that after the 1857 'Sepoy mutiny' and the role played by Muslims, especially artisans, during the revolt, there was a major reversal in the generous attitudes of British colonial rule towards its Muslim subjects (Chandra 1979). Distrust of the state meant that Muslims were edged out of both land and employment. Their economic condition in the immediate post-'mutiny' era in much of North India was quite pathetic (Khalidi 2006). Distrust between the Indian state and its Muslim subjects as also between Hindu and Muslim communities marked all negotiations for a standing in social and political space in the country. The roots of this idea are again found in the colonial discourse whence any aspiration or expression of a different identity by Muslims was branded Muslim/minority communalism (Jalal 1999). This continued even after British rule in India ended with the division of India and Pakistan in 1947 (Hasan 1990). In fact, it was this distrust on which the foundation stone of the Muslim state of Pakistan was laid. The creation of Pakistan reaffirmed a concept which is very evident in the politics of communalism in India today—of Islam as a foreign imposition and that being Hindu was the 'natural' condition of Indians. The concept soon found currency in popular culture representations of the Muslim community in India.

Ravi Vasudevan (1995) opines that mainstream cinema in India also effectively projected the 'Hindu nationalist' viewpoint and 'a symbolic narrative of the Hindu nation was put in place, one which rendered other identities subordinate to this privileged one' (ibid., p. 2809). Embedded within this configuration lies the idea that Muslims are disloyal and not committed to the cause of the nation, and the 'tolerant' values of the larger Indian society. More recent films like *Ghadar* (2001) continue to invoke memories of Partition, highlighting and establishing time and again the 'inherent' link of Indian Muslims to Pakistan (Jha and Sharma 2009).

The matter of Muslim alienation in India has also been mostly blamed on the overt communal violence unleashed by the *Hindutva* groups or *Sangh Parivar* and/or on the apathy of the ruling classes (mainly Indian National Congress among the political parties). The truth that a more deep-seated prejudiced view is prevalent which has to do with a much broader range of discriminations is mostly ignored. MJ Akbar (1988) and Gyanendra Pandey (1990) have charted the chronology of communal violence beginning with the 1962 riots in Jabalpur as being the first one in independent India. Later violence targeting Muslims is recorded as breaking out with considerable regularity in towns and cities all over India—Ahmedabad, Bhiwandi, Jamshedpur, Aligarh, Varanasi. Through these accounts communal violence experienced by Muslims is recorded as tied closely to political contestation between Congress and the Jansangh/Bhartiya Janata Party as an electoral front for RSS.

A few scholars of urban studies have also recognised that communal violence is often connected with claims over resources, markets and city spaces. Patel and Deb (2009) note that many small towns and medium-size cities have become characterised by communal conflict and thus communal riots. They list Ahmedabad, Vadodara, Godhra, Hyderabad, Meerut, Moradabad among such cities and ask whether 'the control of the local governance structures by a majority community aids and sometimes instigates such conflicts? It is important to make a note of Patel's contention 'that riots have become a form to claim a space in the city rather than social movements' and ask why would that be so. While this important question may have been flagged in contemporary studies, the engagement has been fleeting because detailed explanations for it have never been sought.

This trend of commenting on a phenomenon but not engaging with it thoroughly is a discernible trend in most writings on Muslims. For example, Asghar Ali Engineer (1988, 1989, 1985, 1991 b, c, 1995, 2004) has chronicled the intricate terrain of communal violence, the quantum of damage suffered by Muslims and the impact on the victims in each of the instances. Indeed, in the face of the unfortunately long and wide history of communal violence in India, his work has also assumed formidable proportions. Unfortunately though, Engineer's theoretical engagement with his subject has left much to be desired and beyond recounting events meticulously, his work is unable to offer any insights regarding the root causes of communal violence and the connection between violence and other processes. In this tradition of raconteurs of communal violence, Christopher Jaffrelot is another important name. His work (1999, 2005) is marked by insightful descriptions of the genesis and proliferation of the Hindutva ideology and outfits. However, once again the rich descriptions do not extend to sustained efforts at theorisation. In any case, in Jaffrelot's formulations the Hindutva outfits and actors are the main protagonists and Muslims make an appearance only as their victims and those passively impacted.

This lack of theorisation may also be seen as an acutely deficient engagement of social sciences with issues of Muslims and communal violence. In context of Dalit critique, Gopal Guru (2012) asserts that in the absence of attempts to theorisation there cannot be an interrogation of the prevalent frames of debate and no possibility of envisioning an alternative. In his opinion, doing theory is social responsibility that restores agency to those deemed powerless and respect to their experiences, and is, therefore, an emancipatory, transformative and political project (ibid.). While Dalit Studies is now a legitimate and well-established academic discipline developing a Dalit critique of caste hierarchy and oppression, the Muslim experience is yet to be recognised even as an epistemic resource. Among a few works that can be mentioned as attempting theory of communal violence (but not really of 'the Muslim experience of communal violence') is that of Paul Brass (1997, 2005). The recent work of Parvis-Ghassem Fachandi (2010, 2012) analysing the ferocity of violence in the 2002 pogrom is also a step forward in this direction. While Brass's engagement is with the discursive and political processes at work, Fachandi takes a social-psychological route to understanding the 2002 Gujarat pogrom. One common feature of both these readings is that they deviate from the path treaded till now in this genre which was to describe these instances of violence as spontaneous 'riots' which are disconnected with the 'normal-natural' harmonious course of social relations. Ashutosh Varshney (2003) also attempts to provide an alternative reading of communal violence. He proposes that ethnic conflict and ethnic violence be differentiated from each other and that it is in the nature of engagements of the civil society with ethnic communities where the key to ethnic conflict flaring up as ethnic violence rests. Ayesha Jalal (1996, 1999) has also explored Communalism in the broader South Asian context and has made astute comments pertaining to history and the legacy of Partition in present-day communal contestations. In her formulations, a subaltern reading of Muslim history in South Asia is a running theme.

The other popular genres of research where Muslims make an appearance are studies tracing the socio-economic and political status of Muslims in general and Muslim women of India in particular. Most of the available information is quantitative in nature (Kazi 1990; Mistry 2005; Sachar report 2006; Hasan and Menon 2006). Some studies related to caste and stratification among Indian Muslims also exist (Ali 2002). One common theme in all these works is that the problem faced by Muslim communities, people and women (including communalism) are most conveniently ascribed to the religion itself. Engineer (2002) argues that religion may only be considered a factor among many and an instrument rather than the fundamental cause. Nevertheless, this view has not been countered completely and in the contemporary 'globalised' world, Islam as a belief system and a faith, and Muslims on the whole, find themselves in a siege-like situation. Islamophobia undeniably creates a spacious breach between the Muslims' perception of who they are and the ways in which they are perceived by others (Saliba et al. 2002). Misinformed public attitudes/opinions related to Muslims are persistent and deeply held.

While the interest in and volume of research undertaken on various aspects of Muslim societies has grown manifold, the narratives they produce are not always edifying. An examination of Muslim women and their conditions is conspicuous by its near complete absence from these narratives. This phenomenon can be traced back to the colonial period wherein Muslim women were generally not a part of political or academic discourse and were absent from any kind of literary scrutiny (Hasan and Menon 2004). Recent studies into this matter reveal that it was easy for scholars to resort to stereotypes and ascribe this 'absence' solely to the seclusion and *Purdah* practices among Muslims (Minault 1998). Because Muslim women were not seen, it was only natural that they were not talked about, or so went the explanations. Stereotypes were accepted and repeated in various studies and articles by Indian and non-Indian, Muslim and non-Muslim authors alike, and repeated so often that they almost became self-fulfilling prophecies. Misrepresentation and stereotyping of Muslim women is also rampant in mainstream media and popular culture, especially as reflected in Bollywood. The Muslim socials of 1950s and 1960s have contributed a lot to the stereotypical images of women in *purdah* and the culture of seclusion of women in the *zenana* of an Indian Muslim household as in *Chaudhvin ka chand*, *Mere Mehboob* and women being divorced cursorily as in *Nikah* (Bhaskar and Allen 2009). It is a fairly recent phenomenon that the *discursive* 'absence' and 'invisibility' of Muslim women in India is being taken note of by academics. Mahua Sarkar's (2008) study of how Muslim women have been rendered invisible from the history of Bengal is an important work in this regard which illustrates the discursive processes that have marginalised Muslims in India. When accounts dealt specifically with Muslims, Muslim women were relegated to the margins (Sarkar 2008). In accounts dealing with women, Muslim women were again rendered 'invisible'. As Sarkar notes, 'The problem... is not just that the existing scholarship privileges Hindu women and ignores Muslim women as its object of inquiry but rather that it typically *fails to as much as register* Muslim women's invisibility as something that might need some explaining' (ibid., pp. 7–8).

When queries that concerned themselves with Muslim women began to make an appearance, simplistic assumptions about the role played by the 'Islamic-monolith monster' in oppressing and disempowering Muslim women became accepted features of mainstream academic discourse. Hasan and Menon (2004) assert that the mainstream discourses continued to labour, for a long time, under broad generalisations regarding Muslim women in particular and Muslims in general as a continuous singular category. The Ram Janmbhoomi Movement and its mobilised processes provided unrestrained room for articulating and enacting the generalised hostility for this monolithic caricature of Islam in India. This hostility, when enacted in overt violence—riots, massacres—targets women specifically as symbols of 'honour' of the community (Sarkar 2002; Khan 2009). In such a scenario discourses tended to emphasise the 'Muslim' part and underplay the 'Indian women' part in the expression 'Indian Muslim women'. The commixture of poverty and gender disparity in the lives of Muslim women in India did not get its due in these discourses. Adding to the already heavy assault of domestic violence suffered by Muslim women (just like other Indian women) and the struggle for survival and dignity as poor women, Indian Muslim women also find themselves being brutally targeted during communal riots and pogroms against Muslims (Sarkar & Butalia 1995; Panikker 1999; Nussbaum 2007). Some authors have pointed out that, Muslim women, just like women from other communities, are at the receiving end of the complex but fairly broad landscape of gender discrimination in India (Kazi 1999) and that Islam is no more oppressive to women than the workings of the modern secular state (Majid 2002).

Apart from the rampant stereotyping, academic debates and discourses on Muslim women in India have also tended to revolve around specific areas (Fazalbhoy 1997). Stock representations are tied to looking only at the effect of Muslim personal law (Hasan 1994), overemphasising *purdah,* triple *talaq,* polygyny, etc., or concerning themselves only with issues related to education, etc. Considerable stress was laid on the fact that Islam and personal laws are intrinsically related to traditional beliefs and the inequality of Muslim women 'within' the community (Roy 1979 cited in Hasan and Menon 2004). It is these shaky 'representations' and the fractured approach that have actually added to the 'invisibility' of Muslim women. They have repeatedly been presented as victims: victims of Islam and Muslim men.

As has been mentioned earlier in this chapter, numerous studies of the socio-economic status of Muslims exist that make little or no attempt to locate and describe women's position vis-à-vis their inquiry. There exist some quantitative studies on access to welfare services, education, communal violence, Muslim ghettos, etc. They relegate women to either a footnote, a column in a few tables, or at most a small separate section. When we look at empirical studies that concern themselves solely with Muslim women, these are also mostly quantitative. In 2006, the findings of two major quantitative studies were published and made available in the public domain. The first was what is commonly known as the Sachar Committee Report and the other was the Muslim Women Survey (MWS) conducted by Zoya Hasan and Ritu Menon. The significance of the Sachar Committee Report lay partially in the fact that it was commissioned by the state, whereas, MWS was not. Both the studies went in for massive primary data collection. While the Muslim communities were not surprised by most of their findings, the fact that they had been articulated at all was certainly redemptive and even cathartic. These studies also served to generate a lot of purposeful debate in civil society regarding the issues and problems faced by Muslims.

The most proliferating kind of studies that continue to be undertaken on Indian Muslims are the sociological studies on the caste composition of Muslim communities (Alam 2009; Ali 2002; Anwar 2001; Bhatty 1996; Ahmed 1978), their educational status (Mainuddin 2010; Hasan & Menon 2005; Mondal 1997) and their reproductive behaviour, especially on their use (or non-use) of contraceptives (Hussain 2008). Many studies seek to address a combination of these issues (Mistry Ahmed 1993–1996; Faridi et al. 1992; Engineer 1991; Mondal 1992; Ahmed 1983). These studies often essentialise the experiences or attitudes of Muslims as if they are not influenced by the processes at work in the larger Indian society. In most sociological studies seeking to profile them, Muslims are portrayed as a laggard community, loath to change its attitude in the race of demographic transition in India in which other religious communities have reached milestones much ahead of them.

What unfolds in most such efforts is an essentialised identity tag, which pretends to have some operational basis but ends up only confirming the view of the hegemonic gaze. Also, what is discernible in this review of literature is the ritualistic tone and vocabulary of the literature. Much of the journalistic writing on Muslims as well as the sociological studies are conducted and/or written on routine lines. It is as if scholars start with a precautionary inventory which was designed by someone in the seventies and since then not much has changed in the nature and manner of enquiries. Especially among the Muslim scholars it was disheartening to see the extent of 'dumbing down' in research engagements on issues related to Muslims in the last three decades. It is only some recent studies that have begun to initiate alternative enquiries or against-the-grain readings of dominant discourses. Methodology and approach is a key consideration here and we are beginning to see ethnographic and narrative approaches in these recent studies. In my opinion the most important question confronting Muslim scholarship is that of renewed rigour, creativity, and inventiveness in framing and asking questions. Dragging ourselves on the well-treaded path may be easier but it is time to recognise that this has not got us anywhere.

With the controversies around the Shahbano case[1] and the banning of Salman Rushdie's *Satanic Verses* in India there is also lot of literature

---

[1] Shahbano was a Muslim divorced woman who moved the Supreme Court of India to demand maintenance from her ex-husband. In 1985, the court ruled in her favour in a judgement which made explicit reference to the Muslim personal law. The verdict enthused the women's movement to press for the scrapping of Muslim personal law. They were readily joined in this demand by the Hindu right who utilised the opportunity to whip up a strong and wider anti-Muslim campaign. The verdict and these demands were seen as an affront on the Personal Law and fundamental right to practise religion by Indian Muslim religious organisations which have long adhered to a patriarchal interpretation of Quranic and Hadith injunctions on rights of divorcees and widows. Although

around the issue of anti-liberal attitudes of Muslims. While several authors contend that the Shahbano case divided the women's movement in India, my opinion is that it merely illuminated the rifts that already existed (and still exist) but were glossed over by the movement which claimed (and continues to claim) a pan-Indian sisterhood that does not exist in reality. Scholars such as Zoya Hassan (2000, 2006), Flavia Agnes (1992, 1995, 1999), Martha Nussbaum (2001), Nivedita Menon (2001) and Madhu Kishwar (1998) have debated the issues involved extensively. What is interesting is that in both the cases, the left-liberals as well as the Hindu-right converge and chastise Muslims for being irrational and anti-liberal. Both these controversies flared up under the Rajiv Gandhi government. His government's stand on both counts caused the dominant discourses to allege 'appeasement' of Muslims which in turn obliged the government to open the doors of the hitherto locked Babri Masjid[2] for Hindus to worship inside the mosque. This handing over of the mosque to Hindus and later its demolition is marked in academic literature almost unanimously as a blot on Indian democracy, its secular character and so on, but there is absolute silence on what did these events mean to the Muslims of India.

---

the Shahbano case was not the first in which relief had been granted to divorced Muslim women it received unprecedented media and public attention. Shahbano herself appealed to court to withdraw the favourable judgement because, she said she did not want to be a cause for communal hatred being fermented in the country in her name, although she had fought her case for maintenance for 10 years. Later, the Congress government led by Rajiv Gandhi passed the Muslim Women (Protection of Rights on Divorce) Act in 1986, to allegedly set aside the Shahbano verdict and 'appease' Muslim sentiment. Some have questioned the Women's movement for failing to critique the patriarchal elements in the Hindu personal law similarly, for failing to recognise the insecurities of a minority community and responding with a more nuanced position for women's rights, and finally they were also criticised for playing directly into the hands of anti-Muslim groups in India (Kishwar 1986).

[2] Babri Masjid was a 14th century mosque in the city of Ayodhya in Uttar Pradesh. The city is an important pilgrimage centre and is believed to be the birthplace and seat of rule of Lord Rama. The site of the mosque was disputed to be the exact place of birth of Rama. Although the dispute dates from the colonial period it became the epicentre of the communal conflict in India in the early 1980s, and has been the rallying point of anti-Muslim mobilisations and violence in various parts of India by various Hindu nationalist groups and organisations that come together under the umbrella term 'Sangh Parivar'. The disputed mosque which had been locked since after the illegal installation of idols inside the mosque in 1949, was unlocked in 1985 on orders of Rajiv Gandhi's government. The mosque has since been razed (on 6 December 1990).

Following another observation, while there are many studies on Muslim women, Muslim men and masculinity are severely understudied. The studies that do exist are located in *madrasas*,[3] for example Sikand (2005, 2008) and Husain (2004). In fact, the interest in *madrasas* among the academics in India seems to have surfaced only after 9/11 when these were described in the dominant media discourse as dens of terror or radical training. This interest is extending now to girls' *madrasas* too, for example Jeffrey et al. (2004) and Weinklemann (2007) but the representations remain problematic and as ever steeped in a perception of Muslim women lacking agency and Islam being the only point of reference in their experiences.

Another trend is the one that shows a tendency to employ psychopathological frameworks to study Muslims. The title of Rajmohan Gandhi's book on Muslims, *Understanding the Muslim Mind* (1999) is an example of this trend. Presenting concise biographies of eight Muslim men who are deemed by the author to be important personalities that have shaped the destiny of the community in India, Gandhi claims to make a statement about this entity called 'the Muslim Mind'. The singular number, proper noun, 'the Muslim Mind' in the title is an indication of a subconscious motivation to 'understand' a phantasmal, mega and singular-unified 'Muslim mind' by showing some common thread in eight prominent male 'minds'. This is a peculiar way to title a study which hints at a representation of 'the Muslim' as suffering from some psycho-pathological ailment which can be uncovered by psychoanalysis. Numerous works exist that employ this peculiar academic formulation and claim to look into, examine and understand what goes on in 'the Muslim Mind'. Edward Said (1997, p. xii) noted, 'Malicious generalizations about Islam have become the last acceptable form of denigration of foreign culture in the West; what is said about Muslim mind, or character, or religion, or culture as a whole cannot now be said in mainstream discussion about Africans, Jews, other Orientals, or Asians....' In the west, this has led to cognitive psychological approaches in studying Muslim attitudes on the lines of marketing studies. In India, too there is increasingly a trend towards using focus groups and surveys in assessing Muslim attitudes towards various issues such as modernity, contraception, terrorism, etc.

---

[3] *Madrasa* is an Arabic word literally meaning a place of learning, mostly used to mean a school. Lately, and especially in South Asia the word has come to stand for institutions of Islamic learning and has been ascribed the pejorative connotation of being fundamentalist spaces.

In the past decade, there has also been some literature that pertains to Muslims as participants in politics in India. Most of it predictably pertains to electoral politics (Hassan 1990) and controversies regarding the voting preferences of Muslims or the so called 'Muslim vote bank' (Engineer 1995). The debates around reservations in education, jobs and parliament also make references to Muslims (Bhambri 2005; Wright 1997; Zainuddin 2003; Hasan & Roy 2005). Many of these writings focus on caste identities and women within the Muslim community pitting these as oppositional to the larger questions of the Muslim communities (Sikand 2001; Shahabuddin 2002; Jenkins 1999, 2001). Literature pertaining to politics of caste and discrimination among Muslims along caste lines puts forth arguments that remind one of literature on Hindu Dalit movements (Anwar Alam (2009, 2003) and Javeed Alam (1999) Ahmed (2003)). Most studies assume that the caste situation among Muslims is just a replica of the Hindu caste system with some minor variations. Writings which present an alternative reading of Muslim participation in the public sphere have appeared recently which pose questions about how Muslim participation is limited due to the ascribed identities of Muslims (Ahmed 2009; Ali 2001). This factor has also received considerable attention from the state which periodically takes stock of the position of Muslims vis-à-vis the rest of Indian society.

Beginning with the report by W.W. Hunter on *The Indian Musalmans* [2002 (1871)] in response to Lord Mayo's query about the Muslim subjects of the state, the Indian state (colonial and independent India) has commissioned various enquiries around the grievances of/around Muslims (Khalidi 2009). These include enquiry commissions on numerous instances of communal violence as well as enquiries into the developmental status of Muslims such as the Sachar Committee (2006) and the Rangnath Misra Commission on Religious and Linguistic Minorities (2007). These state-sponsored studies have often done a good job of delivering the tasks that they were mandated to but various governments have consistently failed to take any action on the recommendations of any of these enquiries except paying some lip service. It also must be said that these reports have served very well to strengthen existing stereotyped, essentialised representations (Das & Samaddar 2009). In fact, various data generated by the governments through its programmes, census and surveys have done little more than this. Furthermore, Muslims are rarely mentioned in planning documents, and end up being clubbed with all other minorities who are doing well on many of the development indices which see planned interventions. Systematic studies analysing this policy situation are yet to be conducted.

Gayatri Spivak and her work on subalterns and representation offer me a great point of reference to talk of Muslims specifically. The story of what grew into subaltern studies begins with narratives of Arabs whose representations in the western world have long been subjected to caricaturing, exoticisation, and dehumanisation. Spivak (1993) refers to Frantz Fanon and Edward Said, both as writers of 'great texts of the "Arab World"' calling Said's *Orientalism* the 'source book' in her discipline. In this regard, the importance of *Orientalism* (Said 1978) cannot be overstated. The radical nature of Said's work which followed Fanon in a contrarian reading of the history of their people and the way it has been represented by the subjugating, hegemonic west, made possible a new kind of articulation. Said's criticism of Orientalism recognises the discursive processes that produce and control the image of the orient by essentialising, oversimplifying, exoticising and demonising the 'orient'. He argued that regions and people referred to as the 'orient' are far more complex and diverse than the label—short hand for Muslims and Arabs—would allow. Orientalism rather than being the benign study of the orient was shown by Said to be a process of fabrication of identities existing only in western fantasies. The most damning criticism of orientalism offered by Said was that, in effect, it were these phantasmagoric representations of the Muslims and Arabs that were guiding the relationship of the occident with the orient, with disastrous consequences. Orientalism, in Said's own words is,

> ...a *distribution* of geopolitical awareness into aesthetic, scholarly, economic, sociological, historical and philological texts; it is an *elaboration* not only of a basic geographical distinction (the world is made up of two unequal halves, Orient and Occident) but also of a whole series of 'interests' which, by such means as scholarly discovery, philological reconstruction, psychological analysis, landscape and sociological description, it not only creates but also maintains; it *is*, rather than expresses, a certain *will* or *intention* to understand, in some cases to control, manipulate, even incorporate, what is a manifestly different (or alternative and novel) world; it is, above all, a discourse that is by no means in direct, corresponding relationship with political power in the raw, but rather is produced and exists in an uneven exchange with various kinds of power... (Said 1978, p. 12)

The central thesis of Said's entire oeuvre of work is that the measure of control over who gets represented in what manner is a measure of power. This nature of representation as power exercised is the prime task of a postcolonial critic. We may also see Malcolm X and Ali Shariati within this attempt of Fanon and Said at reading one's own history from a perspective that is aware of subjugation but is not subjugated itself (Dabashi 2009). 'Orientalism' as described by Said is still alive and kicking as evidenced by the cultural discourses in western media and the geopolitics of the military interventionist foreign policy of USA and developed countries of Europe. It is also evident in the work of the academia in different measures, by design or inadvertently. And even though Said's critique of orientalism is revolutionary and capable of providing a programmatic content for resistance, it is, in the final analysis, a discourse that is still often interrupted and sidelined by the might of capitalism and its cultural hegemony.

We can discern an indigenised, local version of Orientalism that Said pointed out and critiqued in India. Well-intentioned efforts to argue for social justice and equality for Muslims fall in the discursive traps that do not allow for alternative imaginaries that can actually free Muslims from the discursive double bind to be able to claim social equality and justice for themselves. A close scrutiny of this *discursive* reality shows that the case of Muslim women in India is all the more precarious because they have to negotiate with the anti-Islam posturing as well as with the rigid patriarchal stances and structures from within the community, both of which may well present themselves, on many occasions, as intertwined. The predicament caused by entanglement of feminist politics with Islamophobic politics of our times has let down Muslim women by demanding solidarity from them, expecting them to give up their particularity, and not letting them identify any gains that they might want. This has not only battered Muslim women's defences but also detracted the scholarly gaze from their agency.

Indian Muslim women's criticism of the wider women's movement in India has not registered a significance presence but on the global front Muslim women have come out in clear criticism of western feminists accusing them of ethnocentric or orientalist tendencies, reducing Muslim women to the position of 'inessential Others' (Al-Hibri 1999). These Muslim women emphasise their commitment to their faith and the religio-cultural community along with the belief that these can change. However, they also believe that these changes will have to be brought about by people within the fold of the community and not from without

(Wadud 2006). They believe that equality between genders is an idea not antithetical to Islam, rather it is enshrined in the Quran and *Hadith* (Ahmed 1992). According to Azizah Al-Hibri (1999), Islam celebrates rather than suppresses diversity, and that Islamic law is meant to be flexible regarding time and place. She further argues that *Ijthihad* (the interpretation of the religious texts) is available to both men and women.

It is the contention of Islamic feminists that it is the patriarchal readings of the religious text that have created practices which treat women differentially from men. Embedded within this issue is also the distinction, which Islamic feminists stress, between cultural practices of a community and those that are sanctioned by Islam. They assert that most discriminatory practices have their origins either in pre-Islamic and/or local culture or are imposed by patriarchal conservative elements within the communities. They engage in re-reading the Qur'an and the *Hadith*[4] in order to show that Islam in itself does not discriminate between genders. This re-reading is done keeping in mind that the context in which these texts came into being have dramatically changed.

To the liberal secular feminists this may seem like a contradiction but Islamic feminists in India, as elsewhere on the globe, are convinced that their way is the only practicable approach that can contribute to improving the lot of Muslim women (Schneider 2009). Schneider, tracing the fortunes of Islamic feminism in India, places the Shahbano case verdict and the surrounding debates as a possible point of departure for the Muslim participants of the women's movement in India. She recalls that the demand for a uniform civil code was a longstanding issue of the secular feminists in India but the appropriation of the demand by the Hindu nationalist actors saw feminists increasingly disassociate themselves from it. Critiques of such demands posing as a women's rights issue by Madhu Kishwar (1998) and Flavia Agnes (1996) may serve as a point of reference. At this point the 'secularisation' project as a strategy for ensuring equal rights for all women from all communities became a debatable issue. While the Shahbano case experience was a point of split in the secular overarching women's movement in India, it is this and the adoption of the Muslim women's bill that represent the emergence of a

---

[4] Essentially the pronouncements and practices of the Prophet Muhammad which have been collected by Islamic theological scholars using systematic methods that look into several aspects including the content of the reportage, route of transmission and moral reputation of the reporter of the *hadith*. Hadith are considered important in understanding and interpreting the Quran for practices recommended by the Prophet to his faithful but also in the matters of Islamic jurisprudence.

Muslim women's rights movement in India. In an ethnographic study of Muslim women's organisations in India, Sylvia Vatuk (2008) mentions that organisations like Awaz-e-Niswan operated in a manner which was not differentiable from other feminist/women's organisations but the later activities of Muslim women's groups and the emergence of groups like Bhartiya Muslim Mahila Andolan (BMMA) showed a recognition of the aspirations of Muslim women for reform within Muslim Personal Law. BMMA takes a clear position that the women's movement has failed to address the needs of women from marginalised communities because of its historical domination by upper caste Hindu women, and that there is a need to create a separate movement led and dominated by Muslim women (Kirmani 2009). In BMMA's own literature[5] tracing the history of its formation, the movement articulates an aspiration of Muslim women to lead a movement for the rights of not only Muslim women but for the Indian Muslims as well.

> ...our experience particularly in Gujarat and many other situations of communal violence shows that secularism is the key foundation for working on women's issues and it should be upheld at all costs. We were shocked at the conspiracy of silence in Gujarat in which even women's groups participated even as Muslim women were brutally mass assaulted and burnt alive in broad daylight. Besides the Muslim women's exclusion cannot be fought in isolation without simultaneously addressing the exclusion of the Muslim community. We need a proactive participation of the entire Muslim community, the secular groups, the civil society in order to address Muslim women's rights. We feel that we need to take up the leadership of our issues ourselves even as we work closely with the mainstream women's movement and other excluded people's movements such as the dalit movement, the trade union movement, the adivasi people's movement, etc. We believe in a healthy constructive solidarity and collaboration with secular community even as Muslim women lead the struggle for their rights. *Jiski ladai uski agwayi*[6] is our motto (BMMA 2008, pp. 3–4).

Elora Shehabuddin (2011) identifies what she calls 'feminist imperialism' in western feminists' writings who present the 'change in the Muslim world as possible only with the intervention from the United

---

[5] Unpublished pamphlet dated September 2008, titled *Bhartiya Muslim Mahila Andolan: Journey So Far*.
[6] A popular Hindi slogan in movement groups (literally means 'Leadership to those who struggle') which gestures a protest to often seen trend of movements of groups being led by those who are seen as 'outsiders' to the group.

States—either by force through the violent eradication of oppressive Muslim men or the less dramatic support of 'moderate' Muslim groups and individuals' (ibid., p. 121). She alleges that western feminists are worried not so much about the actual lives of Muslim women but their own positioning as saviours, and that this is merely redirected racism. According to her, they ignore Muslim women's voices struggling for change within Muslim societies and in doing so rule out the possibility of change occurring from within these societies. Shehabuddin calls out the phenomenon of colonial narratives within the stories of Ayaan Hirsi Ali and Irshad Manji, who have been labelled as having 'escaped' the atrocities of Islam and Muslim men. She repudiates the insinuation within these narratives that they are representative of the lives of all Muslim women. It is to be noted that Hirsi Ali and Manji are not just 'victim survivors' but are celebrity authors who have written bestselling books like *Infidel* and *The Trouble with Islam,* respectively. Hirsi Ali (2006) has fiercely critiqued the adherents of Islamic feminism on their feminist credentials and their advocacy of multiculturalism. She argues that the cultural rights of communities frequently come into conflict with the civic rights of individuals and this has a devastating effect on the civic liberties of Muslim women. Hirsi Ali and other Islam detractors in the west like Manji, in turn, have been critiqued for being 'neo-orientalist' in their claim to have written the true and insiders' account of Islam and Islamic societies (Bayoumi 2010).

In the development of Islamic feminism, Nilufer Gole (1996) reports another important trend of women's participation in Islamist movements. While these women became activists in the public domain they stopped short of asking for full gender equality until many of them were disillusioned by the treatment meted out to them by their male Islamist colleagues. Scholar-activists identified as working and writing under the rubric of 'Islamic Feminism' are also debating the label themselves. Asma Barlas (2006) feels that for Muslim women, the Quran is an adequate resource to challenge patriarchal traditions within Muslim societies. She asserts that taking recourse to 'feminism' is unnecessary and she resists the use of the term 'Islamic feminist' to describe herself. Others such as Amina Wadud do not resist the term but do not actively use it either to describe themselves. They accept the use of the term for strategic descriptive and analytical purposes and see it as a position that allows space to include their particularity (Kynsilehto 2002). In my opinion the rejection of the term 'feminism' by Barlas and indeed by many other scholars who have been called Islamic feminists is more because they perceive an orientalist hostility or patronisation folded within western 'feminism'. The rejection is easily responded to by recognising that for Muslim women feminists it is possible to offer resistance to patriarchal norms and practices as an extension to their faith. This is evident in the example of Pakistani teenage Nobel Laureate Malala Yousafzai who resisted using the term 'feminist' to describe herself or her work initially but has recently decided to call herself a feminist. Rafia Zakaria (2013) contrasts Yousafzai's embracing of her Muslim identity and struggle for emancipation of her community and region with the 'renunciation narrative' of Hirsi Ali. Yousafzai fiercely embraced her Muslim identity and contested the Taliban allegation that she and her ilk were not Muslims for wanting education and equality. Margot Badran (2008b) highlights the fact that while Barlas might continue to resist being called an Islamic feminist, her work is more radical than that of secular feminists in Muslim societies who call for full equality of genders in the public sphere but settle for 'gender complementarity' in the private sphere and within the family. Badran credits Barlas (2002) for actually showing convincingly in her readings of the Quran that patriarchy in both public and private spheres is un-Islamic. In another theological endeavour Fatima Mernissi (1991) had challenged the rigid closure of the possibility of gender equality by falsifying fabricated *Hadith*. Wudud (1992) also explicitly positioned her own work within the ambit of *Tafsir*.[7]

Moghadam (2002) accepts the importance of feminist theology and its implications for reform from within but also appeals for a dialogue with modern ideas of enlightenment when looking for resources for change. In particular, she highlights the left influence on the feminist movement in Iran and advocates learning from the Marxist-Feminist perspective. She concludes that, '...if feminism has always been contested, if feminists should be defined by their praxis rather than by a strict ideology, and if a feminist politics is shaped by its specific historical, political, and cultural contexts, then it should be possible to identify Islamic feminism as one feminism among many' (ibid., p. 1165). In further exploration of 'neo-orientalism', we turn to US scholar Francis Fukuyama who wrote

---

[7] *Tafsir* literally means 'to explain' or exegesis of the Quran. It involves looking at the historical context of the revelation, the syntax of sentences, meaning of words as they were used especially in Arabic poetry, Hadith, and other Quranic verses. Tafsir is considered to be an exact science and is said to be prohibited when undertaken solely from the point of view of the commentator without knowledge, although it is widely accepted that the most basic principle of undertaking tafsir is to be motivated by the ultimate Islamic goal of goodness and happiness in life and hereafter.

an article called 'End of History' (1989). He followed it up with a book (1992) following the same argument which was that, 'The triumph of the West, of the Western idea, is evident first of all in the total exhaustion of viable systematic alternatives to Western liberalism.... What we may be witnessing is not just the end of the Cold War, or the passing of a particular period of post-war history, but the end of history as such: that is, the end point of mankind's ideological evolution and the universalisation of Western liberal democracy as the final form of human government' (Fukuyama 1989, p. 162). Fukuyama asserted that only Islam has proposed a political alternative to both liberalism and communism in form of its 'theocratic state', which according to him, is an alternative that holds an appeal only to Muslims. He also spoke of the paucity of viable economic alternatives to capitalism. He claimed that success of some far-eastern economies may be partially ascribed to their non-western cultural values related to work and savings, etc., but that Islam again is the only real challenger to western capitalism because it specifically prohibits certain kinds of economic behaviours and instils 'deeply ingrained moral qualities' (ibid., 1989, p. 5).

Fukuyama's phobic positioning of Islam as a sole challenger of western liberalism could even be well taken if it were to stop at economic and cultural hegemony. But western Islamophobia also has a militaristic and geopolitical content. Around the same time when Fukuyama was sanctifying western liberal democracy and liberal capitalism, another American scholar with expertise in West Asia, Bernard Lewis (1990) wrote an article titled *The Roots of Muslim Rage*. The article depicted Muslims as a threat to the more 'superior' western world. The ideas expressed in the article were already gathering immense favour in US foreign policy and before long Samuel Huntington further formulated these ideas in his article titled the *Clash of Civilisations* (1993) followed with a book with the same title (1996). These ideas not only essentialised 'Muslims' as a homogenous entity but strangely conflated the concept of civilisation with religion. Huntington divided the entire world into several 'civilisations', essentially along the majoritarian identities of a particular region. So Muslims were seen as a homogenous group even when they were in countries in disparate geographical regions. Countries like Bangladesh which have a Muslim majority population were included but India where the largest population of Muslims live in absolute numbers was excluded from the 'Muslim civilisation'. India was labelled a Hindu country in the 'Eastern civilisation'. Similarly, states where whites and Christians are in a majority were all clustered in a 'Western civilisation'. There is so much theoretical incongruity in the conception of 'civilisations' by Huntington that it is difficult not to think that the measure of attraction of this conception is the measure of prejudice against non-western 'civilisations' generally, and particularly against Muslims and Arabs. Huntington prophesied that the battle lines of the future will be drawn along the 'fault lines between civilisations'. This was essentially the framework which lent intellectual legitimacy to the Bush administration and its foreign policy premised later on the 'war on terror' (Dodds 2007).

There have of course been numerous nuanced academic protestations. Amartya Sen (2007) challenged the assertion that diversity and democracy are western values. Edward Said reacted to Huntington sharply, calling his conception nothing but 'imagined geography' in an article titled *Clash of Ignorance* (2001). Said also called Huntington '…dead wrong on every point he makes'. He went on to add,

> No culture or civilisation exists by itself. None is made up of things like individuality and enlightenment that are completely exclusive to it, and none exists without the basic human attributes of community, love, value for life, and all the others. Even Arabs have those things in their culture. To suggest otherwise, as he does, is the purist, invidious racism of the same stripe, as people who used to argue that Africans have naturally inferior brains or that Asians are really born for servitude, or that Europeans are a naturally superior race. This is a sort of parody of Hitlerian science directed uniquely today against Arabs and Muslims (Said 2004, p. 293).

The question that bears asking is why there has been so much hostility against Muslims and Arabs. Are the reasons merely rooted in the historical quibble between the three Semitic religions—Judaism, Christianity and Islam? Commentators do point towards something more contemporary in these hostilities. In his discussion on resistance to globalisation, Frederic Jameson (2000) agrees with Fukuyama in that Islam and, various anti-western-imperialist nationalisms in the third world are the only two forces to offer any resistance to the advent of globalisation, but he points to the 'weakness' of the former's position and the danger in the strengthening of the latter. Interestingly though, on the matter of nationalistic impulses in opposition to globalisation, Jameson opines that communalism in India is only 'Hindu identity politics' and distinguishes it from Indian nationalism. His view on the weakness of Islam as a serious challenger to globalisation lies in the fact that the resisting factions within Muslims are those that are characterised as 'fundamentalist' and, thus, lack universal appeal. Indeed, it is against this background that western Islamophobia must be seen—a manifestation of the process of responding to the next 'enemy' of the capitalist 'west' after the disintegration of communist USSR.

It goes without saying that the discussion that I have presented in a nutshell above took place before 9/11. It is a fact that if Muslim factions or states that challenged western hegemony lacked universal appeal before 9/11, after the event, they also became enemies fit to be abhorred and even annihilated. Huntington's prophecy in the *Clash of Civilisations* became in effect a self-fulfilling one. The contours of militarised western Islamophobia paid lip service to the incidental 'collateral' damage but went on to devastate many parts of the Arab-Islamic world in the guise of striving to establish US-styled 'liberal democracies' in Afghanistan and Iraq while forcing or coercing others in the region to bow down to their neo-imperialist designs. There were terrible fallouts of this in the streets-turned-battlefields of various parts of West Asia but equally debilitating was the phobic, phantasmagoric identity foisted upon Muslims living in different societies and countries across the world (Runnymede Trust 1997; Allen 2010). Thus, 'Orientalism' took a new turn and 'Global Islamophobia' was born.

This also marked a turning point in research interests in Muslims lives, perspectives and attitudes. In Europe, for example, there are studies conducted to calculate a close estimate of the Muslim population, and studies that investigate Muslim immigrants, Muslim citizens of colonial origins and native Muslim converts (Buijs & Rath 2001). There are also a plethora of academic and journalistic writings on the experience of being Muslim in different western countries (Saggar 2009; Pargeter 2006; Schebley & McCauley 2005; Abbas 2007). For the most part these works do express the angst of discrimination and the environment of suspicion and misrepresentation but in most cases these representations mostly fall in the trap of essentialised phobic identities themselves. The questions framed, the behaviours observed, the values probed are all from within the dominant discourses which are, of course, orientalist. The only difference is that from the exotic, erotic, backward Muslim the representations have moved to the suspect, disloyal, fanatic Muslim who, if he is not a terrorist himself, must then be a sympathiser.

With the flooding of media and academia with this kind of literature there have also been incantations from the establishment that 'good Muslims' needed to be distinguished from 'bad Muslims'. In his influential book *Good Muslims, Bad Muslims*, Mehmood Mamdani (2005) analyses this binary. Mamdani asserts that this binary fails to regard that historically Islamic societies and western societies have been in interaction and dispute with one another, and that Islamist militancy cannot be considered a direct and 'natural' product of Islam. Mamdani objects to the formulation of 'terrorism' as a premodern reaction to a progressive modern western civilisation. He contends that terrorism is a 'modern ensemble at the service of a modern project'. Another interesting thing about this binary is that it is not a binary at all because its one pole, the 'bad Muslim' is defined in such terms that essentialise all Muslims as bad. Mamdani further explores how Muslim cultures are not only represented as homogenous monoliths but as premodern, and Muslims as people who do not live and create culture but cast in an archaic-unchanging culture which they can only conform to.

The main problem with the neo-orientalist representations of Indian Muslim women is not that they are entirely false but that these make no attempt to engage with or examine the historical processes that produced the situations. This huge gap in engagement reduces the Muslim men and Muslim women's identity and snatches away from them their ability to represent their own issues in any alternative way. It is the nature and processes of these academic representations too that Muslim communities are kept back in a subaltern status.

Accordingly, while *any woman* may be extended to the epistemic position of representing *all women*, in the final analysis, The Feminist Standpoint in India is that of the upper class, upper caste, Hindu academic. Muslim women and Dalit women 'listening' to the mainstream feminist discourses find that they have already been spoken for. Dalit women have begun to question this but have not been very successful in getting the mainstream to engage with them. They have actually been scoffed at and branded intolerant and irrational. Muslim Women have not dared to make any major moves in this matter. This is reminiscent of white women accruing benefits from their privileges in the racist structure in the US and their habit of not noticing these privileges as such (McIntosh 2008). Works exploring or even mentioning the privileges that women from a certain caste and community enjoy without even noticing them are few and far between. Muslim women in India are burdened with a false universalism of India's mainstream women's movement and by extension the global feminist movement. It cannot be overstated that the communal question cannot be separated from Muslim women's question in India and the fact of global Islamophobia has to be factored in as well.

2
Representation and 'Listening'

Noorjahan is an activist who lives and works in Ahmedabad, Gujarat. She not only lived through the 2002 anti-Muslim pogrom but has stood witness to it every day of her life since then. In the study workshop which she helped us organise, I noticed that every time a girl said that she wants to study, Noorjahan's eyes brimmed with tears. After the workshop was over Noorjahan took me to see the 'border' areas. These walled-in localities where Muslims of Ahmedabad huddle together are bereft of any welfare, any civic amenity. Parents are too scared to send their children to school. In a low voice she tells me about the *dhamaal*.[1] She tells me her four-year-old daughter lives in an orphanage in Delhi. It has been over a year and half that Noorjahan sent her away so she could dedicate more of her own time working with Muslims in Ahmedabad. I think of my own three and a half year old daughter at home in Delhi and tears well up in my eyes, too. If I was carrying a questionnaire I would be hard-pressed to decide which box to tick.

Social researchers have long been itemising social realities in questionnaires—responses are coded, counted and correlated, and

---

[1] 'Dhamaal' literally, means 'chaos'. As in a common usage in Gujarat since 2002 February, here it refers to an anti-Muslim Pogrom was unleashed by Hindu Nationalist groups at various places in the province of Gujarat. Ahmedabad was the worst affected city but Muslim families and businesses were attacked in many other urban and rural settlements across Gujarat. Muslims were brutally killed by murderous and organised mobs in an insane, frenzied death ritual under the protective gaze of the police for over a week. Thousands of families were driven out of their houses to 'refugee' camps and later to cramped Muslim ghettos. The surviving victims did not receive any relief or compensation from the state government. Gujarat chief minister Narendra Modi's BJP (Bharatiya Janata Party, a part of the Hindu nationalist group) government, was alleged to be complicit to the violence. Modi is on record rationalising the pogrom as a 'spontaneous' reaction to the Godhra incident. On 27 February 2002 a group of 'karsevaks' returning from the disputed site of the demolished Babri Masjid in Ayodhya were burnt alive in the train compartment they were travelling in just a few hundred metres from Godhra Railway station near a Muslim ghetto. The train was alleged to have been set on fire by Muslim mobs in a pre-planned move. The charred remains of the activists were taken out in processions while still in the custody of the state administration. In the ensuing violence thousands of Muslims were killed and bodies burned to destroy evidence. Women were also subjected to brutal and sexualised violence.

relationships are established. People are quizzed on the number of children they have, whether they prefer eating rice or wheat, their dietary pattern is shown to be influenced by income data and birth, and fertility projections are made. Statistics, it is often argued, present stark social realities in a shockingly straightforward way: 'Less than 17% of Muslim girls finish eight years of schooling and less than 10% complete higher secondary education. Muslim female graduates constitute less than 1% of all female graduates' (Hasan & Menon 2004). Development plans and policies are borne out of these numbers depicting needs, predilections and aversions of people. But can realities be really encapsulated in numbers? Often when the recorder is switched off, and forms are put back into the bags (and if the researcher still does not leave to rush to their hotel or airports and railway stations to leave towns), people show another side of their lives to the researcher.

Thus, in this chapter I strive to make a case for the relevance of using narrative methods for researching Muslim women to draw more attention to the politics of representation. I contend, learning from Gayatri Spivak, that the much discussed 'lack of voice' among Muslim women in research is only the 'lack of will to listen' among researchers. When the effort is indeed made to listen to Muslim women's voices that have been raised in the course of a research enquiry, the researcher opens out an avenue to understand the cultural context with which women's speech had to negotiate and in which it was created. My attempt here is to highlight the relevance of narrative strategies and the possibility of fashioning an empowered 'self' through self-representation/ articulation.

The positivist and empiricist research paradigms that inspire an 'objective', 'detached' academic demand that intuition, feelings, etc., not be allowed to 'adulterate' the research process and stress for a 'scientific' approach. Underlying this demand is the assertion that anything 'scientific' is completely irrefutable. These studies aim to establish (causal?) relationships and/or define generalised laws to be used to make prediction. Often the research process is trusted with the responsibility of discovering and presenting 'facts' as 'truths'. This envisaging of research as unearthing a 'social reality' that exists independent of the discoverer takes its evidence from the *existence of things*. It is, therefore, prone to becoming a view from *within the existing order of things*. Research is often reduced only to the research findings that exist independent of the process, while the process through which the phenomenon being studied came to exist is not afforded any attention. Add to this the fact that the research process is also made to appear impregnable and inaccessible instead of revealing the power dynamics of the persons participating in research.

'Discoveries' made empirically, relying only on sensory experiences, often preclude the social content of the phenomenon being studied. Thus, it is easy to see why Marx thought that empiricism confirms the status quo because it ignores that behind the so-called 'facts' there is any history, ideology and the relationships which produced these 'facts'. Taking recourse to Marxist vocabulary, this tendency of reducing research to a commodity and concealing its real mechanisms may be seen as a tendency to 'fetishise research'. This is not to suggest that all experience is only a result of *reification* in thought which Peter Berger labels a kind of forgetfulness 'as if they (social phenomenon) were something else than human products—such as facts of nature, results of cosmic laws, or manifestations of divine will' (Berger & Luckmann 1966, p. 89). However, empiricism does stress that there is no rationale in believing any description (theoretical) of a reality that cannot be observed. Just as Althusser criticised empiricism for assuming that what is being observed through sensory experience is the thing itself (Resch 1992). Clearly then, not all processes can be studied empirically.

An oft-repeated argument for quantitative research is that it lends itself easily to the aim of advocating policy changes. It is often argued in activist groups and non-governmental organisations that we need to present 'hard facts' to policy-makers. While it may appear that the policy-makers are still relying largely upon quantitative work for shaping their perception of social realities and required interventions, this view is actually a part of the oversimplified discourse marred by stereotypes that blocks out voices of the marginalised in research. Many activists and organisations advocating for/on behalf of various population groups often do not realise that stories are the life-blood of the policy formulation process. Technocrats, bureaucrats, legislators, lobbyists—all those who influence processes of policy formulation are in turn influenced by (dominant) narratives first and seek (usually successfully) to find statistical data supporting their ideological positions. A specific genre of research termed narrative policy analysis in US has in fact shown that, '... because of their simplicity and transparency, narratives can crystallize and mobilize public opinion, and force an issue to the top of the political agenda' (Hyman 2000, p. 1149). In failing to record the voices of the marginalised, research attempting to influence policy decisions ends up (even if inadvertently) resorting to messages from dominant discourses and negating an important factor creating unjust conditions.

In a stark illustration of this, in their study of Muslim women in India, Zoya Hasan and Ritu Menon (2006) surveyed 9,541 Muslim women across 40 districts of 12 states. In this pioneering work Hasan and Menon debunked the commonly and conveniently held myth that Muslim women are in an abysmal state only because of their personal law and, by logical extension, because they profess a particular faith, i.e., Islam. The study problematised this view and brought into picture the 'disadvantage, discrimination, and disempowerment experienced [by Muslim women] at specific and particular intersection of class, caste, gender and community' (2006, p. 3) Yet, in a work full of tables, pie charts, bar graphs there was no space for quoting even one of these women on any aspect of her life under study. In fact, the questionnaire made available in the annexure has no space for the women to 'speak' and perhaps, the researcher dealing with the pressure of filling his/her quota of the overstretched and belaboured tool would have had no time to 'listen'.

A review of literature on women in Islamic societies points to this

> Type (of monograph) often produced by researchers in South Asia... a statistics-laden description.... In addition to relying on government statistics at various levels of generality, the researcher questions a sample of respondents for a detailed quantitative *breakdown on numerous aspects of life*, e.g., marital status (how many currently married, how many widowed), employment status (how many in what types of work), diseases, delivery practices, household expenditures, and decision-making in the household (Offenhauer 2005, p. 25) (emphasis added).

While debates on the merits and shortcomings of quantitative and qualitative research methods are not new, the play of power in research especially involving women and minorities has also been clearly and repeatedly pointed out by feminist researchers. Notions of objectivity in research which frown upon emotions, subjectivity and intuition are not just reductionist or positivist in nature but also, undoubtedly, patriarchal. Feminist research methodologies do not negate lived experiences of people. They highlight the fact that oppressed people weave, carry and share unheard narratives that have been rendered silent by androcentric assumptions of statistical validity and reliability in social science (Olesen 1994). Questions regarding and issues involved in the 'objectivity' of the researcher and her/his positionality are increasingly being recognised. This discussion exerts itself to elucidate methodological issues that are often, and erroneously, scoffed at in India as being merely those of research ethics.

Representations of oppressed communities are replicated in quantitative research like canned recipes that are routinely opened and served, never really varying in taste and texture as a freshly prepared meal would. This is not just a matter of ethics; all the ingredients in the can may be perfectly fine and free of adulteration but the nutritional and aesthetic values behind a ready, canned meal are circumspect. When we analyse social conditions from the way they appear in personal experiences of various members of the group it is only then that we *truly understand*. The Weberian notion of *Verstehen* may be employed here to stress that human manner or method of 'being in this world' is not so much through experiencing and feeling but through interpreting and 'understanding' (*verstehen*). In Weber's (1993) conception a person seeking to understand a reality is already situated in a context and arrives into the situation because of her/his prior understanding. So for a social researcher with this approach, the main task is to 'comprehend' rather than to 'explain'. Verstehen, as Weber argued, is not an opposite of the scientific, objective method of knowing but actually includes in it all the other ways of knowing employed by humans. In research processes, Gadamer explicitly refers to *verstehen* as the understanding which may be achieved as a result of allowing those who are 'alienated by the character of being distantiated by cultural or historical research to speak again' (cf Flynn 2006, p. 119).

Research focused on gender, and racial communities have beaconed methodological paradigms which are better in tune with the lived realities of ethnic/racial or other minorities. In the experience of this study, methods that are close to real-life situations and involve reflecting, conversing, sharing (projective expression, semi-structured interviews, group discussions, transect walks, and narrative writings) encouraged articulation of narratives and life-histories in ways which are not alien to oppressed communities. The researchers and the research both exercise some amount of control (or lack of it) to shape and be influenced by the research process. The amount of power to shape and the nature of influence on each are a function of positionality and the identities of the researcher that come into play during the research process.

Placing emphasis on the subjective approach and using narrative methods is also to highlight the phenomenon that identity and self are never constant and unchanging; they are rather always in the process of 'becoming', being shaped by personal *as well as* collective experiences. Personal narratives are not merely individual productions; they are fashioned by social, cultural, and historical conventions. By extension, formation and existence of a 'self' is bound with its articulation. It is in speaking of a 'self' that we become it. This is the reason why in most cultures, historically, autobiographical articulation has been available only to the powerful.

In a research situation, narratives also get affected by the relationship between the narrator and the interlocutor (researcher). Experiences in this study indicate the possibility that the telling of life-stories may be a method for empowerment, as the articulation made it possible for the raconteur to express a new 'self' and desires that are otherwise considered untellable.

Narrative methods allow for the voices of the researched to be heard on par with those of the researchers. Consequently, both, the researcher and the researched, can gain rare insights into the motivations, struggles and realities that guide and contour the narrative trajectories. The contents of personal narratives are *not* data to be reduced to content-analysis. Counting the number of times an expression is repeated serves little purpose. Narrative texts are subjected to discourse analysis which involves reading and re-reading the text, so that any patterns of symbolic meaning behind expressions used may emerge. Looking for some kind of intrinsic array or order in mostly unconscious associations of words with words and/or actions of individuals can throw up important comments on social conditions that are relatively independent of these individual actors (Goffman 1983).

While positivist research uses people as guinea pigs to generate an 'objective understanding' of social phenomenon, narratives heal as they explore and bring to the fore feelings and emotions that the narrator may not have articulated even to herself prior to the research experience. Personal/autobiographical narratives can be 'a source of consolation (and)… a way of recovering what is lost' (Eagleton 2008, p. 161) and have a transformative power that frees people to imagine new stories for themselves and move on to more productive lives (Abels & Abels 2001).

In an exercise in this study the participants were asked to articulate their life-story using the metaphor of a river marking out the major events in the journey. The metaphor was provided for its familiarity in most cultures especially popular culture. The participants were asked to imagine their own life in the flow of a river touched and shaped by and impacting upon the two banks of private family life and social events. They took some time to think of and meditate over which events they wanted to write about or depict by drawing. These were then shared in the group by them in as much detail as they felt comfortable with. At the workshop in Mumbai's Mumbra, most girls were college-going and used to writing, but still they sat with their sheaf of paper and markers for a long time unable to write. Mehreen said, 'I cannot remember any incidents.' Another girl Shaheen said, 'I can't imagine what to write, how to start and from where to start.' She later said she was worried that if she started writing she would break down. Muskan (field researcher) told her to just start writing and not stop herself from feeling any emotions. 'If you feel like crying, do not stop yourself.'

It was a hot day and there was no electricity supply for at least two hours during the workshop but the girls did not remove their *burqas* despite repeated requests. Even their teacher who had helped the BMMA activist organise the workshop requested them to take the *burqas* off but they refused. For a while they did not even remove their *naqab*. When asked they said, *'Burqa nikalenge to uljhan hogi'* (we will feel uncomfortable if we remove *burqa*). When the girls began writing they wrote a lot but not many wanted to share what they had written with the group. 'What if someone said something?' Then gradually, they relaxed and began sharing.

> The *burqa* has been made infamous.... We are termed terrorists.... We are not allowed to enter a shop with the *burqa* on; if we enter a non-muslim's shop the shopkeepers are rude to us. Even banks do not allow us to wear the *burqa* inside. They fear that terrorists will attack them in the guise of a *burqa*. After the terrorist attack and train bomb blasts parents are scared to send us to far-off places for studies or classes. After Ishrat Jahan's encounter too the parents are scared... Mumbra is made infamous by terming it a den of terrorists. It is also called *chota* (little) Pakistan.... My parents keep saying, 'Mumbra *ka mahaul bahut kharab hai, is liye kisi se baat nahi karna'* (Do not talk to anyone because the environment in Mumbra is terrible).

Later, in the focused group discussion the girls become very animated talking of the status of Muslim women.

> The Muslim woman is under a lot of pressure, she does not have her full rights.... Other community people say that Muslim women are oppressed which creates some more pressure.... If a Muslim does something wrong it becomes front page news but when a non-Muslim does it, it is reported on the last page.... Muslim girls are not allowed to take up employment, after marriage they have to take permission from their husbands to work. They are also made to wear *burqas* after marriage which is wrong.... The girls do not get good jobs, the parents do not send them for good courses, they are not allowed to travel far for studies or jobs... *ladkiya kuch achcha*

karein to bura aur bura kare to bhi bura (If the girls do something good that is also considered bad and if they do something bad then that too is of course bad).

In another exercise, they share about their dreams and aspirations and many say that while writing about their life-events they felt as if *'hamare jazboon ko zubaan mil gayi. Man halka ho gaya, jaise koi bojh uth gaya ho'* (our feelings have got expression, the heart feels light; as if a big burden has been lifted). At the end of the day when Muskan asked them whether they will be able to achieve their dreams, all of them very loudly and confidently said, *'Insha Allah!'* (God Willing!).

The workshop in Jaipur, Rajasthan was full of similar experiences. Articulating these narratives, being listened to and listening to somewhat similar and somewhat different experiences of others, they confirmed each other's and their own existence. Later Nishat *Aapa*[2] who facilitated the workshop told me that her organisation had been working in the Idgah area for many years providing aid and counselling to Muslim women but had never been successful in getting adolescents and young girls to join their activities despite conscious effort. In a turn around after the workshop, the girls began visiting Nishat *Aapa*'s office on their own, wishing to get together and talk.

In other exercises the girls were similarly provided with projective techniques and spaces for open discussions to articulate their experiences and aspirations. The research experience became for the participants an experience in validation. Through the day their contributions were consciously facilitated by building an atmosphere of trust and support through exercises and discussions. The organisers of the workshops sought to include young women who volunteered to participate. Some young women wished to participate but could not come to the workshop due to the distance, or the date not being convenient for them, or because they had not been given permission by their guardians. They were interviewed at home using open-ended questions that encouraged in-depth, narrative answers. However, meeting the participants together in the workshops was emphasised because of the implications for analysis and insights that they could accrue during group and collaborative processes. The potential of an assembly of individuals in a democratic learning space lies in their engagement with each other utilising methods that stimulate dialogical questioning and critical reflection. It is

---

[2] Honorific for elder sister.

imperative that we enquire at this juncture if the poor and the marginalised are researched because research has the potential of being a liberatory moment for them or only because they are eminently and easily 'researchable'. It is easy to knock at the doors of poor people's houses and ask for answers to sometimes absurd, sometimes obvious questions that will add to some knowledge bank. While, drawing from Paulo Friere's deliberation on the pedagogy of the oppressed, research as praxis calls for 'its consequences [to] become the object of critical reflection.... To achieve this praxis, however, it is necessary to trust in the oppressed and in their ability to reason' (Friere 1993, p. 48).

Muslim women hushed quiet by communal violence, poverty, domestic violence, illiteracy, lack of economically viable skills, etc., are rendered further 'voiceless' by those who study them. Researching Muslim girls' education, Zoya Hasan and Ritu Menon (2005) wrote their accounts of five cities based on interviews with some schoolteachers and principals. The teachers and educational administrators described the problems they faced, breaking them down to factors like 'reality of having to deal with inadequate infrastructure and teaching staff; constraints on expansion which prevent them from meeting the demand for education; poor resources, material and human; financial, social and gender considerations which inhibit girls' schooling and most importantly, the positive changes that have occurred over the past couple of decades' (2005, p. 37). In the last chapter, the authors, dissecting these interviews in light of government data, talk about the gap between state policy and practice. Somehow, in doing all this they miss interviewing even a single Muslim schoolgirl or dropout, probably not trusting in the subjects' ability to say anything of value in a work of research with has their interests at its centre of inquiry.

Friere (1993, p. 49) stresses that, 'When people are already dehumanized, due to the oppression they suffer, the process of their liberation must not employ the methods of dehumanization.' The method that Friere proposes is dialogue. Most research looks at outcomes (findings or conclusions) of the research and disregards the impact of the experience during the research process itself. There is no reason why *concientização*, a process that brings to the oppressed the conviction to struggle for her own liberation, cannot be one of the objectives of research. Narrative methods allow research this space.

In the present study, narrative methods have been used to emphasise the importance of participatory dialogue in research and assume that this will permit the development of mutual collaboration for change as well as co-creation of knowledge. Thus, narrative methods can be termed *transformatory* methods for their role in turning an enquiry into an element of personal and social change. The narrative research process can bring about a realisation in its participants that has the potential to trigger and catalyse the process of change in them. At the end of a narrative research, not only have the participants partnered in the creation of clearer knowledge about their social realities but also actively altered it in some way. Whereas, *Confirmatory* (positivist!) methods curtail dialogue—the researched is reduced to a repository of fragmented information about her own life-situations and targeted by a string of questions by the researcher. Any cooperation which occurs, does so within a hierarchical context and no attempt is made to challenge the status quo within the process. For this reason the conclusions drawn at the end of a confirmatory study would hardly ever bring any new realisations or revelation to the researched community themselves. The 'findings' of the Sachar Committee report or the MWS hardly surprised or held anything new for anyone in the Muslim community, including young Muslim women. In fact, both the studies were hailed as having validated what the entire Muslim community, Muslim women and those who work with them 'had been saying all along'. These studies sought out to describe realities of Muslims and create an alternative discourse but did not 'listen' to them in the process, did not include their 'voice' in the report and only 'confirmed' a status quo in their findings.

At the Ahmedabad workshop, the girls were not able to speak for the most part. There were long intervals when there was complete silence in the group. When I told them to take a break they sat silently, not even chatting with their friends. Blank faces stared back at me. When I met their gaze and smiled, they averted their eyes. But they wrote. After a while, 17-year-old Majida visibly braced herself and nodded to me to indicate that she would share. '2002 affected our families badly and I was taken out of school after that. I was told that I will ruin family prestige if I go out. I was made to drop out of school.' At this she broke down and wept. The others looked noticeably uncomfortable. Then Shaheen began to speak, 'I wanted to study and contribute something for social good by becoming a social worker but I couldn't study because there are no good schools in the Muslim locality. So my goal remains unattained now. They don't teach Muslim girls. There are issues in our stepping out of home. Therefore, Hindu girls get better jobs and we don't.' Even before Shaheen finished speaking, many other girls were weeping. We had to discontinue the discussion.

Later Noorjahan told me that even the girls from the same localities do not meet each other. They hardly ever go out of the house for any purpose. In the aftermath of the 2002 pogrom, a terrified and badly scarred community, destitute families, and frightened parents placed severe limits on women, especially young women, in a desperate, pathetic and counterproductive attempt to 'protect' them (their honour?). The restraint on the mobility of these girls was so severely limiting, Noorjahan told me, that it was a difficult task to escort them to workshop venues as they did not even know how to cross the road. The workshops were able to provide a space to girls in most cities (which were part of the study) to articulate their feelings and perhaps even arrive at some point of breakthrough for themselves, but the more deeply scathed were not able to reach that threshold as easily. During discussions in smaller groups and in interviews in Ahmedabad and Sabarkantha, they talked. But even here they wept more than they spoke.

When I began the study I went ready to hear narratives. The breaking down and weeping did not appear in my schema as 'narratives'. But the intensity of grief expressed during the research process forced me to take a fresh look at the term 'articulation'. Was it not natural that tears would form a part of the vocabulary of grief? Any process that sought out to facilitate the expression of self would need to recognise the language of the narratives of an injured psyche. The grief over personal loss felt by the victims of communal violence may be private but they also share a collective memory of a public tragedy. Burk (2003) in his work on public spaces originating as a symbol of collective voice of women against violence in the1990s in Vancouver explored the importance of expressing private grief by disempowered communities in the public spaces in imaginative, discursive as in physical domains. In this light perhaps, we could see the crying as part of the narrative encounters between the participants of the study and this research as a site for public expression, sharing and possibly lessening of private grief. If I were forced to name the single-most important aspect of personal learning from the experience of leading this study and writing this manuscript, it would be that to the discerning researcher *crying and silence are also speech acts*. Their production occurs when the participants have been through tragic experiences that must not be articulated for selfpreservation. The actual threat or perception of threat from the oppressors may be consciously felt as a source of fear but at the subconscious level the ferocity of atrocities and the levels of cruelty experienced by people triggers a defence mechanism which weakens their will or the need to articulate it. I am reminded of a philosophical problem conceived by Jean-Francois Lyotard, *differend*. Differend is an instance of injustice in which redressal requires that the oppressed represent their position in the manner and form which is actually excluded by the very act of injustice that they are seeking redressal for. Lyotard relates this with the example of a holocaust sceptic who insists that he would believe that the extermination in Nazi camps took place only if the one who was exterminated testifies it (Malpas 2002). A Differend requires a frightfully totalised instance from which there is no escape because in it the terms and conditions for dispensation of justice are set by the oppressor and the victim's true testimony cannot be formulated within the boundaries of the conditions so defined. If we take away the totalising omnipotent oppressor and the denial of any other avenues of justice but the oppressor, if we also take away that 'speaking' of the experience of injustice is not always a testimony aimed at dispensation of justice from powers that be, then, we can learn from this neat little philosophical formulation.

We know from various experiences in history that whether justice is delivered is not the prime motivation for victims of atrocities to testify. Holocaust survivors and families of victims, those impacted by the violence of apartheid, victims of the Partition in South Asia and victims of the nuclear strike on Japan and other far too many examples of pogroms and genocides, know that there could hardly be any 'justice' for them but this does not bear any impact on their need to bear witness and testify. The human need to 'speak' and craving for other people to know what they have gone through is paramount. It is in this sense that even tears and silences are testimonies if the witnesses can listen and attempt to understand.

Representation as Speaking *and* Listening

In her seminal article 'Can the Subaltern Speak?' Gayatri Spivak (1998) maintains that the position of subalternity has built into its definition, a *political inability* to speak. This is not so much to do with the capacity to 'speak' *per se* but the dominant system's unwillingness to 'hear'. In an interview clarifying her position, Spivak points out that in Gramsci's original and covert usage of the term 'subaltern', it signified 'proletarian', whose voice could not be heard, being structurally written out of the capitalist bourgeois narrative. She further says that in post-colonial terms,

> ...subaltern is (not) just a classy word for oppressed, for Other, for somebody who's not getting a piece of the pie... everything that has limited or no access to the cultural imperialism is subaltern... a space of difference. Now who would say that's just the oppressed? The working class is oppressed. It is not subaltern (de Kock, 1992 pp. 45–46).

In Spivak's usage, which is of pivotal importance to this work, 'subaltern' is not another synonym for 'marginalised'. When she says they 'cannot speak' she means that in the space of difference that the subaltern occupies no one is responsible to listen and respond.

For the analysis in the present work, the very nature of Muslim women's subalternity hinges on their voices being subsumed by hegemonic narratives and thus, Muslim women cannot 'speak'. Essential to this understanding of 'speaking' is the presence of a 'listener'. Often listeners (researchers) do not recognise a self-representation because it does not fit their expectations and their methodological requirements. This is due partly to the fact that the moment the act of 'speaking' has been committed (with the necessary corollary of 'listening') casting-off her subalternity becomes possible for the narrator. The positionality of the 'listener'-researcher is another important factor in the contents of the representation process. The listener's identity influences the extent to which she has access to the meaning behind the 'self-representation' of the narrator. Herbert Gans (1997) emphasises that the researcher and their identity should not be left out of the analysis. A heightened sensitivity of the researcher's position on the gender, ethnicity, class, caste continuum and how it influences the representation can actually turn out to be the strength of a research endeavour. Hegemonic representations may not be completely pervasive and may be available to the people. Thus, this reflexivity is the only way in which persistent power imbalances that prevail in the society can be prevented from being replicated within the research experience of the participants. Further, personal narratives as self-representation may be the only ones able to subvert/challenge its force. This is finally the reason why Muslim women's true representation by any delegated or self-appointed advocates is nearly impossible. Thus, as Spivak suggests, instead of the academicians and researchers trying to give voice to the subaltern, the attempt needs to be to 'clear the space' to allow them to speak.

Philosophical moorings of this work lie in the Critical Theory's call outlined by one of its founders Max Horkhiemer (1831) for research that has emancipatory aims. For this purpose it must not only raise the issue of physical violence, dominance and deprivation but also pay attention to how ideology and consciousness play a role in maintaining dominance within social, political, economic and cultural processes. Methodologically, critical theory requires a recognition of how these structural processes are embedded within everyday experiences. Critical theory provides necessary tools to overcome the dilemma of choosing between macro and micro, or little and grand narratives. It allows for building 'macroexplanations' over 'microfoundations' (Little 1986, p. 127). Drawing from it, in this work, I have attempted to demarcate stable and continuing structures through which people experience their everyday.

Philosophical works such as *Being and Time* (Heidegger, 1962) and *Phenomenology of Perception* (Merleau-Ponty 1945, 1962) emphasised perception and 'being-in-the-world' in what is known as the phenomenological framework. This gives precedence to the practical, bodily experience understood through tasks and actions, over any theoretical or philosophical view of reality (Tilley 1994). Tilley further opines that this approach turned its attention towards how interaction with landscapes, monuments and such other material 'things' shaped human lives and memories. This move, even though criticised by Tilley for privileging visual perception and contemplation, is recognised for its accommodation of 'contingencies of history and embodiment' (Polkinghorne 1983, p. 205). This existentialist and historical turn in the understanding of the reality gave rise to the possibility of recognising that ultimately all material culture is imbued with social meaning and that material culture may therefore be read as text. Also, the emphasis on perception made it important to realise that any reading is not final because it depends on the readers' perception as much as on the context in which the text was produced (Tilley 1991).

In psychological terms, each life has a script that might be discernible upon analysis. In fact in most therapeutic interventions, disclosure and analysis is the process of discovering, reading and interpreting this script. The conception of 'the unconscious' and 'the collective unconscious' in psychoanalysis and other approaches to human development and behaviour are indicative of an overall structural pattern in human conduct which can be scrutinised and explained (read?) as if it were a text. Just like in a literary text things might not be what they appear at the first instant. The literal may be read as metaphorical and the most contrary phenomena may share some similar properties. Similarly, contradictions may be contained within a seemingly unitary phenomenon. Indeed, as Marx asserted, everything might be pregnant with its contrary. This sort of reading does not deny the importance of exact words and events but rather emphasises the possibility of different readings in different spatial, cultural and temporal contexts. So while reality is textual, its 'meaning' is positioned on a tapestry woven out of location, history, language, identity and psyche. This 'meaning' of a narrative is not uniquely inherent in its precise content. Neither is it wholly created by its speaker, not is it entirely a creation of the listener. The content is contextualised by the manner in which issues appear in it or remain unacknowledged in their absence. The speakers and listeners are situated in their respective contexts, too. In other words, the boundaries of the context may also be difficult to pin down and clearly define. While a reality may mean something in a given context, it may also contain extended significance to explain events occurring in different contexts. Or the context itself can be extended through emancipatory and imaginative practices of reading. Thus, the practice of reading the text of everyday life can be limited to noting its situated meanings but has a potential to be extended such that its significance may illuminate related, wider concerns and patterns.

When narratives of everyday acquire a textuality they may be characterised as 'cultural texts', that—like popular cinema, architecture, economics—contain a 'political unconscious'. Frederic Jameson in his book titled *The Political Unconscious: Narrative as a Socially Symbolic Act*, suggests that this political unconscious in these texts may be read for embedded political and social assumptions (Jameson 1981). Jameson points out that while this reading may lead to accessing 'symbolic solutions to real historical problems' held within the texts, contemporary society has no vision to see its own reflection or representation contained in these cultural texts for what it is. Using Jameson's explanation of the mechanics of this process we can deduce that the textuality of everyday has a *surface* narration which arbitrates with the unconscious reality of the link between an individual life and history.[3] Extending the notion of

---

[3] Instead of its commonsensical usage of a linear story of the kings and conquerors, Jameson, as Marxist theorist, uses 'history' more in the sense of a messy, multidirectional, non-linear account of oppression, power struggles and contestations for dominance. In this usage 'history' is not the full story-until-now situated in 'the past' but rather a presence that lingers on continually impacting and interfering in the conduct of 'the present'.

'Real' as historical, Jameson says that this embedding of history is there in every text of a time. For our purposes then, the narratives of Muslim women created also contain history, but not apparently and on the surface, rather it is embedded in the *unconscious of the narrative* and needs to be uncovered with attentive criticism.

Let us understand, drawing from Jameson further, why this link between a (personal) text and history is not apparent and buried hidden in the unconscious of the text. In a different book, Jameson (1991) investigates the so-called postmodern nature of the contemporary realities. He explains that rather than the end of modernity, post-modernity is merely a cultural justification produced to veil the infusion of all aspects of life, including consciousness by capitalism. It is this veil, created to hide the internal contradictions of capitalism, that does not allow a society to see its true image and blurs its vision for the solution to its problems.

I want to highlight that this is a powerful argument that must alter the way research in social sciences decides on the methods with which to grasp the present realities. If we see a human being as a *whole,* her identity may be seen as a representational model that presents her by highlighting certain features. In a representational text, different identities of a person may then be seen as ruptured pieces of the whole, but the whole—the human being—is always something more than the arithmetic sum of all the identity pieces. Social relationships, interactions and experiences form the very substantial and critical glue that holds the whole together, the lifeblood that makes this whole a person. Again drawing from Jameson (1981), I make a renewed plea for interdisciplinarity in order to preserve this 'wholeness' of human existence from disciplinary fragmentation. The study of gender, class, religion by scholars (including feminists) such that these are disparate phenomena that may be separated from one another.

> ...social life is in its fundamental reality one and indivisible, a seamless web, a single inconceivable and transindividual process, in which there is no need to invent ways of linking language events and social upheavals or economic contradictions because on that level they were never separate from one another (p. 40).

For Jameson, narratives are the symbolic representation of social reality. It is in the narrative that the apparently individual content exists alongside the unconscious content drawn from the larger society, but equally importantly, the narrative mediates between fragmented representations of society and the underlying wholeness of human society.

When researchers believe that individual actions and everyday experiences of people have their own meanings and there is no overarching explanation for it all, they reify human society as having a logic of its own, while it is but a product of human relationships of power. Critical theory's approach on the matter of emancipation allows for an escape from reification. It neither implies that structural forces have no influence over any individual action nor that hegemony is a blinding pall over all social reality.

Being mindful of and armed with these reading practices, I proceed to read and analyse the narratives weaved in the workshops and other conversations that took place in the course of this research. I wish to place this study also in the discursive realm of representation which goes beyond just a 'more accurate' representation of a marginalised culture. I hope that messages encoded in the structure of everyday narratives may be decoded such that they may be used for theory-building purposes and not just description. But representation can never be perfect and is limited by the power imbalances between the ones attempting to represent and the ones being represented. The debates related to these are discussed in more detail in the next chapter but the awareness of the researcher of their own perspective arising from class, gender, religion and other identity positions is a crucial factor in the representation. An argument not too unfamiliar to feminist researchers draws from the above discussion—that human life and even a limited view of experiences and opinions are far too complex to make all-encompassing 'true' representations. Any representation, however close to a facet of human existence, is at best 'a' *representation of* 'a' *facet of human existence*.

Geertz (1973) and Goffman (1971, 1974) in their interpretive and dramaturgical (respectively) approaches to culture, emphasise the public, collective, and performative aspects of social life. In other words, these approaches contend that culture is being shared by people while they *produce it together*. In the workshop setting, the production of narratives also emphasised this public, collective and performative aspect of peer culture among the participating young women. It also aimed at invoking 'Practical Consciousness' (Giddens 1984) and bringing its contents to be expressed by the participants. Giddens terms 'Practical Consciousness' that reflexivity which exists among a people sharing a culture. It enables them to have a tacit knowledge of their practices and the reasons behind the same even though they may not be 'able to give them direct discursive expression' (1984, p. xxiii). Reflecting about and articulating their everyday engagements in the workshops brought to the fore this practical consciousness—collective knowledge and experiences of people that infuse everyday routinised cultural practices. Just as the cultural practices are formed through their performance, the narratives about the same are also created in performance. And it is in this process again that the space is created for resisting, subverting and altering these practices *collectively*.

A subject of research also 'reads' the text of her reality from her situated position and 'speaks' to represent her interpretation to the researcher. The researcher 'listens' and again interprets it to 'comprehend' and 'understand'. The entire process of knowing can be encapsulated as 'comprehension of comprehension'. An act of interpretation and representation may be deemed successful, if not final, in a fusion of three instances of 'understanding'. First, being the prior-understanding of the researcher on the issue. Second, being the understanding of reality held by the researched. And third, being the understanding of the researcher of what others have comprehended and narrated to her.

— —

In this chapter I tried to take a fresh look at understanding the portrayal and representation of Muslims in congruence with the methodological choices in the rest of this work. Inspired by Moghadam I have attempted in this work to build a framework which draws on postcolonial feminisms, especially Islamic feminism, while looking at Critical Theory (Frankfurt School) for clues to achieve a feminist and emancipatory approach in which Indian Muslim women could address their issues and problems. I have undertaken the analysis of the narrative data collected in the course of research utilising the Marxist tradition of *engaged* analysis, which is a form of analysis that aims at emancipation and not just description. The underlying assumption in this approach is that uncovering discourses and their ideological content can have emancipatory impact. It is in this light that I shall undertake, in the second section of the book, to analyse the narratives of the participants of this study utilising a semiotic approach in combination with discourse analysis. As stated earlier a little differently, my concern was not just with the contents of a text but also the meanings and significance of my readings of the signs appearing in a text. In the process sometimes we can also discern the conventions and structures that direct the formation of these texts and the shaping of their meanings for all the participants. This issue of conventions directly relates to perceptions and disciplinary practices and thus to identities. This work makes no attempt whatsoever to quantify the presence and presentation of particular content in a text, but only reads it for its meaning and significance. In some ways, the select voices which have been recorded and 'heard' in this work tend to demonstrate the dialectics of *the struggle to be seen*. This *struggle to be seen* is not just a metaphor coming out of contentious politics experienced and encountered by women in our society. A literally real struggle whose layers were folded-unfolded during the enquiry emanates out of the analysis of interviews, discussions and other interactive platforms the researchers had an opportunity to engage with. From their manner of talking about everyday life, its suffering and denial, its trials and celebrations, we understand that these were, in fact, the descriptions of the larger and complex social realities in which individual lives are embedded. When words failed to express the experiences that these young women had gone through, silences and tears came to the rescue. We stood witness to those. In each act of seeing, listening, witnessing and recognising and recording, I felt relieved that our efforts to facilitate the young Indian Muslim women to represent themselves and thus mould a new 'self' were not worthless, and our endeavour to 'listen' has not been entirely fruitless. Beneath the discourses on lack of access and opportunities, and behind the veil of stereotypes, there appears a discernible craving for recognition, an unwritten memorandum that Muslim women be *heard*, and not just be *counted*.

3

Portrait of a Researcher as a Muslim Woman

Where human beings are 'subjects' of an enquiry, can 'power' be behind? Karl Marx asserted that the ruling ideas of a time are the ideas of those who are in power. At the same time social researchers may alert themselves to the pitfall of the understanding in which, Marx says (1976, p. 60), 'we detach the ideas of the ruling class from the ruling class itself and attribute to them an independent existence, if we confine ourselves to saying that these or those ideas were dominant at a given time, without bothering ourselves about the conditions of production and the producers of those ideas'. In this chapter I scrutinise the issue of *producers* of the ideas such that it opens up the possibility of articulation and empowerment of Indian Muslim women. This exercise draws from the first chapter where the dominant and hegemonic discourses on various counts related to Muslim women have been discussed and countered. And it continues from the second chapter where I had focused on the conditions of production of ideas by discussing the methodological approaches and epistemological choices of studies on Muslim women including this present work.

It is a truism that the religion or faith affiliation of the subjects of research are not necessarily of consequence in every kind of inquiry. But it has been frequently seen that regardless of the nature of the questions that frame any inquiry on Muslim women their Muslim-ness is always interpellated or called into question. In most studies if the subjects are Muslim, their faith identity would become the pivot on which the entire analysis would hinge, otherwise their religious identity would not be invoked. Further, when a Muslim woman researcher conducts a study, she is expected to 'shed' her Muslim identity and 'act neutral' in service of 'objectivity' in research, while the dominant identity is assumed to be 'objective' by default. As a result 'Muslim women' as a category have been essentialised as *eternal subjects of research*.

From the experiences of the participants in this study and from my own work in this research study and others, I discuss here the possibility of Muslim women transgressing this eternal subjecthood and position as researchers and creators of knowledge about themselves. In other words, my effort is to paint a portrait of a researcher as a Muslim woman. This is done by placing our experiences within an exploration of standpoint epistemologies and must be read as an extension of the preceding discussion on colonisation of discourse and approaches that achieve this hegemony. It is quite evident that research producing statistics and figures that have to fit within the existing dominant discourses is ineffective. The need is to challenge the dominant discourses and proffer alternative explanations. While writing this research my effort was to produce a political work which also attempts to create a niche in the existing theoretical knowledge. It is a project in re-assigning my faith in making sense of life and reality as a whole with all its contradictions, even if the end result is a pessimistic picture. The pessimistic assessment of the realities of Indian Muslims fills me up with just enough distaste to enthuse me for resistance, action and praxis. After a brief discussion on Muslim women's experiences as researchers I come back to critique the issue of standpoints of researchers and its impact on the contents and dynamics of research, the politics of consumption of research, and the overall aims or research activity. It goes without saying that after making an all out attempt, I leave space for fallibility, disagreements, further learning and possible revisions.

I

In conventional quantitative research, 'objectivity' is often propped up as sacrosanct. When research projects, designs, methods and tools are conjured there is hardly any thought spared for the possibility that the research process also implies a power imbalance between the two kinds of participants, the researcher and the researched. Subjective rationales and motivations are deployed but not acknowledged. I argue that it is impossible for human beings to enter into an interaction having completely transcended their social boundaries and I emphasise that a 'view from nowhere' (Longino 1993, p. 137) does not exist. The only recourse then available for a study like this is to be mindful of these boundaries and positions (termed 'positionality' of the researcher), and how these can influence or shape the interaction. The term 'positionality' was coined within feminist theory to describe the situated positions from which subjects come to know the world. It includes a recognition that any knowledge creation is valid only if the *process of finding out* and the *findings* are placed in context of relational positioning of researcher with the researched (Maher & Tetreault 1993). In feminist theory, the positionality of researchers is emphasised both to challenge the proposition that there is objective knowledge and to sensitise researchers to how analysis is shaped by her 'social situatedness... in terms of gender, race, class, sexuality and other axes of social difference' (Nagar & Geiger 2000). Conceptions within feminist theory emphasise a number of aspects of positionality that are essential for understanding the concept. First, positionality is a relational construct; possibilities for an individual depend on her or his position with respect to others. Second, positionality involves power relations, both in the sense that some positions tend to be more influential than others and in the sense that emphasising the situated nature of all knowledge challenges the power of those who claim objectivity. Third, positionality is continually enacted in ways that both reproduce and challenge pre-existing configurations. That is, one's positionality is persistent, because in most settings the prevailing power imbalance will keep getting reproduced. At the same time, there is a possibility that unexpected change can occur because each repetition is imperfect (Rose 1997; Valentine 2002).

The practice of reflecting on these effects, analysing and critiquing them is called reflexivity. In this work, reflexivity in practice was sought to be achieved by a conscious creation of sites that could host dialogues in which the researchers reflected on their status in the power imbalance.

Effective dialogue, thus, is a phenomenon that may get informed and shaped by identities—class, gender, age, etc., and also experiences of those communicating. Drawing reference in the research process from the feminist position 'personal is political', it becomes imperative for a researcher to connect the 'personal' and to be aware of her positionality in order to make her politics transparent. This laying out of the personal opens up the possibility of reciprocity between the researcher and the researched rather than just 'enacting' a neutral-sterile relationship. This chapter is part of my attempt to write myself and other researchers in the team into the narrative accounts and analysis presented in the following chapters. The concern here is to present an account of Muslim women traversing the boundary of researched and researcher, out of the role of 'subjects of research'. It is a montage of images and impressions of our experiences strung together to form a reflexive narrative of Muslim Women researchers.

I identify myself as a Muslim and have lived all my life in two Muslim localities in Delhi. It can safely be claimed that I have always been 'immersed' in the 'culture under study'. Even for formal purposes my conscious registering of the distinct realities of my existence as a Muslim woman as such began much before I began this study. I must point out that right from the beginning of my career as a development worker and social researcher I have always remained aware of my Muslim identity. It can perhaps also be said that I was never allowed to forget it. Nevertheless, I did increasingly register an awareness of how I might put my identity to use for mediating my interactions. In professional capacities I found myself interacting on dual tracks. I would be addressing the issue or the task at hand and I would also simultaneously be catering to sensibilities of people through which they were 'filtering' my positions and work as a Muslim woman. The fact that I am also a Muslim woman made it possible that their speech acts made sense to me without the speakers having to make everything explicit. At the same time this shared identity allowed the participants in my study also to feel that they could communicate to me some of the experiential complexities of being a Muslim in India. Much of the insight afforded to me in this study was possible only as I had access to the use of my identity. For me and the team of researchers, our identity of being Muslim as a heuristic device enabled a cognitively complex understanding of participants that would be difficult to develop for others who did not have access to this device, given the nature of research methods and the limits of engagement during the workshops and interviews.

In the research situations I took care of the need to be sensitive to the sensibilities of my study participants in my dress and communication, but I also realised quickly that the issue would not be simply resolved by noting the 'similarity' of my religious identity. After all people do not discuss these issues all the time, and they do not ensue or pursue these discussions with anybody and everybody. I perceived that differences in my position as a researcher and differences in my demeanour needed to be downplayed a little but there was no need to try to eliminate them entirely. One reason, of course, is that Muslim communities across India are so diverse that a Muslim woman from Delhi cannot possibly hope to completely obliterate all differences. The other reason was that the familiarity with organisers, facilitators and other participants, the trust-building via mutual sharing, a sense of shared comfort, and the novelty of the situation all came together in intriguing ways for the experience to be truly facilitative of the aims of the workshop. We can easily agree that two persons sharing one identity do indeed share many differences, that all identities of all the persons in one designated 'group' or 'community' do not perfectly coincide. Having set out this fact I feel I must go back to the issue of the researcher being an 'insider' or 'outsider' to the group under study. The debate on whether an insider researcher enhances the effective use of research methodology or an outsider has been taken up by different researchers who have in different cases concluded in favour of both. Indeed, if the effectiveness of utilising the methods and tools is the criterion, then it has been argued that too much identification can be detrimental to the overall research process and interfere in effective research data collection due to 'role confusion' (Asselin 2003, cf Dawyer & Buckle 2009). On the other hand, some researchers (Adler & Adler 1987, cf Dawyer & Buckle 2009) have even suggested that during fieldwork the identification of the researcher with the participants during fieldwork for effective data collection is more common in practice than the proponents of objectivity would care to confess and that this 'objectification' mostly occurs during analysis and writing. This insider-outsider debate needs to be explored further not just within the confines of enhanced effectiveness of research methods, but also questioning whether it is only effectiveness that is at stake.

In this study, some field researchers spoke from the point of view of an 'insider', the researcher being like the other young Muslim women she was studying. For example, Muskan in Mumbai, who saw herself as a person who had experienced everything that the young women were talking about or had observed them from close quarters in her own everyday work with Muslim women in Mumbai slum communities. But, she was also aware of her difference in being more articulate, and capable of facilitating articulation of those like herself. At another level the difference also lay in her being in a position to reflect on the process and this 'difference itself'. In her report Muskan was able to write about everyday lives of girls in Mumbai with deep insight but at the same time she utilised the writing device of being a distant observer, creating this distance consciously as an epistemological device.

There were others who were to realise that even a lack of difference can be overwhelming and difficult to surmount. Shahda, who came from a lower middle class family from Patna and was pursuing an undergraduate degree course at the time, found herself continually questioned on her motivations by the interviewees. The participants asked her what they would gain if they answered her questions. On several occasions she reported being chided or laughed at for her naiveté at posing some of the questions that seemed too obvious to the women. The tone of the reports sent by Shahda was serious and it seems that the 'difference of positions' was too wide in the face of her youthful inexperience. She took her 'position of difference' a bit too seriously and as a result found that her 'subjects' held her to it. They demanded from her an evidence of some special ability that would prove to them that she was indeed different from them. Her experience hints that it helps a researcher to be similar to the participants but it helps more when just enough difference is also maintained. Paradoxically, the difference needs to be highlighted *and* underplayed simultaneously.

Bringing knowledge and awareness regarding a situation to the fore is one of the core aims of research. It is absurd to believe that this is a one-way process. Naghma, talking about her experience of participating as a researcher in this study in Bangalore, says,

> I saw this girl—weak, scared to talk, sad eyes... and wondered why were we born as girls? Made to feel insignificant by our own families and considered throughout our lives as someone who is good only for cleaning and washing. But I spoke to her and I felt good about being born a girl because, I could understand her situation even when she could say only a part of it in words.

In her position as a young Muslim woman researcher from Delhi slums, Sabiha found that she needed to challenge her own self-proclaimed shortcomings. '*Dimagh bhi thoda kamzor hai baaji mera*' (I'm not very sharp in the brain, sister), she had told me in the field researchers' training. Three months later, I asked her how the interviews were going; she told me,

> *Bol nahin paati ladkiyan... in sab sawalon ke jawaab dena bohot mushkil hota hai unke liye... apne barey mein, apne khwabon ke barey mein kabhi baat hi nahin kari kisi ne. Mere abba khud kehte the ke ladkiyon ki aawaz nahin sunai deni chahiye, yahan tak ke hame koi aisa zewar pehnna bhi mana tha jo khanak kar aawaz karey. Ab bhi mein kabhi zor se bol deti hoon toh khud hi dar jaati hoon.* (The girls find it difficult to speak... these questions are so difficult for them to answer... none of them have ever spoken about themselves or their dreams. My father used to say that girls should not be heard, we were not even allowed to wear any jewellery that could clink and make any sound. Even today, when I sometimes speak a little loudly, I get startled myself.)

From her own experience of having to be a person who lacked intellect and must never be 'heard', Sabiha instinctively knew the difficulties faced by the participating girls in speaking of their aspirations. Her report of the workshop was so meticulous, treating each word uttered there as invaluable.

Is it sufficient to deduce that Muskan and Sabiha's success in engaging and facilitating articulation stemmed from the fact that they hailed from similar backgrounds as the girls they were interacting with? Perhaps, it also mattered that both of them were slightly older than our definition of young in the study (15–25 years)… and that both had been working as community workers for several years now. Shahda was a new recruit and still had to establish her credibility as someone who was truly interested in knowing the Muslim girls and being sensitive to their situation. This factor is also reflected in the incident when at the end of the field researchers' training Nishat *Aapa* shared that she felt that she could depend on me to lead the research study with 'understanding and sensitivity' as I was a 'girl from within the community' and felt assured that my education and confidence would contribute towards building the community stronger. I realised that the other participants also needed a confirmation that I possessed qualities that set me apart, that they could put their trust in my ability to represent them, and that our discussions were not part of a futile, empty exercise.

But this was not enough. My experience in Gujarat added another dimension to this exploration. The workshops in Ahmedabad city and the Sabarkantha workshop were organised by Noorjahan. She was assisted by Beena who made many arrangements possible. Beena has worked extensively with the urban poor in Ahmedabad for many years. She also worked in the relief camps during the 2002 anti-Muslim pogrom in Gujarat. In an environment when communal relations are still incendiary Beena's tireless work has won her enormous goodwill and the trust of Muslims. As mentioned earlier in the book, at the Ahmedabad workshop, the participants came wearing *burqas*, with only their eyes open. Once at the venue, they uncovered their faces but they did not take off the head gear and the *abaya*. I asked them to take these off so that they may feel more comfortable. They were shocked by the suggestion; I could see them visibly recoil. I continued and added that there was no male presence in the hall so it was okay to take *burqas* off but my reasons did nothing to persuade them. Noorjahan seemed uncomfortable too but began verbally 'encouraging' them. Beena intervened. She spoke to the girls in a very intimate tone and seemed to have reassured the girls when she said that if they did not feel like it they need not take off their *abaya*. With this intervention everyone immediately relaxed a bit and we could proceed further.

From my position as a middle-class Muslim woman from Delhi visiting Ahmedabad for the first time, I was an outsider to the group in the workshop and Beena, who is a Hindu woman but had been with them through a lot of the traumatic experiences during the 2002 genocide and the subsequent struggle for life with dignity, was an insider. Obviously, sharing the 'Muslim' identity was not enough in this case but it did have some value; when the workshop was formally closed and I began getting ready to leave, the girls crowded around me and bombarded me with questions about whether I was married and how did my family give me permission to travel without them. In a way, these questions and my answers only highlighted how I was not like them and did not know much of their lives. On the other hand they were interested in getting to know my background (for example, more than a non-Muslim researcher accompanying me for assisting in documentation) because *I was like them* in being a Muslim woman, despite our differences.

Fieldwork in social research can be both, muddled and intricate, simultaneously. But, the 'writing' of research at its conclusion is equally, if not more complex. The (re)creation of data by the writer-researcher also needs some reflection. Every production of knowledge has a particular context and it is relevant to ask who formed this knowledge, where, how, and why (Harding 1987; Stanley & Wise 1983). In most positivist researches, the researcher obsessed with objectivity and neutrality feigns controlled emotional involvement not just with the process of research but also the product of the research. This means that the writer of the report himself/herself is 'missing' from it. Feminist research has now quite an extensive history of the researcher writing herself into the research product. In this way I (the researcher) also act as a research tool (Al-Hindi & Kawabata 2002), injecting my own insights that stem from my personal experiences into the recorded narratives. During the time I was writing this text I was asked by a senior scholar if during the workshop I did not feel any rage or anger at the 'plight' of the Muslim girls in Ahmedabad. I thought for a while and had to answer in the negative, 'No, I did not feel angry.' He could not believe me and cajoled me for a more 'honest' answer. Honestly speaking, I only felt despair. As a young Muslim woman myself I had watched the horrors of the 2002 Gujarat pogrom on television news channels. Almost eight years since then I felt that justice was nowhere near being delivered. How long can an individual sustain anger while coping with the demands of everyday life? The repression of anger into a defence mechanism is inevitable. For most people anger gave way to despair and cynicism. And this in turn, got channelled into other manifestations such as simply a resolve to continue to live life and infuse it with as much dignity as possible. This strange mix of despair and resolve is as much a constituent of my shared identity with other participants of this study, and it is this as much as, if not more than, other markers of identity, that bound me to them.

In social psychology, identity is understood as a form of self-concept. Accordingly, Charles Cooley (1902) described the process of acquiring identity as a response to their perception of how other people see them and named it the looking-glass self. Mead (1934) expanded this 'other' into a more nuanced 'significant other' and 'generalised other'. He also asserted that this individual-self is in relation to the selves of other members of the same group, reflecting and expressing broadly their outlook and behaviour. Mead also stressed that this self is not static or biologically given but rather a negotiated, cognitive entity 'poised between an evolutionary notion of the creative, open, spontaneous, but potentially conflictual, individual and group action and an "instrumental rationality" which attempts both practical and progressive social outcomes' (Roberts 2006, pp. 36–37). This description of identity formation though valuable, supposes that the process of identity formulation of individuals and groups takes place with their consent. This view was countered by Giddens who, through his dramaturgical view, pointed out that social identity is a process of role-prescription, essentially a categorisation or typification based on definite 'social criterion' and may contain a disconnect between what they prescribe and what actors actually carry out. Thus, identity roles contain within their scripting the conflicts that reflect broad structural features of society and linked to structures of domination (Roberts 2006). It also means that my intuitive methodological tightrope act of balancing insider-outsider roles, and the reciprocal navigation of complex interplay of identities by the participants, afforded to me a situated view that threw up deep insights and helped me access the embedded knowledge of people about their own lives.

Thus, as far as research is considered to be a value-neutral task which can be and needs to done effectively, the worth of being an insider or outsider may be judged in its ability to deliver. As can be deduced from the above discussion we may argue in favour of an insider's view as to bringing out a deeper and truer understanding of the subjects and issues at hand but that is clearly only a matter of skilfully traversing and transgressing various identity boundaries that are of importance in the inquiry and keep intersecting each other. But this is only an instrumental view of research and knowledge production. In this view it does not matter who produces knowledge as long it is done well and effectively. This is exactly the argument of a Brahmin intellectual Sharmila Rege, when she asserts that the 'Dalit standpoint' is something that can be adopted by anyone for 'avoiding' what she insists is an epistemologically narrow position implicit in 'direct experience-based authenticity'.

The dalit feminist standpoint which emerges from the practices and struggles of dalit woman, we recognise, may originate in the works of dalit feminist intellectuals but it cannot flourish if isolated from the experiences and ideas of other groups who must educate themselves about the histories, the preferred social relations and utopias and the struggles of the marginalised. A transformation from 'their cause' to 'our cause' is possible for subjectivities can be transformed. By this we do not argue that non-dalit feminists can 'speak as' or 'for the' dalit women but they can 'reinvent themselves as dalit feminists' (1988, p. WS-45).

The instrumental rationality of Rege's suggestion is disturbing. In fact, the entire article reads like an apologia for Brahminical appropriation of Dalit women's voice in the women's movement while pretending to expose it. The Dalit feminist standpoint is by Rege seen merely as a pedagogical device that can also be utilised by Brahmins to educate themselves about Dalits. There is also a hint of contempt and thinly veiled threat here that unless Brahmin women articulate the Dalit feminist standpoint it would not 'flourish' in the Brahmin-dominated discipline of Women's Studies.

As all instrumentally rational arguments do, this one too side-steps the matter of morality. It does not consider the moral imperative of the appropriation of Dalit feminists' voice, which Rege insists has erroneously been conceived as 'different'. The tone of the article remains passive-aggressive throughout, beginning with chastising white feminists for allegedly having remained silent and letting black feminists assert their 'difference'. Her reading of 'colonial' is so narrow that it becomes possible for her to call the application of Edward Said's postcolonial framework to the Dalit movement and women's movement problematic, only since both had 'utilised the colonial law, justice and administration as a major resource'. For Rege, the value of defining the Dalit feminist standpoint in such terms lies in its potential for building a consensus in the women's movement by 'transforming individual feminists into oppositional and collective subjects' (ibid.).

So then, is the 'standpoint' of the Dalit feminist woman (or any other feminists) just a 'place' to which anyone can go and stand and they shall be it? Could the knowledge formation and truth content of the representation from this *standpoint as a 'place'* be the same no matter who the producer was? The temptations in such a viewpoint for members of the dominant groups are obvious. It allows them to present and believe that the drawing and redrawing of the insider-outsider boundaries is a strategic move rather than a move towards truth (Haraway 1988). It is astounding that even in feminist movements in India it is possible to claim a scientific objectivity that is disembodied and devoid of authentic experience, as feminist. Haraway asserts that standpoints of the subjugated offer accounts of the world which are closer to reality and the ones that can transform the world because 'in principle they are least likely to allow denial of the critical and interpretive core of all knowledge. They are knowledgeable of modes of denial through repression, forgetting, and disappearing acts-ways of being nowhere while claiming to see comprehensively' (ibid., p. 584). But the ability to see from the margins or from below requires, according to her, not only intellectual or technoscientific vision but also a skill with body and language. In other words, the subjugated standpoint is necessarily an embodied experience and to claim 'equality' of positioning is oppressive re-appropriation of not only language but also the body.

The pedagogical instrumentality of standpoints of the marginalised is the other consideration. This potential cannot be limited for the consumption and learning of the dominant groups about the subjugated or the marginalised. Unfortunately, that is how it often is. Research has been a part of imperialist practices and still remains subservient to neo-imperialist projects. This is not to say that it cannot be subverted and utilised by the marginalised and the subjugated to understand their positions better, and for attempting to counter their marginalisation and oppression. It is this hope that has motivated the conception and execution of works such as the one being presented in this book.

4

The Everyday of Inhabiting Margins

Even as religious and gender identities are at the centre of this analysis, it would be a fallacy to pretend that we are scrutinising a reality where class has ceased to matter. For an analysis of communal and gender discrimination to be meaningful, it must take cognisance of the material logic of the structures that inscribe these discriminations into the everyday lives of individuals. In its Marxist usage, the term 'alienation' refers to the loss of control that people experience in capitalist society over their own labour and the resultant loss of the ability to define themselves. The exploitative nature of relationships (a combination of poverty and communal prejudice) permeates everything in the Indian social structure and alienates Muslims such that their marginalisation and alienation prevent the realisation of full humanity. It renders them socially non-existent and produces in them a 'way of being' such that they cannot be themselves. This way of being is enacted and experienced in everyday life. The everyday is also the only site where this marginalisation is fully registered and critically understood.

For Lefebvre, everyday life is not doomed to consist of unchangeable, dispirited and dispiriting routine, it is rather the space where change is understood. In the everyday life of marginalised people it is clearly experienced that although the larger society may have progressed and become affluent, it does not aim to assist everyone in realising their full humanity. How much qualitative improvement there is in the everyday life of people is the measure of the possibility of reversing the process of marginalisation. Lefebvre argues that it is in daily life that human beings realise their full humanity, but often it is the contingencies of daily life that hamper this possibility.

> I clean my home in the morning, make tea for all and cook food before I go to school. Sometimes I wash clothes also. After I am back, I sleep for a while, watch television, cook food for the night and then go to sleep after putting everything in its place.

During the interviews and in the workshops we often heard the remark, 'A woman's work is never done'. The repetitive nature of

The Everyday of Inhabiting Margins 53

household chores is especially crushing for a young woman in a poor or middle-class household as there is little possibility of respite from it. Girls everywhere told us of their routines, which included tasks such as cleaning the house, washing clothes and utensils, cooking, taking care of siblings, going to school or/and jobs outside the house, working at home for meagre wages—stitching, applying sequins, embroidery, packing incense sticks, giving tuition to children, etc. When they were asked which of these chores/tasks they liked or did not like, many responded with, 'What is there to like or dislike?' Others replied stoically that they liked all their work. Some were more expressive of their dislikes....

> I don't like washing clothes and dishes but I don't have a choice... it has to be done....
>
> I don't like cooking, especially in the summer.
>
> I come back from college and immediately go into the kitchen after changing my dress to help my mother. I feel tired, but if I rest everyone becomes angry and starts shouting.
>
> When I get married I will have to do all the work. I have to learn....
>
> I hate getting up from my studies for some mundane work.
>
> If I don't do housework Ammi will have to do it all... as it is she is so tired.

But most young women carve out small niches of enjoyment in their tasks:

> I like cooking rotis. I make almost 50 in a day. They are perfect.
>
> I like trying out new dishes to cook.
>
> I like to go for my tailoring class.
>
> I like talking to my elder sister.
>
> I like visiting my nani's house, she lives nearby.
>
> I love talking to my cousins. We have so much fun when we are together.
>
> I like getting my children ready for school.
>
> I like reading. I start reading everything... even a newspaper bag!
>
> I like teaching my tuition children.
>
> I like to offer namaaz. It gives me so much respite... when I am praying no one disturbs me.

For the most part, pure recreation is a rare privilege available only to a few. Leisure, for the young Muslim women participants of this study, is a complex phenomenon beset by a combination of choice and constraints. What people do when they 'work', and activities considered appropriate to pursue when at leisure, is already gendered. For men, work and leisure are completely separated from each other. For women, however, leisure has been a problematic construct and they challenge the demarcation between work and leisure as an untrue dichotomy (Wearing 1998). Women feel a lot of pressure to enjoy, or claim to enjoy, what they have to do. During the discussions in the study many girls said that if they complained about housework they would be considered bad and incompetent. In many cases, girls reported a sense of pride in keeping a clean house or doing other chores efficiently. Proficiency in cooking and providing a good meal to the family is considered the mark of a nurturing woman.

Examination of their everyday life shows that leisure cannot be completely severed from the rhythm of the rest of everyday life. There is no 'pure leisure' that can be judged by standards that do not apply to the broader experiences of the individual. Leisure is worth studying because what people like to do in their free time stems from their socialisation—what they have learnt from family, friends or elsewhere. It may also give us a glimpse of the various boundaries that may limit the choice of leisure activities available to a person—gender, age, caste, class, etc. Finally, there is the matter of choosing from among the available options or even the act of creating new choices. As a methodological concern Blumer (1969) suggests that choice should be used, not as a defining concept, but as one that sensitises the query. Following this suggestion we become alert to the fact that the participants of this study do choose leisure activities in order to first learn what these choices are and then to describe how they are constrained in making these choices. Muslim women who are being further pushed to the margins within their communities and families are at a vantage point to grasp fully their position. While Lefebvre, interestingly, called for studying women's lives because in his view these were the more 'unknown' sectors of life, our experience in this study indicates that even though the choices available to people may be dismally few, they engage in choosing from what seem to them accessible alternatives.

Almost all the young Muslim women who have not dropped out of formal education are aware that continuing to go to school/college and to computer/tailoring classes is not something they can take for granted.

They enjoy it, even savour it, they work hard at it and wish to prolong this 'privilege' as much as they can.

Across the country, TV is the most common source of recreation in everyday life. It is an accessible choice—television sets are now available in most homes. Watching serialised dramas and reality shows is seen in most households as acceptable recreation for women. While most media studies literature finds fault with the *saas-bahu* dramas for being regressive, it cannot be ignored that for an hour or two in the evening the remote control is in the hands of the women in the family.

Many participants in the workshops in Delhi, Lucknow, Bhopal, and Patna reported reading women's magazines like *Mehekta Aanchal* in their leisure time. These magazines contain romantic stories that are set in Muslim households. Marriages and other functions among relatives and friends are also occasions for getting together and recreation. Sleeping is an often cited pastime, and considering the ages of our participants (15–25), this is not surprising.

Labour is their only true resource, but not being able to exchange it well enough to afford a decent lifestyle, and in the face of their complete stereotyping/reification, people try to convert their misfortune and suffering into a resource. They can transform a portion of their misfortune and suffering into forms of piety. Praying and reciting the Quran is an activity that many young women reported enjoying in their free time. In many cases, for example in Tamil Nadu, young women reported that they enjoyed going for *Bayaan* or *Waaz* (lectures where women are taught religious practices or where stories with some moral lessons are recited).

Clearly these words, sentiments and choices of young Muslim women do not suggest that they are not aware of their situation or that they believe that their situations and choices are just, though they may seem inevitable. For most young women who participated in this study, families and household chores do not exactly fit the liberal description characterised only by caring, affection, etc. These 'private' spheres are actually where social status, economic marginalisation, and political power play themselves out in subtle ways. My purpose is to portray the everyday lives of young Muslim women such that we can see what looks like pre-ordained for them as an alterable situation. Leisure is not just relief from the humdrum everyday. Work and leisure are dialectically united. The rupture between the two is itself symptomatic of the alienation. One way to patch up this rupture in studying work and leisure is to also give close scrutiny to 'leisure' activities and the spaces for them. By doing this we can remove the cover of uniformity, homogeneity and mediocrity that covers the everyday, uncovering the 'marvels' that lie ensconced within the ordinary everyday.

In the aftermath of the violence of World War II and the atrocities that took place inside the Nazi concentration camps, Lefebvre's view was that the critique of everyday life needs to be approached as an act of rehabilitating everyday life as the essential ground of human existence. De Certeau argues for building a history on the everyday and the unremarkable, which are often discarded in such enterprises. The narratives of history are mostly hinged on events that are extraordinary and its chief ingredients are epochal events and figures. Not only in history but even in social science research, ordinary everyday experiences are not given as much importance as 'event'-based particular experiences. We may do well to remember that Marx, who insisted on historicizing ideas, human nature and human needs, had said that 'the strangest things are often the most trivial', to which Lefebvre quipped that 'the most extraordinary things are also the most everyday' (quoted from Merrifield 2002, p. 79).

The richness and value of studying the everyday for Lefebvre is in the possibility of providing details of what is familiar but not necessarily known. He insisted on a critique of everyday life as 'sensory'—that which needs to be 'perceived' rather than 'thought' of. The study of the everyday could contribute towards lessening the fragmentation of human existence if it is imagined as brimming with wholeness. Lefebvre recognized that the everyday is indeed characterised by routine and ritual, but he was also fascinated by the fact that on close scrutiny it seemed to be punctuated by festivity, delight, pain and suffering. At times when the routine is disrupted and the monotony of the everyday is broken, a possibility arises for people to know of their alienation and lead to its re-evaluation. For Lefebvre, the scrutiny of the everyday involves discovering the unrealised possibilities in it.

Through such critical practices the sensory space of the everyday can be transformed into a discursive space in which we can discern the structural forces too. In the study of the quotidian we may catch glimpses of the structure but we must be wary of fetishising the concept of structure itself. Lefebvre claims that the everyday is appropriated as a medium where realities merge and evolve. He characterises the everyday as the 'nourishing soil' of higher activities such as religion and art. But he also sees these higher activities and routine activities as intertwined in the everyday with a possibility of transmutating into each other. What is routine and banal to an observer can be deeply spiritual or creative to the one performing it, inversely an act familiar as religious to the observer may be emptied of all its spirituality and reduced to routine or given a new meaning by its performer.

Another important feature of the everyday is that it resists total organisation and control. There is always a residue that cannot be controlled in unforeseen circumstances, under bureaucratic or state control, familial or parental control, religion, etc. Resilience and resistance are integral to the everyday. To a distant observer what seems like dull, grey routine often turns into high drama: but neither the routine nor the drama can be said to characterise the everyday.

The everyday is the site of uneven development. Technological developments further cause interference and interruption in the natural and traditional rhythms of the everyday, but new rhythms are not established. The everyday is treated like wrapping paper: it covers everything, but when we wish to study anything the first thing we discard is the everyday. Gendered enquiries such as time-budgeting surveys and studies of access to and control over resources, conducted by NGOs in India, are what Lefebvre (2000) might call 'pseudo-everyday' because they caricature and fetishise the everyday.

Often the 'everyday' becomes a site of enforcement and encroachment by the 'private'—shrinking further the space for 'public' within it. This sterilises everyday community life by presenting only the individualism, cut off from history, it encourages the cult of the material and impairs its capacity to act as a site for resistance to powerful historical forces. The individualisation of everyday private space must be resisted. This can be done by treating everyday life creatively such as a piece of art, made creatively, loaded with meaning through historicising it, and contextualizing it so that it transforms spaces of alienation and marginalisation. If people are able to see their lives as something they make, a creation, a work of art, it may contribute towards ending their alienation.

De Certeau (1984) distinguishes the study of everyday life from studies of popular culture. My reason for choosing to undertake the study of the everyday life of young Muslim women is essentially to avoid being trapped by the stereotype of the 'tyrannical Islamic monolith' enmeshed in mainstream popular culture. It is from within the study of everyday practices as a repetitive, rhythmic and non-premediated set of activities that we receive our clues to how young Muslim women, who may seem to be steeped in a subjugating culture—rituals, representations and rules imposed on them—often practise these differently from what the imposers had in mind. A positivist enquiry may conjure up the impression that these women are neither rejecting nor altering the rules because they have no choice but to accept them. To become acquainted with everyday acts that alter *the interpretation of the meanings* attached to these repetitive activities, we need a more microscopic view, which is afforded to us by a critical approach. This will let us see that 'they were *other* within the very colonization that outwardly assimilated them; their use of the dominant social order deflected its power, which they lacked the means to challenge; they escaped it without leaving it' (de Certeau 1984, p. xiii).

Certeau further stresses that the changes that are set before us by dominant discourses—by intellectuals, clergy, educators, and media—as standards of measuring socio-economic advancement tell us nothing about their meaning for those whose lives will be affected. In other words, the study of everyday life allows us to analyse the manipulation of these representations from the point of view of those who are impacted by it. In this way, everyday practices (talking, reading, moving about, cooking, shopping, etc.) can 'bring to light the clandestine forms taken by the dispersed, tactical, and makeshift creativity of groups or individuals' (ibid., p. xiv). Certeau calls these 'tactics' or 'ways of operating'; victories of the 'weak' over the 'strong'. James Scott (1985) called these practices 'weapons of the weak' in his path-breaking study of everyday forms of peasant resistance. Applying some of Scott's ideas is useful for my analysis, such as his insistence that on the basis of their daily experience, subordinate classes have a fair level of consciousness of their own condition, that they hardly ever make the mistake of accepting the inevitable as just, and that because no hegemonic ideology can be perfect, its imperfection supplies the vocabulary for its own criticism. In becoming aware of alienation, relative freedom from alienation may be attained. Sometimes just continuing to live is an act of resistance. Lefebvre calls for studying those aspects of individual lifestyle that express human needs as well as everyday life, not just as a means to something beyond the ordinary everyday, but as its own end.

Agency

Transgressing the expectation of smooth and 'normal' functioning of the household threatens the social well-being of the family and disrupts domestic life. When the girls speak of their responsibilities, of how they discharge these, and of how it makes them feel when they meet expectations, they give an account of their agency and their conflicts and negotiations with social and cultural norms. But often the 'agency' of the Muslim woman subject is judged by the mainstream feminist adjudicator only in open and militant resistance to the designated enemy and oppressor by this adjudicator.

I have seven siblings and, being the oldest, I have to take care of all of them. My father pulls a trolley and my mother doesn't keep well. I take care of all the household work as well as my all siblings. I study through an open school and go out to take tuition and stitching training. I really enjoy my classes and talking with friends there. All of us try to take our learning seriously. I love to study, but I have to do a lot of work and by the time I go to bed, I am too tired.

I teach at a primary school in our locality. I dislike going to school every day and teaching because my own study suffers. After the job and all the household responsibilities there is no time left for study.

The entire day I work at home cutting zari pieces clean. My younger sister does all the housework as she likes cooking but hates sitting in one place all day to do the job work. I do not like it much myself... but someone in the family must do it. Most Muslim girls in our neighbourhood do skilled work at home like making lac bangles and zari making, and they earn five hundred to one thousand rupees in a month. I wish Allah gave me so much money that I could do something for them. I wish everyone to think positive, because negative thoughts take the person nowhere. I end my thoughts by greeting all Indian Muslim girls like myself and wish that my thought reaches all of them.

I wanted to study but we aren't economically sound. My father opposed my education. He argued that education is not important for girls. But I was also adamant and I got myself enrolled. I also stitch people's clothes to continue my education. I work in the house all the time as I do not want anyone to say that I'm not doing my work. I do not want my father to turn this into an excuse to stop my studies.

I used to study in a private school. My father took me out of school because neighbours would criticise him for encouraging me and giving me freedom. They told him not to spoil me and that no one would marry me. But my mother supported me and I sought admission again. I am again in a school because of my mother. I wish my father would support me.

I get up very early and finish all the work at home before going to teach children in a private school. When I come back I do the housework, rest for a while and then study.

I hate receiving 'free lecture' from a teacher in my college and sweeping the floors in my house as I am allergic to dust. I like reading the Quran, offering namaaz, reading the newspaper and giving tuition to children.

If I could turn back time, I would bring back my childhood and play a lot. Now there is no time even to draw a breath. I really hate that the work is never over. In my free time, I now watch serials. Ammi and I love them.

I dislike being scolded by anyone.

I remember when I started working. Sometimes I would wear jeans and talk to boys. For that, the neighbours criticised me and the boys of the locality taunted me. I started getting prank phone calls. But I persisted... I continued working and ignored them. That shut them up.

If we are strong, societal policing and restrictions will not be able to stop us.

I study very hard and am the topper in my class. Sometimes I help my sisters and brothers with their homework. I like to watch television, listen to music and read 'risaley' (magazines) when I am free.

My father is always beating my mother. He also does not give enough money to take care of the family. My mother works here and there in order to earn for the whole family. The behaviour of my father has changed my life entirely. I am extremely disturbed. Now I am working and earning a little and helping my family. Due to my efforts, my family is living somewhat peacefully. I love going to marriages and I try to buy little things for myself like artificial jewellery with my money.

I do a lot of work but I hate washing clothes. I love music, so when I wash clothes I put the music on.

When no one is at home, I bolt the door, play loud music and dance.

I used to study in a private school but my father, under the influence of another person, had my name struck off as he believes that girls should not get higher education. However, with the help of my mother I got admission in a government school. I also work as a volunteer to administer polio drops and earn something. I feel that the mother is the best friend and guardian of a child.

I do not study any more. I dropped out of school two years ago. I learn stitching and embroidery from my neighbour and keep myself busy with work. I have made many beautiful covers and handkerchiefs and similar things. I don't really like embroidery but I feel happy when everyone praises what I make. I like praying. I remember many duahs. My friends are always asking me which verse they should read to ask for a particular duah.

People are neither completely autonomous entities who exist in a context-less vacuum, nor are they automated machines whose choices and actions are predetermined by the social structure they are placed in. Bandura (1989) stresses that the capacity of people to exercise control over their own motivations, thought-processes, and actions is a distinctive human characteristic. He calls this capacity to intentionally make things happen by one's actions, *agency*. Central to the idea of agency is that it enables people to play an active part in their own self-development, adaptation, and self-renewal (Bandura 2001). On similar lines, Giddens talks of *structuraion,* a middle path between the impacts of human agency and social structure on determining social action. He explains that it is the repetition of the acts of individual agents which reproduces the structure. This view reconciles the views that social structure—traditions, institutions, moral codes, etc.—shape ways of doing things with the possibility that these can be changed when people (agents) reproduce them differently by defying them or altering them. The term 'reflexivity' is commonly used by social scientists to refer to the ability of an agent to consciously alter his or her place in the social structure.

It has been mentioned earlier that Muslim women have been mostly represented as 'victims' who have no agency. Even their faith and related everyday practices such as their attire, praying five times a day, reciting the Qur'an, is portrayed as something that is *done to them* as inanimate objects, rather than *by them* as active agents who exercise their agency.

Laidlaw (2010) contends that in standard anthropological usage, agency refers to an inner ability of individuals to resist social structure to achieve freedom. He criticises this view as being far from reality and suggests a reconceptualisation of agency as arising out of unusual circumstances rather than being born of individual responsibility and directed intentionality. Using the example of women accused of witchcraft, Laidlaw points to the circumstances in which agency may be ascribed to persons without intentionality, responsibility or even the evidence of an actual act. Agency, then, is in the eyes of the adjudicator. It is in their inclination to attribute agency to an act and withhold the label from others. And this act of attribution or withholding the agency is a strategy used for examining the lives of potential 'agents'. This strategic process itself is embedded in the power relations already existing in society and may be used by researchers to ascribe agency to an act while the actant herself may not read any resistance or revolt in her actions, while on the other hand the researcher-adjudicator may call an actant submissive and lacking agency when she sees herself as taking charge of her life and shaping it as she desires. Following from this, we can see that mainstream feminism in India has defined 'agency' for Muslim women in such a way that rejection of the values inherent in their faith is a necessary qualification for being judged agents.

In this context, Saba Mahmood (2005), in her book *Politics of Piety: the Islamic Revival and the Feminist Subject*, argues for a particularised conviction that there are other experiences of meaningful and fulfilling life than those envisioned by Western liberal feminisms. In her study of an Islamic revivalist movement in Egypt, she finds that although those in the movement in their activism may end up challenging patriarchal modes prevalent in their society, their intentions are not rooted in the secular feminist tradition of individual liberty or even in a personal connection with Allah. Their wish, rather, is to fashion and perform a more pious self as prescribed in their faith. Their agency is directed towards the realisation of a potential rationality- and emotionality-informed Islam which is not read by them as an affront to their personhood.

This is not to allege that Muslim women's agency is to be defined in either of the two extremes, in resisting or submitting to Islamic mores. My attempt is to point out that the feminist project of struggling for the equality for all women is not served by a denial of recognition to agency of certain kinds because they do not fit a fixed scheme of things. This position may be utilised to analyse and understand the reality that while no woman aspires for inhuman treatment and a subhuman position in society, not all women extend their solidarity to mainstream feminist aspirations unreservedly.

Structural Violence

Across India, Muslim populations live in localities which have some similarities. Most are segregated enclaves and have real or tacitly understood but well-defined boundaries. Often these segregated enclaves are in the older quarters of cities. While it may appear that the residents choose to live where they do, they feel compelled to reside in these enclaves because of a combination of discriminatory real estate practices and their fear of communal violence (Jamil 2014). In addition, they are compelled to remain within these bounds because of their poverty and the absence of liberty to practise their faith without evoking aversion among the majority community to their 'Muslimness' and possible threats to it. The exacerbation of poverty and fast transforming needs and aspirations in the globalised world also prompt the migration of more and more Muslim people and families from semi-urban and rural areas to these enclaves in the cities.

> *'I was born in 1991 in the dark city of Mumbai.'*—Sumaiya, resident of Mumbra, Mumbai

It may be that Sumaiya is using the word 'dark' as a metaphor, but narrative after narrative told us that living where Sumaiya lives, it literally is dark. Mumbra, a Mumbai suburb, has been subjected to 10 to 12 hours a day of unscheduled load shedding for many years now. But 'darkness' is a metaphor too. According to another study (Jha & Shajahan 2009), there is not a single government school there for eighth standard teaching in any medium. After children from the economically weaker families in Mumbra have passed the seventh standard school examination and are unable to afford education in private schools, they drop out of their studies. Eighty-five per cent of the population of Mumbra is Muslim, a vast majority of which has migrated here in the aftermath of the post-Babri Masjid demolition riots in Mumbai.

> Earlier I used to study... after we moved to Mumbra my parents could not arrange for me to go to school. I had to drop out. Here water and electricity are always in short supply. Most people are unemployed. There is garbage everywhere. The stink is awful and bothers people living around here, but no one has the guts to take any action. We only silently wish for things.... But until when? On Election Day we are the first ones to step out of our houses and go to give our precious votes to our leaders with hope.... (sneers and pauses) Nobody should be treated like this.

This story, with some variations in the dates when instances of overt communal violence and riots took place, the number of people killed or the quantum of damage to property and businesses, etc., repeats itself in many locations across India where Muslim populations are concentrated. Civic negligence and the callous denial of very basic welfare services characterise these Muslim enclaves. In Ahmedabad the structural violence takes the extreme form of spatial exclusion, being under social siege and economic sanctions. Muslims in Ahmedabad have literally been walled in.

People understand that while the State may not always be a benevolent maintainer of the public good, it is an important arbiter in struggles over the interpretation of needs and the allocation of resources. Even though the State is not a given, ontological reality, its subjects come to *know* it only through its institutions and practices, and through its absences. People examine and evaluate the effectiveness of the State in being the guardian of their interests by looking at its *everyday practices*, seen in routine ways of functioning and representations, and by looking at *the states of exception* manifested in practices pertaining to violence and law. People also tend to evaluate the State both by its intent and its public posturing.

They wish for a public recognition by the State of their subordinated status and the demonstration of a will to address it. A close scrutiny of the everyday can also afford us a critical 'way of seeing' that can discern State practices of neglect, omission, and blatant discrimination in its institutions. The splendour of urban skylines provides a perfect foil for the squalor of the slums and squatter settlements inhabited by Muslims. Load shedding, roads full of pot-holes, inadequate water and sanitation, children dropping out of school, all are read by people's practical consciousness as anomalies that help them conjure up an image of a State which should have been doing something about these conditions. For those who 'have', the State may remain an abstraction: but the marginalised 'have not' subjects of the State can very well decode the abstract idea of the State through a critical reading of the messages embedded in its images. They know that to truly benefit them, schemes of social protection need a more proactive role of the State.

> I do not like the environment of my neighbourhood because it is full of people quarrelling and swearing at one another all the time. I did not do well in my SSC exam because I was getting disturbed by the ruckus all the time. I hate this life.
>
> We have some people in the neighbourhood who are always interfering in other people's business. There is this woman who behaves very badly with me when I get a bit late from school or anywhere else as if I have done something bad.
>
> One of my neighbours was fighting with another once. They were abusing each other and saying very dirty things to each other. My father intervened and tried to make peace between them, but one of them started abusing my father. Abba was very upset and went back into the house. It made me so angry I wanted to kill that person. I love my father.

When the rains start the drains and gutters in our locality begin to overflow. There is so much damage because of this. The water gets into all the houses and that makes people really annoyed and stressed. All the filth reaches people's bodies. Because of waterlogging, sometimes people have to go hungry. It becomes difficult to live, sleep, sit. It is impossible to study during the season, but this is a part of my life. I can do nothing about it.

To understand this aspect of everyday life on the margins of society, we resort in this discussion to Johan Galtung's concept of structural violence. Galtung (1981) identifies forms of violence that are not carried out by identifiable individual actors and which are hidden to a greater or lesser extent in structures, as structural violence. He includes in this conception anything that may impede self-realisation. It would be useful to note that he uses the term 'structural violence' almost as a synonym of 'social injustice'. Thus, much of the discrimination inflicted on and experienced by Muslims in India, like limited access to public welfare, low representation and participation in political affairs, public matters and jobs, and spatial exclusion, is structural violence with a communal colour. The lethal mix of hate, fear and mistrust pushed by the Sangh Parivar presents Muslims as barbaric, uncivilised and lacking democratic values or even human characteristics. This aggressive pushing results in the positioning of the entire community as 'disparaged others' (Jha 2009).

The structural violence experienced by Muslims has many implications for their everyday lives. One implication is for their experience of being citizens of the country. In a democracy such as India, citizens take part in decision-making regarding their lives as subjects of the State not just by voting but also by communicating with one another about their interests. This requires, first, the acquisition of knowledge regarding the decisions concerned and then the exchange of ideas regarding the decision.

Habermas [1989 (1962)] introduced an important concept, that of the 'public sphere', which is a realm in society which is public or shared and not private. The public sphere is not a geographic place. It is a socially constructed site where people can come together to analyse their private experiences in an intersubjective background. Through open and free communication in the public sphere, personal problems can be contextualised into broader issues of general public interests. Habermas also elaborated on situations in which specific types of public spheres arise or decline. It is a concept that has proved very influential and useful in understanding the way social or public discourses change. Further, his idea of *communicative action* (1984) implies that social life is a reflection of people's ability to communicate with each other. The social life, for Habermas, does not merely refer to doing things and getting others to do something *but* to represent or change by communicating a symbolic status. Habermas [1990 (1983)] took the position that modernism's emancipatory potential was not over and should not be given up just yet. His view of communicative action and the public sphere, though called 'naïve' and 'extremely idealistic', has proved to be immensely influential in analysing the contemporary social realities as also in offering a performative, programmatic content to ethical dilemmas of the times we are living in. Also, the idea of communication gave rise to further work by other scholars who held that the public sphere is mediated by mass media (Bennett & Entman 2001).

Among his critics, Nancy Fraser (1990) merits a special mention because she pointed out that the public sphere in liberal democracies is severely and forcibly limited for many categories of people whose identities 'deviate' from the norm in the given society—women, minorities, the poor, and so on. Fraser conceptualised counter-publics as those multiple spheres which are often depicted in the dominant discourses as undermining the effectiveness of the 'idealised' and 'unified' public sphere. Todd Gitlin (1998) also furthered this idea of multiple spheres and called these *public sphericules*. According to him the fragmentation of the public sphere is occurring because intense specialised and personalised use of the Internet and digital mass media has made the possibility of a shared world recede further.

I feel that public connection is unlikely to break down merely due to media usage. Since the public sphere ends up reproducing the already existing inequalities in society, its fragmentation is not necessarily a negative development in a world where normatively citizenship is a measure of the capacity to consume and make loud claims. It may not be seen as detrimental to democracy if the various different sphericules have the opportunity to foster robust dialogue within their bounds and at some later point come together with a well-informed argument and stronger symbolic status. The boundaries of a private world and the public sphere for performative democratic politics are then quite real, even though changing and historically determined. And between these boundaries are also the boundaries of the public sphericules fostering discussion between citizens of shared identity and/or interests.

Further, I should like to also discuss the connection between the public sphere and public space. We have seen that the public sphere is best imagined not as a place but as a collectivity of conversations. Public spaces are physical spaces required for human forms of collective living and commuting between private spaces. It needs to be highlighted that all public spaces are potential spaces for collective communication, therefore potential parts of the public sphere. Even though verbal communication might not be contingent, the presence of difference in public space is also a gesture at conversation and turns public space into public sphere. In Habermas's formulation of 'public space as visibilisation', the *burqa/hijab* in the public space is a visibilisation of the Muslim woman who, thus far, has been 'invisible' (p. 11).

Much of the literature on gender and public space rues the dichotomy of public space and private space. It is not so much a problem that these public and private spheres are separated or severed from each other as the fact that they are already gendered. The ease in appropriation, or the power to assign or exclude people from public and private spaces going by gender, is contingent upon the positioning of the community in the larger society and the positioning of women within the community. A blanket statement that all men can freely appropriate all public spaces and women cannot, is misleading. The concern is not to obliterate the difference between private and public spheres but to render the public sphere more open and inclusive.

If people have no access to the public sphere it is inevitable that they will not be able to access opportunities to formulate, phrase and articulate their particular concerns as general public concerns. It is not surprising then, that they become concerned with safeguarding their personal interests such as security of jobs or wages or property and take no interest in the prevailing social situation to challenge patriarchy, violence against women, and so on.

The participants of the study complain of being under constant informal surveillance by unemployed men in the neighbourhood. But the women are also aware of the predicament of the men: lack of employment and lack of religious piety (*kaam karta ho, deendaar ho*). They tried to be empathetic to the behaviour of men in their families even when it hurt. The subordinated position of people in the public sphere brings on self-censure in public space. They regulate their own behaviour, conduct and demeanour.

Because of want and uncertainty coupled with different forms of everyday discrimination, Muslim men and women lose their confidence in public spaces. In addition, Muslim women are even less confident due to their unfamiliarity with these spaces because restrictions are placed on their mobility by patriarchal practices which seek to 'protect' them, seeing them as fragile receptacles of community honour. Urban myths/ stories of the horrific fate of women/families who dared to break the norms also prove to be powerful disciplinary tools. Muslim women are thus kept away from public spaces and develop a relationship of discomfort with them.

Our participatory workshops became public spaces, which have been variously defined as spaces for public action and democratic practice (Arendt 1958) and public communication (Habermas 1989). They also qualify as alternative public spaces because they consisted of and were created by marginalised people who had been excluded from existing public spaces. They also facilitated what Burke (2003) describes as the expression of private grief by disempowered communities in the public spaces in imaginative, discursive and physical domains.

In this chapter I have explored family, culture and conduct manifest in everyday life, previously deemed part of the apolitical sphere. Nancy Fraser (1997) explains that activities belonging to this sphere, which she calls *discursive-political*, involve transformative political practices that reveal the 'contingent and socially constructed' nature of what is portrayed as 'necessary and natural'. The contents of this sphere are often left out of demands for change, whereas demands in the *official-political* sphere take priority. The latter is the sphere of participation in processes which direct the way public and civil society institutions exercise their authority on Muslim women and the wider Muslim community. Interventions in this sphere are mostly demands for legislative or 'official' support for proposed changes. Activities that seek equality for Muslim women must be located in both spheres.

5

Dreaming in Shackles

Human beings are creatures of needs and desires. It is our desires that bring to us the motivation to work. Work or labour is a vital human activity which is mediated by meeting needs and creation of new desires. Marx believed that this constant creation of new desires and needs gives rise to human consciousness and leads to human development. Human society as we know it could not have functioned if desire was not the synthesising force that it is. Aspiring to be something occurs through wishing for a certain kind of work. Aspirations and dreams for the future are basic to the human essence of self-definition. We want to control our circumstances such that we may be able to shape not only our life-situation but also our true 'self' in the image of our inherent potential. Self-definition needs are a function of success in the project of self-actualisation or realisation of one's aspirations. If we achieve what we aspire for and become what we wish to we receive an affirmation of our human existence.

Experiencing oppressive poverty, alienation, communal prejudice and violence, Muslim women dream, forge, negotiate and reformulate their aspirations amidst conditions that are not of their choosing. Nevertheless, these aspirations need to be studied and nurtured for two important reasons. The first reason is that against large odds these aspirations could become powerful propellants for ejecting families out of miserable conditions in the slightest of conducive conditions. The second reason is that people measure up the conditions of their everyday lives against these aspirations and conceive of a reality contrasting it with appearances in hegemonic narratives.

The social position of an individual in the system of social relations is enacted and re-enacted not only in the structural dimensions of work in which wages, jobs, work conditions and the larger economy is organised, but also in the cultural dimensions of work concerned with values, norms and attitudes manifested in career and future aspirations. The realities that thwart the realisation of their true potential, as imagined in their aspirations, are dealt with in several ways by Muslim young women. While the mainstream discourses practically shut out or invisiblise their real problems, the young women respond with an attempt to redefine their problems such that they can find an alternative way to affirm their 'selves'. These alternatives are also not simply their individual 'choices'. They are conversant with the social, economic and political environment around them. The awareness that the alternative chosen may be far from an ideal choice produces distress and dissatisfaction. It may also have an unintended impact of the women buying into the prevalent ideological belief, the backwardness and inferiority of quality of their life caused by their faith and communitarian practices. When they compare their life with how a liberal woman's life ought to be, satisfying and egalitarian, and find theirs wanting, it is a shaming and humiliating experience. As the economic development proceeds in society the doctrine of increasing misery gets operationalised. Poverty and misery are accompanied by shame. The romanticisation of the poor and working class no longer operates in the public sphere and popular culture in India. The welfare state is marked mostly by its absences. Working-class solidarities are utterly inadequate for a class of people who feel they have not been able to make it. Other social relationships that were well entrenched in the traditional Indian society and sometimes also based on the power inequalities and oppressive social structures are also disintegrating. If we look at the caste hierarchy in India, this 'breaking down' of social relationship, notwithstanding its progressive nature, is beset with violence and anxiety too. Hindu-Muslim solidarity based on principles of bhai-bhai (brotherhood) and Ganga-Jamuni tehzeeb (shared/syncretic culture) has also incurred much damage. Women are more and more commodified and face increasing violence in both private and public spheres despite mediation in both the spheres by State and civil society. The overall impact of this scenario on young Muslim women from poor families can be demoralising and disempowering when they realise that the image of the 'self-made' person is mythical.

Mera khwab hai ke mein Samandar ke kinare ghar loon, thandi-thandi hawa mein rahoon. (My dream is to buy a house on the beach and live in cool air.)

Mein chahti hoon ke Abbu gaanv ka ghar achchhe se banaa saken. Ham sab wahan khushi se rahein. (I wish my father is able to build a nice house in our village and all of us live there happily.)

Let us examine briefly how aspirations have been understood and studied in social science literature so far. Aspirations have been defined in the literature variously, such as 'achievement motivation' (Ritchie et al.

2005), 'personal goals' (Nurmi et al. 2002) or 'life plans' (Schneider and Stevenson 1999). Bell (1963) has theorised about two types of aspirations, real and ideal. He defined real aspirations as those which a person will have achieved at some future date. This concept is also commonly referred to as plans. Ideal aspirations, on the other hand, are defined as that which one would like to achieve, as wishes and desires (Harrison 1969). Earlier research has mostly been quantitative in nature and laboured to establish relationships between socio-economic status of the subjects and their aspirations. In case of youth/adolescents, performance in school has also been a factor that has been given lot of importance in determining the level of aspiration. In research conducted with immigrants and persons of colour in the US, it was suggested that social class has an effect on the real aspirations of people, whereas the ideal aspirations of people belonging to different classes did not show much difference (Merton 1938, quoted in Hyman 1953). Some researchers have reached the diametrically opposite view through their findings. They found that people belonging to the lower classes have lower aspirations (Hyman 1953). All in all, seen together, this family of research has failed to establish a relationship conclusively.

Researching aspirations is a tricky proposition because often these have to do with people's values and are not demonstrable. Although aspirations lie in the arena of future choices and speculation largely, they are likely to be influenced by a person's context and experiences in the past (Farber 1989). Therefore, it is worthwhile to engage in a discussion of aspirations of young Muslim women to understand better their own assessment of their situation as it is on the basis of this assessment that they formulate their aspirations.

For the purpose of exploring aspirations in this study the young Muslim women were asked about their 'dreams' for their future, intending to discover what their ideal aspirations were. They were also asked more specifically about their career goals or aspirations. They were asked to share what they would you like to become and what their short-term life plans were: 'What would you be doing in five years' time?' (*aaj se paanch saal baad aap kya kar rahi hongi?*). In a bid to understand a little better how young Muslim women in India wish to fashion themselves they were asked about their role models. And last, but not the least, they were asked about their mothers' dreams for them.

> I wish I could buy some new clothes and new sandals. My dream is to go sightseeing somewhere.

Mein ek khuddar ladki hoon. People used to blame me for going out to work alone but I would tell them and convince them about my work and so they stopped bothering me. Now they respect me. I arranged for my siblings' education. People now give my example saying that they also want their daughter to be like me. I take all the responsibility of home and work for my family.

My mother is very worried about my elder sister's marriage and mine. We are not rich... both of us studied hard but we could not continue our education even though we were in a government school... you step out of the house and there are so many things you need... and I'll try solving all my problems with utmost courage

Everyone at home loves me because I'm the youngest but they don't know what I want. I dream of becoming something after getting an education but it seems that my dream cannot be fulfilled.

My father is a labourer... we often go to sleep hungry... sometimes I wonder how can we ever progress....

When I was in the tenth standard my father passed away... all my dreams just stopped and I got married. Now my life is just cooking and other household chores.... It's not that my husband would stop me from doing anything but we just don't have the money....

Society thinks that it can progress when boys study... a girl would cook if she doesn't study and she would have to cook even if she is educated so there's no point getting an education.

I want to stand on my own feet but I think I would not be able to fulfil my dream as I belong to a Muslim family. I want to become a software engineer but due to financial problems I would not be able to fulfil my dream.

My dream is to become an engineer; it is also my mother's dream. She is supportive but the economic condition at home is not very good. Now, I am trying to become a teacher, which is affordable.

My dream is to become a good English teacher so that I can teach students in an interesting way. But I do not wish to be famous because Islam doesn't let women grow very high.

I want to be a teacher. My mother's dream is that I should be a doctor, but I have no interest in science. Both, my interests and my mother's interests are different. I don't know how to convince her.

I want to be a doctor but my mother's dream is that I should be a teacher as she wants me to strictly follow the rules and regulations of Islam. Her wish is much more important for me so I gave up my wish of becoming a doctor. Now I have started to prepare to be a teacher.

I would like to become a teacher, but my parents want me to get married after completing my 12th as in our society girls should not study much.

It is also one of my dreams to be able to walk alone and be strong. When we are alone there is peace in the mind. No need to face any problems. Just look at the poets, writers and artists; only when they were alone were they able to write. We get good thoughts, new insights. Writers and poets sit under the tree, walk on the sea shore, then they get new ideas and their art is stimulated without any disturbance. Then art comes in the form of poems, stories, novels, etc. We must be able to stand on our feet without depending upon anyone.

Parents do not stand up to the gossip and opposition of neighbours, or society's pressure against girls' dreams. They give up and then the girls have to do so too.

I wish I had more confidence. I am so afraid to even speak to strangers. I wish to stand on my feet. If I gain something I will feel more confident... I want to feel pride in fulfilling all my dreams.

Sometimes I feel life is just too tough. After a long struggle and search, I finally got a job. We have to face many hurdles as we go ahead. But when we walk ahead with full faith, we reach high in our life. Society puts stumbling blocks to our desire. In the search of a job, I got hurt so many times and these incidents remain fresh in my memories.

I want to study hard and become a teacher, teaching is liked by everyone in the society.

I wish I could get my childhood back just to play badminton and I would study harder this time.

I want to be a teacher.

I want to send my kids to a good school.

I want to be a teacher. But I got married and now I cannot be a teacher. Now, I am planning to learn tailoring so that I can stand on my own feet.

If we do not want to wear a *burqa*, we shouldn't be forced to wear a *burqa* and time restrictions should not be there on our mobility, so that we can work. The girls from the low income group should be given free education, books and clothes, and a fellowship of Rs 500 should be given to them every month. So that parents are motivated to send them to schools for incentives.

I want to open the closed gate and walk ahead. I want to clear the civil services. Sometimes I talk of my liberal ideas and my friends say I think like a man. I want to do something to make my country proud. I'll open every door that closes before me.

I want to walk without any restrictions and make my mark.

I want to learn stitching so that I don't burden my family and become self-dependent. I want to look beautiful.

Zid ho to sab kuch kar paungi, warna kuch nahi (I can do anything if I am adamant, otherwise nothing).

What shall I dream of? If only I can change the past.... I would have changed all the bad school teachers, I would have refused to marry.

I cannot become a doctor now because I could not take the subjects of my choice, so I would become a teacher and teach kids like myself who are poor and want to study. I wouldn't get married till I get a job. I am scared that my father will not listen, it will affect my career. I have made my thoughts very clear to my mother.

I got married at a very young age. I was 15 and my husband was 30. My husband had extramarital affairs and his relatives were not cooperative. They would fight with me and beat me. I have three children. I tried to oppose my husband and his family for the way they treated me and my children but it only made the situation worse for me. I was thrown out and sent to my parents' home. I began rag-picking. My aim now is to be self-dependent and start my own business. I don't want to give up on life and I fight every obstacle that comes my way.

I teach children in a private school and take care of my family with that income. My conviction is that we should not let poverty stop us from getting an education. Howsoever poor a person is they should go ahead with their education as I feel that is the only way to get liberty.

Education is what makes a person human. I dream of getting married to a good person in a good middle-class family. I dream the same for my two sisters. I want my future husband to be there with me at every step. I want my first child to be a girl.... I'll work hard at my studies and become a good officer or a doctor.

I think I need efforts and some monetary support to achieve my dreams. It is our society which keeps a check on dreams and aspirations of Muslim women and drags them behind.

My parents and brothers discriminate against me, and by brothers make fun of my dreams to do something. But I want to rise like the sun and show them that I can do well.

I wish I had a scooty and I could go out to places and enjoy like boys. I wish to be born as a boy. Time should be no restriction on our mobility. The boys of the locality shouldn't disturb girls. I want to wear jeans and t-shirt and goggles to school. I want to be so rich that I erase poverty and make houses for everyone. I hate poverty. I feel sad to live among all these.

I want to make my career in IT and have also received scholarship from GNIIT. Our financial condition is not good as my father cannot afford money for my studies. I also played basketball for my state but later I was not allowed to go outside. Society never gives any opportunity to girls to move ahead. They always stop us. For this reason, a girl's dream remains a dream.

I love painting. I did not get any training but developed this art through practice. Due to financial problems, I was removed from a good school. I used to face difficulties in studies but there was no one to help. My brother did not help me and my mother used to get angry when I asked questions. They withdrew my name from the school. I want to do something in life and show that there is no difference between boy and a girl.

Women are not seen as capable of most work. Girls are not given permission to take up jobs. Some girls wear the *burqa* when they leave home but they take it off on the train. When people see all this they don't allow their own girls to go out for jobs. When they do get permission Muslim girls do not get jobs.

Most of the participants expressed that in five years they dreamt of becoming a teacher, professor, nurse, doctor, model, airhostess, singer, pursue their B.Ed./BA, get married and own homes. Most also quite clearly articulated the realisation that their dreams are very difficult to achieve. One participant said she aspires to become a professor but she knows that it is impossible as she wouldn't be able to study that much. Many participants who had dropped out of school shared that they would have liked to become teachers but said it was impossible to realise this aspiration. Dropping out of school is made easy for girls. In most cases of drop-outs no one pushed them to do well. Failure is tolerated well; they are simply told that they can discontinue their studies.

Further, they shared that they are not able to fulfil their dream as they don't have any resources; their financial condition is feeble, they have no freedom and there is no provision of training for them. A participant said she cannot achieve her aspiration of becoming a model as she is not allowed to step out of her house. Another participant said she was very passionate about her singing and wanted to be a singer; she wants to participate in the television reality show, Indian Idol, but she said she knew that nobody would bring her to Mumbai and she would never be able to participate. They need the support of their parents, society and the government in order to accomplish their aspirations. Apart from the perceptions of parents and other family members, and due to economic circumstances, limitations also come from within the perception of what is permissible within the faith. There is also an inherent assertion in the narratives that their lives are shut away from the real world in which others operate. Many then go on to put a caveat on their expressions and sadly share that it will not be possible for them to realise their aspirations.

When asked what they see themselves doing five years from now, everyone was certain that they would be married and have children. Marriage is considered as natural a part of the life-cycle as puberty, or getting older. With such inevitability surrounding it, the husband (or future husband) is an important figure who sometimes becomes the carrier of their aspirations that have not been/cannot be fulfilled in their parents' home. Aspirations about the husband then assume a different kind of importance. The husband should be above all, non-abusive, loving towards the wife, and capable of supporting the family. In an age of suspicion, he also needs to be even-tempered and expected to stay out of trouble.

All the narratives were one in holding poverty or limited finances at the disposal of the family as a major impediment to realising the young women's aspirations. Some of them feel, and they told us, that their families are often sympathetic to their desires; they just do not have the means to help turn their dreams into reality. Some girls shared that poverty makes their families assume sceptical attitudes towards educating girls and towards helping them become more able. Quite a few reported that they have been told of the futility of expending any effort in this direction. The frustration felt by the unemployed women, who do have qualifications that should have enabled them to find jobs, substantiate the scepticism of parents and the significant others in the young women's lives. Muslim women report being discriminated against when they go looking for jobs and being made to feel out of place because of their different appearance. The situation for Muslim young women from poor or lower middle class backgrounds is one of a vicious cycle double-bind.

Young Muslim women adjust their aspirations against realistic and hopeless knowledge that the prevailing conditions shall not drastically change in the foreseeable future. Family attitudes towards careers and actual resources accessible to girls are the two main markers of career aspirations/choice. Some participants who did not believe that all was lost said that they would try to talk to their families and make them understand their aspirations; some even said they would fight for their rights. Some others said that if they face opposition from within the family regarding their aspirations, they would compromise and work towards a goal that the family approves of. Needless to say, mothers can also impact the life and career choices of daughters in light of their experiences and values. The cultural norms against formal employment of Muslim women within Muslim communities and families are strengthened by structural discrimination of their labour power. The result is that Muslim women are more likely than not to be involved in home-based labour and being paid low wages.

As seen in the earlier chapter, suffering does not necessarily have to lead to damage. It can actually turn into a resource for building resilience and determination to improve life circumstances. In resisting being powerless, isolated and silenced, many Muslim young women develop the competence to manage everyday affairs despite continuing to endure adversity. The competence so developed allows them to cope by providing physical and mental escape from the routine, by creating order within familial chaos, by enabling them to develop and execute safety plans and protect and comfort mothers and siblings. Surviving adversity is resistance enough.

Living in the suburbs, urban slums and peri-urban areas, most poor Muslim girl participants of this study also knew of other Muslim or non-Muslim girls from well-to-do families who are getting an education, and daring to dream about future lives. Most of our participants craved certainty of basic comforts in their future, even if not of plenty. They actively and realistically assess their powerlessness and make decisions in tune with this assessment. Adaptive strategies are borne out of such decisions. Many participants ascribed their 'unattainable' aspirations to someone who is, in their view, more capable of carrying these through to fruition like a younger sibling, especially a brother. Many downgrade or relegate their aspirations to something that seems more attainable like becoming a tailor, getting married, learning to apply mehndi, and so on, instead of becoming a teacher, a professor or a lawyer.

> My life is beautiful. I have many dreams; I think I will figure out what I want to do. My sister is my ideal as she is doing what she wanted to. It was very tough for her but she did it. I want to do some good work in my life so that people will remember me forever.

I want to be like Jhansi ki Rani[1] as I dislike taking help from anyone for anything. I somehow want to become strong enough to support and protect myself. I hate it when people help a little and later take all the credit for one's success for just that tiny bit of help.

I am doing my graduation. After finishing my studies, I want to get a job so that I can make my parents proud. I have two dreams; first I want to teach drop-out students and bring them back to school.

We shouldn't change and mould ourselves completely according to the wishes of people. But if we thought only of us, it would not benefit even us. We have to think of others too... take everyone along.

I want to make a house with my own earnings where I can live with my parents, siblings and grandparents.

I am confident of becoming a good lawyer in five years. Given a chance to go back in the past I say I would have stopped the division of India into Pakistan and Bangladesh. I think the power of Muslims got divided through this.

I want to be an air-hostess and consider Sania Mirza[2] as my role model. I want to marry a handsome and educated boy who would love me immensely. I need monetary and family support to fulfil my dreams. I am the eldest of all my siblings and so have the responsibility to take care of them. I am not allowed to go out alone as the society outside is not so good. I am very bubbly and have a lot of dreams to share. I left my imagination free in this meeting and talked a lot about what I want from this life.

We cannot be happy alone. I look around me and apart from my life there are lives of so many people.... It is not enough for me to think of only my life... I go to school, I will succeed in life but if I look into the other person's life only then would I know how they are managing it.

In these articulations we can see that behind a wish for individual success there are aspirations for the family, community and the larger society. In all the workshops in this study we could discern a keen awareness that personal success symbolises for the participants prosperity for the family and relatives as well. Another impulse that is discernible is that for the participants social acceptability as a success is as, if

---

[1] Laxmibai, queen of princely state of Jhansi who fought the British to resist annexation of her Jhansi into British India. She was a part of the rebellion of 1857. Culturally, she is a popular figure for breaking the mould of traditional roles for women.
[2] The most successful woman tennis player from India, Sania Mirza.

not more, important than individual achievement. Probably because of the explicitly stated purpose of the workshops, considerable thought was also spared for formulating aspirations for the entire community.

Arjun Appadurai (2004) has discussed 'the capacity to aspire' as contingent upon available resources and from these to reach the desired outcomes. In his view it is also contingent upon the ability of a person to revise unrealistic goals and substitute these with new ones, which involves experimenting with means and ends. Appadurai asserts that these abilities are developed in the interactions among members of a community who have also faced similar difficulties and may have devised ways to navigate the course to the realisation of aspirations. While participating in the social community and discussions, an individual member needs to find a 'voice' which can articulate and thus contest and respond to the impediments. This voice is found through accessing a sense of the good life shared by the social community within which the individual is located and formulating concrete aspirations out of these. This process is repeated again and again with adjustments each time in the shared and abstract ideas of what constitutes the good life as well as in the individual's desires.

For Muslim women coming from poor backgrounds, access to those networks of people who may have succeeded in achieving their aspirations and the opportunities to experiment are severely limited owing to a complex interplay of neo-liberal economic regimes, cultural conservatism and widespread communal discrimination. For this group, the hostility displayed towards their mobility through public spaces is substantially increased when compared to how much all women in India are actively discouraged from traversing public space. We can deduce that young Muslim women face, what Appadurai calls, a 'brittle horizon of aspirations' where goals are almost certain to be broken as they are formulated out of an unattainable sense of the good life while the knowledge as to how to reach them is flawed and sparse. These young women are more likely to short-sell themselves and their dreams as they become more and more aware that they lack the wherewithal to develop an attainable horizon which is replete with ends and means.

Having the opportunity to develop their 'capacities to aspire' is contingent upon avenues for engagement with a social community in whose construction many stakeholders may play a vital role. These could be successful role models from within the community but considering that those are in extremely short supply we may not insist on necessarily limiting ourselves. In fact, with the backdrop of the ever widening rich-poor divide in neo-liberal India, the lack of political will to make affirmative action policies and programmes actually accessible to Muslims, and an increasingly belligerent and hostile strain of Hindu nationalism, the creation of a social community of viable and resourceful role models in its widest sense is an urgent need.

Many participants named their mothers as their role models mainly because they know that their mothers have sacrificed a lot, gone through many hardships, and yet remain a source of support for them and the rest of the family. Elder sisters, aunts or teachers were also role models for many of the young women. In several instances, the role model is a female relative who is admired because she manages to balance religion and 'worldly' life. Across India most participants also chose public figures as their role models. Also, while most often women role models were mentioned in this regard as well, two men were named as role models by quite a few young women in the study: Mahatma Gandhi and ex-President Abdul Kalam. Many participants named Kiran Bedi as their role model. On several occasions Kalpana Chawla, Benazir Bhutto, Priyanka Gandhi and Rani Lakshmi Bai were also named. Razia Sultan and Sania Mirza were also quite popular; however, a clear favourite was Sonia Gandhi. Many of the participants shared that Sonia Gandhi was their role model because of her balancing of her gender roles as mother, wife and daughter-in-law, her traditional, dignified attire and demeanour, combined with a very powerful public persona.

Many participants also said that they looked up to their mother as a source of ideals. One such young woman said, 'I would like to become an IAS officer, a leading woman in politics and internationally. My mother would support me for any career I chose and she always teaches me to be a strong believer in God.' Another shared that her dream is to become a journalist but her mother thinks careers make no difference, '... she just wishes that I am known as a good person in the world.' Others share the following about their mothers:

> I am divorced and have a two-year-old daughter. My mother doesn't want me to go out but I'm learning computers. I need to stand on my own feet.

> My mother doesn't want me to spend time with my friends... she does not give me permission to visit them. She says it is unnecessary, a waste of time.... I have so much work to do. I enjoy talking to my friends but I don't visit them often.

Islam gives an eminent status to the mother. A girl is most obliged to her mother. No matter how much we do for our mother it is still not enough... even a small fraction of the debt cannot be repaid.

Maine ammi ki maut ke baad koi khawb dekha hee nahi. Bohat gharibi ki zindagi ji hai, humara toota hua kiraye ka jhopda, sigdi pe khana pakana, kabhi kabhi toh ek waqt ka khana milta hai. Aise me kya khwab dekhungi, padhai khwab nahi tha waqt ki jaroorat thi, magar usse ab phir se karna bohat mushkil lagta hai. Har cheez ke liye tarasna padta hai, kisi tarah se ghar chalana padta hai. Aise pe khawab pure hona mushkil hai (After my mother passed away I stopped dreaming. I have lived a life of deep poverty, a broken shack on rent, cooking on a sigri, sometimes I get to eat only one meal a day.... What shall I dream of in a situation like this? Education was not even a dream... it was a necessity... but to start again seems so tough.... I have to long for everything, I make the household function somehow... fulfilling a dream in this scenario is difficult.)

I want to be a computer engineer. I want to make my family members happy; I have dreamt of this since my childhood. I want to spread happiness all over. My mother wants me to be so empowered that I can go anywhere at any time like men do. My mother also wants to do something to earn money but we don't have any facility in our village.

The saddest day of my life was when my Ammi passed away. I cried so much. I thought I would never get over it. I was scared of all the responsibility; how would I be able to take care of so much work. I did not even know how to cook. Even though I was scared I managed to learn.

I lost my father when I was very small. My mother educated me and brought me up really well. But people think I cannot do well without my father, they think what can my mother, a woman, do alone. I want to ask them why a single mother can't take care of her kids. I want to be an IPS officer like Kiran Bedi. My mother has a lot of dreams for me. I want to work for the weaker section of the society.

My mother wants me to excel in my studies. She also wants me to follow all the rituals on time, like doing Namaaz properly, being punctual about Zakat, do Roza. Along with this, she wants me to be away from all the sins of the world like fraud, corruption, deception, etc.

My mother has worked hard all her life for her in-laws. She wants my life to be better and would do anything to support me. I love Ammi... she is so fragile and unwell. I try to help her as much as I can.

My mother and I are the best of friends. When I want something I tell her. My father always says no but she somehow finds a way to buy nice things for me. She never gets really angry with me; even when she scolds me she ends up laughing. When I grow older I want to take care of her all my life and not leave her behind when I get married.

A daughter is a mother in training. She is also a perfect foil for the mother. Mother and daughter share their dreams and often their destinies. The mother-daughter relationship has an immense and lifelong impact on the lives of women. The complexity and quality of this relationship determines not only the gender role-identification among women but also the practical tasks and choices, and the very well-being of the mothers and daughters. While sons are also 'mothered', it can be easily observed and agreed upon that daughters are mothered differently from sons. Scholars differentiate between 'mothering' and 'motherhood' (Chodorow 1978; Rich 1986). 'Mothering', of course, is not a noun but a verb. Unlike 'Motherhood' it is not a marker of who one is but an indicator of what one does. It is argued that in an ideal situation where patriarchal 'motherhood' is not foisted upon women they can indulge in gender-neutral mothering. Freudian psychoanalytical theory provides

> a theory of social reproduction that explains the major features of personality development and the development of psychic structure, and the differential development of gender personality in particular. Psychoanalysts argue that personality both results from and consists in the ways a child appropriates, internalises and organises early experiences in the family—from the fantasies they have, the defences they use, the way they channel and redirect drives.... A person subsequently imposes this intrapsychic structure, and the fantasies, defences, and relational modes and preoccupations which go with it, onto external situations, the re-externalisation is a major constituting feature of social and interpersonal situations... (Chodorow 1978, p. 193).

Chodorow talks about how theories across perspectives are open to the possibility of a 'perfect' mother who embodies a fountainhead of human needs for love, nurturing, protection and reassurance. In the initial stages of childhood a mother is idolised by a daughter who imitates her. In psychoanalytical theories this imitation is understood as an unconscious internalisation of maternal values and behaviour, while social learning theorists believe that it is the positive reinforcements to learnt behaviours emulating the mother that characterise this stage.

During adolescence the daughter goes through a process of self-definition accompanied by the initiation of separation and the resultant anxiety. The separation or individuation of the daughter from the mother is understood to be the daughter's attempt to represent herself. Most theorists agree that it is in the later stage in life when the daughter grows into an adult woman herself and especially when the daughter has children herself that there is a revival of identification. Carol Gilligan (1982) points at a general denigration of mothering. She also goes ahead to explain the mother's bond with her daughter as designed to meet her own emotional needs that are unmet by their male partners. This is a tendency in the mother to reproduce in the daughter a desire to mother. While mothers are often seen in literary and academic literature as 'giving', daughters too give and respond and the distinction of who is a mother and who is being mothered is often blurred.

My own impression from the literature is that while a lot of exploration and explanations exist about mothering, daughters' experiences are not so well theorised; the mother in the mother-daughter relationship is privileged. Mothering is something done unto the daughter and the 'daughter' is just a label or passive status for which there is not even a corresponding verb. In feminist literature it is believed that mothers play an important role in the socialisation of a girl child as a submissive, subordinated entity, a woman. In western psychoanalytical tradition of writing on the mother-daughter relationship, Matrophobia is an important concept. Literally, the word seems to suggest a fear of the mother but matrophobia is not the fear of one's mother or even of motherhood; rather, it is the fear of becoming like one's own mother. According to Rich, it is a kind of resistance to self-hatred being taught by the mother to the daughter for not having a penis and being a lesser human than a man. The troubled relationship between a mother and daughter has also been explained as a result of a contest between the two for the affection of the man between them, the husband/father.

> Matrophobia can be seen as a womanly splitting of the self, in the desire to become purged once and for all of our mothers' bondage, to become individuated and free. The mother stands for the victim in ourselves, the unfree woman, the martyr. Our personalities seem dangerously to blur and overlap with our mothers'; and, in the desperate attempt to know where the mother ends and daughter begins, we perform radical surgery (Rich 1986, p. 236).

Matrophobia is understood as a given in a mother-daughter relationship, and severance is understood to be an inevitable outcome of these 'matrophobic' feelings in a daughter. Rich (ibid.) considers it inevitable that a mother would incur a loss of her daughter and a daughter would have to lose her mother.

Many daughters live in rage at their mothers for having accepted too readily and passively, 'whatever comes'. A mother's victimisation does not merely humiliate her, it mutilates the daughter who watches her for a clue as to what it means to be a woman. Like the traditional foot-bound Chinese women, she passes on her own affliction. The mother's self-hatred and low expectations are the blinding-rags for the psyche of the daughter (p. 243).

Citing Nancy Chodorow's work among the Rajputs and Brahmins in India, Rich (ibid.) contends that the existence of a special bond between a mother and daughter, 'though far preferable to rejection or indifference, arises from identification with the daughter's future victimisation. There is no attempt on the mother's part to change the cycle of repetition into which the daughters' lives are being woven.'

But what of the daughter? Can she be a passive recipient of the mother's affection due to the identification of her future victimisation or feel rage at her rejection by the mother borne out of self-hatred? The participants of this study seem to be making more of their daughterhood than western theorists would allow us to believe. Rich says that an alternative is possible which involves women's (mothers') respect for their own bodies. But she strikes down this alternative herself as a utopian possibility that she probably feels would never materialise in a patriarchal society.

In a response to this analysis, women of colour in the US have pointed out that differences among the women are also a factor in their differential experience of motherhood. Black children are often mothered by many women and not just their biological mother. This reality grew out of their specific needs which were different from white mothers who were likely to be full-time mothers intensively caring for their children alone and finding the experience oppressive and stifling. Black mothers, on the other hand, nurtured into their children a meaningful racial identity to face a society that denigrated them (O'Reilly 2004).

On similar lines, I contend that a Muslim woman is constructed by her situatedness as a Muslim in a communally discriminatory milieu. A Muslim mother in India intervenes in and influences the transactions of her children, but especially daughters, with the communally hostile landscape. A Muslim mother who encourages her daughter to fulfil both their dreams is going a step further than a feminist mother. Perhaps afraid to 'delude' her daughter into thinking, 'you can be whatever you want to be', a Muslim mother is informing the daughters of the expectations, stereotypes, prejudice and discrimination that they would have to face. Certainly, they are weighed down and 'oppressed' by this knowledge. But they develop a capacity to 'read' their encounters in everyday realities intertwined with the facts of being a woman and being Muslim. Muslim mothers and daughters possess a tacit awareness of the society's reaction towards them even though they might not be articulating it thus. The limits, the quiet courage, the resilience all emanate out of love, in an attempt to protect. Patriarchy wins hands down because it is aided and abetted by communalism and poverty.

The daughters attempt at somehow alleviating the material sufferings of their mothers by assisting in the housework. A poor Muslim daughter uses her agency to lend dignity to her mother who has been held 'unworthy' by everyone else in a patriarchal society. Motherhood as a status of 'value' can be pegged differently in the judgement of evaluators. On the other hand, in the Kantian sense, dignity is rooted in agency intrinsic to humanity. Could it be that while patriarchal society continually devalues the female, it is the faith Islam that lends a helping hand in allowing the Muslim woman to hold on to the belief that the female being human as well is worthy of respect too? This conferring of dignity by the daughter to her mother is not dependent on any active capacity to exercise autonomy either by the mothers or the daughters; it is rather drawn from the basic tenets of faith practised in everyday life. In bestowing dignity to her mother the Muslim young woman is not just doing something unto her mother, but for herself too. In regarding the mother as worthy of being held in dignity, she endorses her own worth. It is in this way that she ensures the well-being of each other and of all women in the face of patriarchal devaluation and oppression.

Ultimately we are like our mothers, or so we have been told. But can daughters also aspire to and permit their mothers to be whatever they want to be? It appears from our limited data that the poor and young Muslim daughters in India might be helping their mothers fashion a new self that the mothers were not. Unlike their western and more well-to-do counterparts, these youngsters are helping their mothers overcome (instead of holding them responsible for) their defeats and compromises. While few women growing up in patriarchal society can feel mothered enough, perhaps, we can safely speculate that a poor Muslim woman is a motherless woman and has to contend with a perpetual lack of mothering. This impedes young Muslim women from poor families from actively pursuing their own needs and dreams even as they fall into a status of motherhood, looking after and providing for other people's needs. Mothering men in the family but also mothering her own mother. Many scholars believe that in marriage, women continue their quest to find nurturing and mothering that they were not able to find from their own mother. In this study too, we find evidence that young Muslim women's aspirations from marriage and from their (future) husband are to meet yet unfulfilled desires and aspirations. Marriage in India is also seen as a new beginning almost akin to re-birth. The girls dream that marriage and life with their husbands might be open to a new possibility of autonomy and individuation that has eluded them thus far. Watson-Franke (2004) has suggested that some women might see the opportunity for the sexual manipulation of the husband as an opportunity in the new family to deal with patriarchal boundation, while it was not possible for them to push communication and contestations beyond a certain point with fathers, brothers or uncles in the familial home. Although this aspect was not explicitly raised during the discussion with the participants of this study, it might be seen as a plausible explanation of these articulations.

I want to be a good daughter in-law and want to stay always with my husband and children.

Mein chahti hoon ke meri shadi ho jaae... saas sasur sab mujhe pyar karte hon..., shauhar bohot achchhe hon, kaam karte hon... (I wish to get married... and I wish my in-laws are loving, my husband is kind and nice, he should be working).

I dream a lot, I wish my husband is like a king and treats me like a queen. We should own a big garden, with lots of trees. I want that every Muslim girl should plant a tree on their name and take care of it. So that all girls feel related to the green environment. The supply of dirty water to kacchi basti should stop and we should get safe drinking water.

My future husband should be friendly, he should not stop me from going out and should dislike eating chapattis because I don't like making chapattis.

Mera Naam Nisha hai, umr 19 saal hai. Mein sochti hoon ke kaash meri shaadi achchhe ghar mein ho... badey ghar mein ho. Shauhar har baat sune, sharif ho, deendar ho—namaaz reoze daar ho, maar peet na kare, achchha kaam karta ho... kamata ho (My name is Nisha, I am 19 years old. I wish to get married in a good family, a well-to-do house. My husband should listen to me, he should be dutiful and polite, religious—he should pray and fast, and he should not be violent and abusive. He should be well employed and earning well.)

I wish for a husband who is loving and soft-spoken. I cannot stand violence, men who beat up their wives. He should not get involved in fights. If he has a good job a man would keep to his own family. He would leave home in the morning and come back home on time. He should occasionally take me out.

In the end, it can be said that dreaming and aspiring are basic to the human spirit. Even in the worst and most oppressive conditions, the existence of aspiration signals the existence of a critical life-force and fortitude. People have an innate sense of the reality they are in although the alienating conditions they are in may not allow for a formation of conscious articulations of their tacit knowledge. From their situated positionality in the Indian society, young Muslim women are doing the hard work that 'dreaming' entails. Each time an aspiration is frustrated, alterations and negotiations come into the picture. Their own experiences and experiences of the others—mothers, role models, people whose dreams came to fruition, people who have encountered defeats—create knowledge and a possibility of a more realistic assessment. Young Indian Muslim women may be extended the courtesy of acknowledging the hard work involved in continuing to nurture small and noble dreams while they feel the weight and might of the shackling structural forces and conditions that they live with/in.

6

Memory and Experience of Violence

Direct and overt communal violence is easily recognisable as such by any observer. Thus, overt acts of violence against Muslim women in communal riots and pogroms are chronicled and documented in various formal inquiry commissions and unofficial fact-finding reports. But very few academicians and media observers realise as Jha (2009, pp. 60–61) notes, that while communities engaged in comprehending 'the meanings and consequences of the new spate of violence defining the intercommunity relations, (...) contemporary episodes of rioting were in fact writing a new script for violence itself.' In other words, violence not only harms communities and alters inter-community relations, but the way various forms of violence interact and combine also prepares ground for the continuation of violence. In this chapter, I share reflections which point out that the impact of acts akin to ethnic cleansing during communal riots, or violence by the state agencies directly, does not get obliterated with time. Long after the incidents of overt violence have been perpetuated, young Muslim women continue to be subjected to individualised and collectivised forms of violence. The impact of violence is not limited to the victims and survivors of direct violence, but extends to those young women who have not experienced the violence themselves but share the collective memories of the acts and incidents of violence.

In an earlier chapter in this book we have engaged with Galtung's notion of Structural Violence as causing and abetting further overt violence. Galtung later introduced another concept: Cultural Violence, which bolstered and made more comprehensive his account of violence. He linked Cultural Violence to those aspects of culture that are used to legitimise the use of violence. The process explained by him is akin to the ideological account of reality in Marxist terms. It includes manipulating the morality and reality of an act such that people do not see it for what it is and accept it for what it is not. Cultural violence makes it possible for structural and even direct violence to masquerade as dispensation of popular justice. It makes it easy for perpetrators of violence to assert that the victims are only getting what they deserve.

It will tend to become a self-fulfilling prophecy: people become debased by being exploited, and they are exploited because they are seen as debased, dehumanized. When Other is not only dehumanized but has been successfully converted into an 'it', deprived of humanhood, the stage is set for any type of direct violence, which is then blamed on the victim. This is then reinforced by the category of the 'dangerous it', the 'vermin', or 'bacteria' (as Hitler described the Jews); the 'class enemy' (as Stalin described the 'kulaks'); the 'mad dog' (as Reagan described Qadhafi); the 'cranky criminals'(as Washington experts describe' terrorists'). Extermination becomes a psychologically possible duty (Galtung 1990, p. 298).

In a powerful point regarding Cultural Violence, Galtung likens 'alienation' to 'spiritual death'. Wide social and cultural distance between communities evidenced in segregated Muslim enclaves coupled with their unequal class and citizenship status produces Muslim subjects as socially dead or non-human entities. Direct and collective violence against these non-human/socially dead entities is something that does not attract adequate legal sanctions against the perpetrators and normatively does not merit justice. The victims, survivors and others who share the victims' identity see justice denied also as an act of violence. Galtung also points out that the language used to describe the experience of violence is also often toned down and sanitised such that it fails to capture the true intensity and quantum of violence experienced by the victims. He likens this to a form of violence too and advocates that 'mega-versions' of the usual 'pale words' be used to describe violence accurately such that it aids memory of the act and event of violence. While some may not like to use harsh words such as 'genocide', 'holocaust' and 'extermination', preferring instead 'killings', Galtung argues that there is no grounds for wariness in utilising these terms as these events/acts are something that are known to humanity having occurred earlier in history too. Indeed, we cannot hope to confront and address a reality unless we can dare to name it truthfully and precisely. Paul Brass's (1996) work on Hindu-Muslim violence in post-Partition India also concurs in this respect. He is more explicit in including the language games as a continuation of violence. He says that mislabelling the acts of violence is a diversionary tactic employed by the perpetrators of violence or their sympathisers who are often the ones responsible for naming the crime: journalists and reporters, law-enforcement personnel, intellectuals and researchers studying the phenomenon.

Further, violence is power exercised, force exerted or social sanctions imposed such that these impinge on basic needs. Galtung (1990) identifies four of these basic needs and their negation. According to him, the negation of survival needs leads to death and mortality; negation of well-being needs leads to misery and morbidity; negation of identity and meaning needs leads to alienation; and negation of freedom needs leads to marginalisation and repression. With regard to Muslim women, direct violence is experienced on inter-community but also an individualised/domestic form of patriarchal violence from within the community.

In different ways, both at the domestic front and at the inter-community front, violence is a method of exercising social control. It presents anyone deviating from a norm prevalent in/defined by the majority or the powerful, with explicit harm. Direct violence is not only used to punish an individual/group deviating from a norm but is also used to threaten into submission those who entertain the possibility of 'digressing'. In the immediate personal domain most young women could easily and vividly recollect instances of overt and psychological domestic violence experienced by mother, elder sister or an aunt. Those who were married had their own tales to tell. Most characters housing these narratives are husbands who do not work or bear the burden/responsibility of the family's well-being and beat up wives who show any discomfort with the situation. Young unmarried women narrated discrimination and violence faced by them at home.

> Bhai kehta hai tu padh kar kya karegi (My brother says what will you do with education).

> Abba ne mujhe maara aur kaha ke ghar baith (Father hit me and told me to sit at home).

> Men in the house want everything ready, all their work done speedily—meals, clothes washed and ironed on time. Women do two-penny jobs at home and keep food ready and warm. Man does not even get himself a glass of water. Women do not want their home lives to be destroyed.

The violence is so prevalent and young women felt so strongly about the issue that when they were asked about qualities they wish for in their future husbands many said, 'Marta peetta na ho' (he should not hit). It was striking that many girls also reported some horrific story of extreme cases of domestic violence which they had heard repeated somewhere as a 'lesson' (sabaq) for those who would even contemplate to defy some code of required behaviour. A woman poisoned by her in-laws, a wife beaten to death by her husband, another maimed for life—these narratives would mostly be shared in grave, low voices and hushed tones. Occasionally, some narrators would become angry and raise their voices. 'Lessons' were then replaced by 'questions' that demand explanations and contain expectations that women be regarded as human and equal.

> *Allah ta'ala ne aurat ko bhi insaan banaya hai!* (Allah has created woman too in the human form).
>
> I was fed up with restrictions and violence in my family. My father stopped my education. He would always beat up and abuse my mother. My family lived in so much tension because of my father. Now we have come to live with our maternal grandparent. And now we are free.
>
> After all we are not born in this world just to get beaten up....

In the Cuttack city workshop, young Muslim women were asked what they think is the reason for the present state of Muslim women in India.

> Most Muslim families are conservative in thinking. They do not care about girls. They imprison the women and girls in the name of purdah. And do not bother much about education and do things without giving it proper thought.
>
> Girls and women are not allowed to go out of their homes hence they don't know the wider society and can't walk ahead in life. A few who want to go ahead in life are pulled back by others. The girls who go out to work also face problems in their marriage. People in society at large suppress girls and women in the name of religion. They claim it is written in the religious books that women should not be left to go outside on their own and that they should remain at home only.
>
> If one girl from the neighbourhood does something wrong, it affects all the other girls in the locality. Independence of all the girls is curbed in turn. Neighbours start talking so much about the girls who go out to study and work and are in their adolescence that the girl or the family gets disturbed and she is forced to withdraw from the work she is doing. The girls get married at a young age. This hampers their education and shatters their dreams.
>
> Men don't understand the feelings of women. They don't appreciate her wisdom and suppress her opinion and thought. Women and girls have become so weak that they don't raise their voice for their rights at home and outside. Men show their physical power and independence. And do

what they wish to, without any regulations and inhibitions. Muslims like to be called Muslims but don't know anything about Islam. If we concentrate on our work and action we can do better in life. We don't cooperate with each other and collectively voice our opinion over things, hence we are not heard.

Douglas (1966, pp. 163–64) argues that 'the body provides a basic theme for all symbolism'. Thus not only are Muslim women's bodies sites of perpetuating direct violence but also cultural violence of both the patriarchal and communal kind.

I have never seen my father as he expired before my birth. My mother brought up me all alone. My mother is everything for me; I can share my joys and sorrows with her. My mother struggled a lot to educate me. I also studied well. When I was in the 8th standard I attained puberty. Attaining puberty is a joyful occasion in a girl's life. But my mother became sad and cried thinking of my future. My mother had arranged for me to be married with great difficulty and she borrowed money and gave a dowry of Rs 75,000 and fifteen gold sovereigns of. I thought that my husband would be a good person but unfortunately he is not. So my married life became miserable. My husband is a suspicious person and an alcoholic. Scolding, beating became routine in my life. Despite this I managed to live with him and gave birth to two children. I did not convey my difficulties even to my mother because I thought let these sorrows die with me. One fine morning he left me and the children and ran away with my money and jewellery. Till now I do not know of his whereabouts. My mother brought me up without her husband and the same saga continues in my life also. Despite all these difficulties I would like to bring up my children with good education and also I would like to support my elderly mother; I am therefore searching for a good job. I hope the Almighty will give me strength to realise my dream. I did not have any problem until my puberty. After that my parents stopped me from going to school, saying that 'you are not supposed to find a job, you only have to do the household work. For that this much education is enough.'

Since I began my periods I am not supposed to go out of the house even for relatives' marriages or functions or for shopping and I am not allowed to talk to my friends. I could not even attend my paternal uncle's marriage. My parents destroyed my ambitions... they are going to stop my studies at 10th standard. I wanted to become a doctor/engineer. I cannot overcome their voices. I used to go to school by bus; one day my uncle came and said that I had spoken to a boy on the bus. This was a lie, but my parents did not believe me. I was beaten at home.

My name is Alima. I am a single girl child of my family. My mother was very affectionate and loving towards me. She fulfilled my desires when I was a child. She sent me to school when I was 5 years old and I was studying well. I also wanted to study more but unfortunately when I attained puberty my mother said she wanted me to stop going to school. She says the reason was that the neighbours began criticising my mother saying 'why should you sent her to school after puberty?' I convinced my mother to permit me to continue my studies up to 10th standard. I have finished my 10th standard and have stopped going to school.

Among Muslims in Tamil Nadu attaining puberty is not just a stage that one passes through, it becomes a bane in the life of a girl. It is as if the event marks the transformation of a person into a lesser human being, a woman. In most narratives the young women of Ilyangudi a town panchayat of Sivagangai district in the south east of Tamil Nadu marked attaining puberty as the point in their lives when all the troubles began.

Young women are not allowed to go out even for buying daily necessities. There are many private schools but educated women also adhere to the same principle. The new generation is studying up to the 12th standard and after that they are expected to focus on family life. The main roles of the women are child caring, cooking and housekeeping.

The *burqa* was introduced as recently as in the past 10 years, but now almost all the young women wear *burqa*. The latest trend is to keep even the face covered; this was popularised by the *haafiz* women who teach the Holy Quran in the *madrasas*. Young women are not allowed to interact with men. When someone visits the house the women are expected not to speak to other men and to go to another room inside the house. Men or aged women are supposed to entertain the visitors. Even married women of middle age not supposed to go out shopping in the home town. They can go outside the home town and shop in nearby towns and cities. Married women do not go out shopping with their husbands; instead they go with other women as a group.

Generally at homes, girls are told the attributes of homely and good girls repeatedly: they should not step out of their houses; they should take care of each and every household member and should make them happy.

Time and again, these words are reinforced so that they can become 'ideal Muslim girls'.

Sisters of Ishrat Jahan

When asked about some incident which was not restricted to the personal domain but had affected them significantly, most girls dug into their memories of communal riots as created via family discussions. In Mumbra the haunting spectre of Ishrat Jahan's abduction by the Crime Branch of the Ahmedabad Police and her subsequent killing in custody in June 2004[1] looms large over the everyday lives of young women.

It is now well-established in literature regarding communal violence in India how women come to symbolise honour (*izzat*) of an entire community. To violate them by way of the act of raping and killing them is to violate the honour of the community. As Badran (2009, p. 171) points out: 'Chaste woman's body must bear the weight of patriarchal honour. The honour of men is not produced through their own chastity but through association with the chaste bodies of their women—the women in their families.' When people begin living with their past experiences of overt communal violence or as news travels and memories build, sanctions against young women tighten and become more debilitating. The memory of sexualised communal violence against women in its aftermath continues to wreak havoc furtively but surely in the day-to-day lives of young Muslim women. Patriarchal structures from within the community employ these opportunities to accentuate the need for stricter restrictions. The narratives in this chapter and previous chapter establish that where financial conditions allowed it, patriarchal control was manifested in secluding Muslim women into a private space but where financial conditions required women's labour power to be used for the subsistence of the family, control was manifested in community sanctions and surveillance. Domestic (patriarchal) violence confronted by young Muslim women within the family gets exacerbated after instances of overt communal violence. The overall effects on the psyche and everyday lives of Muslim women, especially the young, are dehumanising and incapacitating.

---

[1] *The Hindu*, 8 September 2009, http://www.thehindu.com/2009/09/08/stories/20090908 56670100.htm retrieved on 3 March 2010.

Direct Collective Violence

'2002 riots were disastrous for us. Our home and basti were all shattered, schools were shut down, shops were burned, women and girls were raped. Men became wage labourers.'

While it was that the narratives coming from Mumbai and Delhi were constrained, punctuated by frequent break-downs and silences, nothing prepared us for what we were to experience and confront in Ahmedabad. The ferocity of the overt violence of 2002 and the intensity of continued onslaught by the Gujarat state government has left the girls' psyche badly scorched if not completely charred. At the Ahmedabad workshop the girls are not able to speak for the most part. There were long intervals when there was just complete silence in the room. When I (researcher) told them to take a break they sat silently not even chatting with their friends. Blank faces stare at me. When I met their gaze and smiled, they averted their eyes. But they wrote.

Today young Muslim women (like the entire Muslim community) in Ahmedabad live a literally walled existence in various Muslim ghettos. Muslim women are acutely aware of different forms of direct violence—communal and patriarchal, as also of structural and cultural violence. The forms of violence experienced directly by them, of course affect them, but they are also able to articulate the impact of violence that is targeted at all members of the community because of their identity and the impact of this violence on their men.

> In the Hindu-Muslim riots it is the Muslims who bear the maximum damage. After each riot, hearts grow more apart from each other. People's hearts get filled with fear. I think people should have a little compassion in their hearts. Muslims are blamed for everything. They are the first to be suspected of wrongdoing. We are also Indians. We have lived here, we have studied here. The politicians incite hatred among Hindus and Muslims for each other. Muslims feel forsaken. The police support Hindus. They do not support Muslims. Muslims do not get any support, any jobs. If people have adequate means of livelihood the question of Hindu-Muslim would not arise. We should not believe rumours but we need to be alert all the time. So many people are killed in riots, I ask you but what about their family members who are left behind after the riots. Who takes care of them? Riot survivors get no support. Politicians and the police are squarely responsible for this situation but the general public is also responsible

because they do not trust and have no compassion. Violence leaves such an impact on the mind... deep impact... people cannot work, they cannot function. Tell us why would decent men fight? All they want is to work and take care of their responsibilities.

Hindu and Muslim residential areas are almost clearly segregated. But sometimes people who have lived together for long also help each other.

There is now little less use of religious symbols. When people ask me my name I get nervous. I know they immediately judge me negatively as a Muslim. There is always a sense of fear and terror. Police can pick up young men any time. Sometimes there are round-ups at night. Bhai, Abbu always keep some identity proof with them. I suppose some Muslims are responsible for some wrongdoing but not to the extent the media would have everyone believe.

Even when Muslims behave compassionately it is considered fake and not trustworthy. Politicians are responsible. They cannot agree on anything and look for reasons to drive wedges among people. The police is predominantly Hindu. They do not listen to Muslims. They tell us, 'go to your own officers'. In 1992, the police fired on unarmed worshippers in a mosque. People cannot forget because the discrimination continues.

Riots are always a possibility. We may go anywhere, on the road, in the train, at work... the fear is always at the back of the mind. Once you have borne loss of body and things, fear never goes away. After a riot a person's perspective changes. There is a perpetual tension that never eases. My father says he finds it difficult to trust Hindus. I feel afraid to mention my name, behaviour changes once it is known that I am a Muslim. This is the biggest impact. It is on our daily social life... we hear of compensation, but I don't know if people get that or not. Leaders, governments they are sure to know of these things... but they never warn people, they never protect them. No matter what happens they only wish to save their positions. People may live in fear or die, it is of no consequence to them (*log darein, marein, kuchchh bhi karein*).

Muslims who lived in Hindu settlements or Hindus who live in Muslim settlements left, they sold their houses at very low prices or even abandoned them if they could not sell.

I cannot believe that if the government wanted to provide security to people it would not be able to do that. If they are serious about it they can do it. How do people get bombs and weapons? This must be stopped. The police can stop it if they are not partisan.

So many people were ravaged in the 1993 riots. They have not emerged from the trauma even today. If there is a riot elsewhere in the country or a Muslim is arrested somewhere on charges of terrorism, my heart fills up with fear. As a woman, rape and dishonour are very real fears; but also think about the education of children being stopped, poor families losing their meagre sources of livelihood, neighbours who have lived together like a family for years starting to see each other with suspicion. Neighbours looted their neighbours. When people fled their homes for survival, neighbours squatted on their properties. The police used to beat up people after asking them whether they were Muslim or Hindu. Even today if there is any survey in the basti, I get frightened whether this might be followed by violence. With so much tension after the violence people moved to live in Muslim localities. When neighbours behave like this, who can you trust? I would not trust a Hindu. I cannot bring myself to trust them. If I go to a Hindu locality I am afraid to mention my name; it is sign that would tell them that I am Muslim.

If I choose not to see it I won't see it but when I look carefully, I see that all around me are the after-effects of violence. Of course, people lose work, property, things, but the loss of education, mental health are no less important. Poverty makes people weak. Boys, men are under so much mental stress. Without any reason the police would drag them out of their houses and beat them. I know in Jogeshwari women used to wear many clothes one over another in their attempt to deter rapists. With my own eyes I have seen the same local leader assure us in the day but attack us later at night. From Dharavi children were sent to stay with relatives who lived in Muslim areas. Young men were being picked up by the police so they were told to go away to the native villages, run away anywhere... my sister used to live in Bandra; she died of fear soon after the riots and my brother is still in Thane Mental Hospital.

How can I tell.... Muslims have been so affected by the violence. People were rendered homeless, childless. So many lives were lost, people were shot and innocent people are still being punished, in jails and in mental hospitals. Even today I urinate in my sleep when I get nightmares of the violence that we were subjected to. Everyone says, forget about it. Do you think I do not want to forget? But there is a corner of my mind where the visuals of violence are still so fresh. This view has found a home in every Muslim area.

Hindus have moved from mixed bastis to Hindu localities. But Muslims are told that they have absolutely no right to live in India! The locality has virtually been partitioned. When the violence is happening, it is complete chaos, people cannot make sense of what is happening. There is no time to think if this is injustice and whether we are being oppressed but surely at some point the people must think of a sane, effective response to this madness. How can we hold leaders answerable to the consequences of violence?

> My father works hard but he never gets his salary on time. Even during ramzan he fasted and worked without asking for any concessions for himself. So many people work but their employers do not pay them in time for Eid. It is as if we are deliberately prevented from celebrating our festivals. Local committees are defunct. Police picking up boys and putting pressure on them is an everyday occurrence. No procedures are followed while making these 'arrests'. Boys lose their jobs. With no livelihood their emotional ties with the family become tenuous and there is much bitterness and resentment in relationships. What kind of mad person would say that they do not want peace? The government is creating so many police posts but they are not treating our men as if they were citizens of this country. Sometimes I think this is how people must have felt under British rule.
>
> Is the future for the Muslim young men jail or unemployment? Once the label of terrorist is pasted on a person what other future can they have. Police picks up the husbands then they start harassing the wives and family as a routine. My husband applied for a passport; so much time has passed and we don't know the reason for delay. Can we even dare to talk to the police? We actually need security from the police.

Their questioning of the patriarchy in Muslim women's family life is halted by the communal hatred directed at them and felt by them and their men in their everyday interactions in the public sphere and in their relationship with the state. The common experience of communal discrimination along with violence (or the anticipation of violence) binds Muslim women and Muslim men together more strongly than the common experience of patriarchy binds Hindu women and Muslim women. The problem is that in the public sphere the Indian Muslim women's voice is merged, dissolved, and, thus, lost in the Muslim male voice, while the Muslim male voice is effectively silenced except when it is raised to curtail Muslim women's rights and freedom.

In her book *The Will to Change: Men, Masculinity, and Love*, African American feminist bell hooks (2004, p. 99) says:

> Although women with class privilege such as Susan Faludi or Susan Bordo who write about men express surprise that most men do not see themselves as powerful, women who have been raised in poor and working-class homes have always been acutely aware of the emotional pain of the men in their lives and of their work dissatisfactions. Had Susan Faludi read the work of feminist women of color writing about the poor and working-class men whom we know most intimately, she would not have been 'surprised' to find masses of men troubled and discontent. Women

with class privilege have been the only group who have perpetuated the notion that men are all-powerful, because often the men in their families were powerful.

The tragedy of the situation is that true to their patriarchal positions, while Muslim women have extended their care-based agency in the private sphere and to a limited extent in the public sphere to ameliorate the subaltern position of the Indian Muslims and thus also the Muslim man, Muslim men have failed to return the courtesy. Demands for justice in cases of (sexualised) violence against women have been raised but strong voices against domestic violence, and for better provisions of education and employment of Muslim women have not been forthcoming. This complaint is not only directed at the religious and political leadership of the community but also male Muslim academicians, scholars and intellectuals. In my experience of interacting with Muslim women in higher studies they have mirrored my own experience that on university campuses, Muslim men have shown little inclination to mentor and support Muslim women scholars. In fact, Muslim men's response to Muslim women scholars, colleagues and students can be plotted on a scale ranging from uncomfortable, uncommunicative, discouraging to hostile communication.

Memory

I have invoked the role of memory several times earlier in the discussion. The preceding narratives clearly illustrate the continued survival of events in the past, especially significant tragic and traumatic events, in memory. In the case of collective violence targeting a community for their subjugated identity considered deviant and/or profane by their significant Others, memories do not remain only in the minds of the individuals who have experienced a trauma or a significant event. They are also collectivised. Pierre Nora (1996) talks of sites in which memory is produced. In his view, building memorials, establishing or expanding museums, and popular representation in films and books are vehicles or sites of memory. Memory is not something that is just there (ontological entity); it comes into existence in the deliberate acts of its production. Memory and commemoration are prisms through which we negotiate our past. Collective memory is produced by the public commemoration and active participation of a large number of people 'doing the work of mourning and public remembering themselves'. Memories according to Halbawchs (1992, p. 38), 'are recalled by me externally, and the group of which I am a part any time gives me the means of reconstructing them.' The memory of an event in the past is constructed by not only conjuring a picture of the event but it is also habituated by ways in which people reach these images. It might be that they experienced the event themselves, or that they were witness to it. But consigning an event to memory may also be done through various other methods such as interacting with victims, retelling or recounting experiences through different methods, including mass media. Based on the narratives of young women in Kerala, Karnataka and Odisha recounting the horrors of 2002 Gujarat, I can say that a factor that seems to facilitate collectivisation of memories of collective violence is that memories can also be borrowed or imagined such that they are not really a remembrance of experience but are rather a pictured act of empathy. Although invoking a memory is a mental faculty of an individual, it is neither merely biological nor exclusively personal. Commemoration, as well as creation of memory, is firmly located in the social and cultural realms.

Indeed, theorists of collective memory agree that it is located in the brains of individuals but it exists independent of an individual brain. It depends upon the group that remembers an event, as much as (if not more), upon the nature of the event that is being remembered. According to Halbawchs (1992) the most long-lasting memories are those that are in harmony with (or find resonance in) the memories of others. If our memories lack this resonance, we tend not to trust them as true memories and relegate them to the category of 'better forgotten'. It has been argued that this view is a functionalist view of commemoration and forgetting, but other authors have disagreed, pointing out that Halbawchs actually brings to light the interplay of conflicting narratives fighting for a share in collective memory (Barnier & Sutton 2008). It is a play of power of groups that decides which version of the narrative goes into the collective consciousness. The continuity of our past in our memories and its impact on our present is why history-writing is always such a contentious project. If collective memory seems to be a function of inter-community conflicts in a given society, we can imagine that in deeply divided societies such as India the collective memory is also not a singular device but rather several fractured entities. The Muslim community's memories that are challenged by the dominant narratives in not being acknowledged or contradicted cannot get access to the dominant collective memory. Obviously, not all are simply forgotten and they survive the force of relegation to oblivion. At the same time, forgetting too is not a seamless phenomenon. When people seem to 'move on' or 'forget' certain significant events they often say that it is because in their everyday lives they find their memories to be of no use. Some of this frustration emanating from the task to remember is to do with the denial of justice and continuity of violence in different forms. But, as Benedict Anderson (2006) asserted, to know that which has been forgotten is also an act of remembrance. Members of communities on the margins of a society or the alienated minorities often live with this dissonance. They know that their memories are out of sync with the memories of their significant Others but they do not relegate all their memories to 'better forgotten'.

Although this resistance and the very existence of a *subaltern collective memory* is significant, it would not do if I do not point towards the hegemony of not only the ideas of the powerful but also the memories of those who are in power. This is the only way to account for how even certain Muslims buy into the argument of fundamentalist, irrational and violent Muslims. Not only is it true that the remembrances which will be successful for making into collective memory is a function of power of those holding the memory, but also who gets to conveniently forget what is also a function of power.

One would imagine that living with a 'faulty' subaltern memory would have its own repercussions. Being the purveyor of this subaltern collective memory but also being subjected to the dominant collective memory with all its contradictions can be a big burden, especially considering that there is so much discord between the two. This discord brands the collective memory of the oppressed as unreasonable and is experienced by the members of identity groups declared profane in a society, as a moral and existential problem that further alienates the bearers of these identities.

To understand this problem further let me question the very purpose of existence of a collective memory. Collective memory is needed because personal memory is 'ephemeral' and fleeting. It cannot be trusted with ensuring the continuity of life and, somehow, with the idea of continuity of 'humanity' itself. Thus, collective memory is metaphorically but intrinsically connected to reason, meaningfulness of life and immortality in the face of death. Collective memory is a powerful device for the Muslim community in India in the face of horrific death as a result of direct collective violence but also a 'spiritual' or 'social' death caused by the structural and cultural violence faced by them.

Death is a break in the narrative of life, which is remedied by religion because it brings hope of the possibility of continuity of existence. Death is also morbid because of its association with forgetting. It is indeed possible for individuals to cope with the pain of loss because it is possible to forget. One of the most spectacular fears related to death is that it induces loss of space in the consciousness of the living. Immortality is sought if not physically then as a permanent space in the collective consciousness. To be remembered is to be honoured by rising above the limitations of human existence. Heroes and martyrs pass from a brief physical existence to a transcendental eternal existence in the collective consciousness.

Meaningful death is the loss of the individual whose life experiences are held together adequately in the collective memory. If this memory makes it easier for the group to live their life then the death is meaningful, but if the space required by the remembrance of the dead person in collective memory does not aid the identity-formation of the group then the death is senseless.

Collective consciousness is public space—being remembered by a collectivity is being in the public realm. This is probably the reason why exemplary figures who are propped up in communities to be remembered for eternity, are mostly men. The act of remembrance is also gendered, as by being remembered a woman brings disgrace upon herself. In most cultures, narratives of extraordinary women are often recounted to suggest that they must not be followed or cannot be emulated because they portray examples of tragedy and caution. Remembering and forgetting are both selective exercises of social sanctions that are designed to help us compose a past and a present that we can live with, or stay alive in.

Halbwachs asserts that the controlling role of collectivities sharing a remembered past cannot be over-emphasised. In Islam, for example, Prophet Muhammad clearly indicated that the memory of his life and how he led it be a source of a code of behaviour for his followers. This memory is now inscribed in the behaviour pattern in little or big ways in the collective memory of his followers. In more secular ways what is remembered, who remembers it, and how, is inscribed into our daily lives. The consciousness of a group of its identity is mediated through its awareness of its past. The identity of a group and indeed its existence as a distinct group depends upon this particular collective memory of its own past. When the nature of collective memory of a group changes, the group ceases to exist, as it were. The members form a new group with a new identity. This is the reason that history and memory are potent sites where most contentious conflicts often unravel but memory could also be construed as a site which a community inhabits to attempt metaphoric continuity and actual safety. Collective memory can also be a source for 'metis' described by Scott as practical knowledge that is embedded in concrete situations and develops intuitively in interaction with institutions and other actors (Scott 1998, p. 316). It is clearly replete with lessons that bolster the resilience of a community experiencing violence. Diane Davis defines 'resilience as the ways that actors and institutions at the level of the community actually cope with or adapt to chronic... violence' (Davis 2012, p. 5).

Despite the limited space for agency, community, religious and intellectual leaders must work towards providing means and creating spaces for processes and rituals necessary to deal with pain. Commemoration and performance of pain facilitate a better grasp of the reality when blinded with pain. Performance gives meaning to events (Goffman 1959) when one cannot make sense of violence and everything seems meaningless. These rituals can include something similar to the methods employed in this study. Voicing their story of injustice in public, even if it is by remaining silent or through tears and crying, may help people perform resilience in crisis. We may remind ourselves that social disarticulation of the powerless in a society is like social death which paves the way for actual killings.

While we must name the forms of violence and the perpetrators of violence, truthfully, we must also insist upon the analysis of suffering to be historical. Any analysis of violence must keep in mind that not only direct violence but also extreme suffering in its structural avatar is a result of agency on part of someone who has power. It is to be noticed that some forms of violence like domestic violence and rape, and subsequent suffering are almost exclusively feminised, while others are not. For example, restrictions on mobility arising from fear and hostility acts both on Muslim young men and women, although differently. This fear stems from overt State violence by the police or by its failure to act to prevent violence.

We should also pay close attention to the empathetic witness people can provide each other and share the pain in suffering. From being just isolated and helpless bystanders, we need to become listeners and counsellors. We need to find solace in coming to an understanding that our individual suffering is not unique but shared. And in this shared suffering we can make sense of not only what we are going through, but also find resilience in crisis and the agency to name it. If the agency to express and articulate can be inculcated and nurtured, it could give people an agency to prevent violence. The articulation, when listened to, may lead to sensitivity to the needs and acknowledgement of the humanity of the subjugated. As a beginning, we must seek to create safe spaces where articulation and recognition is not interrupted, as it is in the real world, due to power concentrations or asymmetry.

7

I Speak, Therefore I Am: Articulation as Shaping of 'Self'

> Human existence cannot be Silent, nor can it be nourished by false words, but only by true words, with which men and women transform the world. To exist, humanly, is to *name* the world, to change it. Once named, the world in its turn reappears to the namers as a problem and requires of them a new *naming*. Human beings are not built in silence, but in word, in work, in action-reflection.
>
> Paulo Friere (1993, p. 88)

The after-effects of overt violence and the continued onslaught of structural-cultural violence do not stop at affecting daily living and functioning. The overt, structural and cultural forms of violence continue to deeply affect not only young Muslim women's aspirations for their future but also the formation of their self-concepts. This view finds support in Galtung's (1990) contention that the structure of violence not only leaves its marks on the human body and material aspects of life, it also impacts the mind and the self of the affected. Structural and cultural violence together strengthen the oppressive elements within the structure and aim to avert the awakening and mobilisation of the critical consciousness of the exploited with which they could fight the prevailing violent conditions.

The first casualty in this regard is the expression and articulation of experiences that may raise critical consciousness. The dominant discourses of what Muslim woman should be like and how they should behave impact their own ideas regarding their 'self'. What constitutes 'self'? What good is 'self'? How is the 'self' that can speak more valuably than that which was non-discursive silent/not heard-only spoken for/about?

Cooley suggests that 'self' is fabricated as a looking-glass self [1902 (1964), p. 184] '... has three principal elements: the imagination of our appearance to the other person; the imagination of his judgment of that appearance, and some sort of self-feeling such as pride and mortification.' Further, according to Cooley, how the society appears to the individual becomes her 'immediate social reality' (ibid., p. 119). It influences and is influenced by the mental construct 'I'. Thus, 'there is no separation between real and imaginary persons; indeed to be imagined is to become real, in a social sense' (ibid., p. 95). In other words, people behave the way they think they should appear to other people. If Muslim women construct a social self from an understanding (of how they should be) derived from dominating discourses, by corollary, they can also conceptualise an alternative sense of self and bring it into existence. This is the reason that the question of self is so important to feminist thought and strategies.

In most philosophical literature 'self' has been understood as the ability to reason and often been defined in masculine terms. This masculinised 'self' is acknowledged as a real thing, as embodied, while the women, who are merely the other and irrational, are ascribed a status of a shadow of the masculine self. The ascription of an apparition-like self to women is inscribed in the intonation such as 'behind every successful man is a woman'. It is then not surprising that selflessness and self-sacrifice are considered feminine virtues. The problem of an unreal and invisible self for women cannot be solved by their putting on or mimicking a rational-masculine selfhood which is defined in a way that women cannot have it. Carol Gilligan (1987) provides a way out of this challenge by redefining the issue of morality arising not solely from the demands of rationality and justice but also from the demands of care. The care ethics conceptualised by Gilligan allow for an agency that operates in a climate of empathy, trust and interconnectivity among humans. In the intra-personal development of morality and agency, and thus of self, this account of care ethics points to the inescapability of dependence that traditional non-feminist philosophers ignore.

In Chapter 5 of this book, I discussed how work is a way in which we define ourselves. This notion of work, or the reproductive activity of human beings as a self-definition is of course not the only way to conceptualise it. Hannah Arendt in her book *The Human Condition* (1958) says that through labour people can express their sameness, i.e., their humanity, but it is only in interaction, using action and speech, that human beings display their unique individuality. It is the revelatory quality of speech or communicative action that helps the ascription of individuated personhood onto an agent.

'A self' is not a singular entity. Individual subjects do not have a singular 'self'. It is the differences and collectivities in the social that account for plurality and change in 'selves'. The 'agentic subjects' do not together form 'social', they are formed and shaped by it. Their positioning in social circumstances not of their choosing, and their constant negotiations with interpersonal relationships with other people in such circumstances inscribes structure in their everyday actions. Speaking out in a manner, at a time, in a space such that one is heard may catalyse the interplay of identity and power. It is upon the identification of these circumstances that a self may emerge which is capable of agentic action for political change.

Following this suggestion, in this chapter I explore a consciousness of self as discerned from the narratives of Muslim women and their observations. I have read in the narratives, self-consciousness among young Muslim women as comprising of several things—their ability to represent themselves through voice, expression of self and difference through dress, wider self-definition in recognition of identity through participation in collective forums, and completion of the speech acts of self-disclosure through acknowledgement by others.

Just as we have seen that violence incapacitates voice, we see that education facilitates it. In the experience of this study it was seen that self-disclosure is something that came most easily to those groups where participants were from more well-to-do backgrounds, for example, in Calicut, Kerala, and in one group in Delhi. On the other hand, girls who had dropped out of school and were struggling with the vagaries of acute poverty took time to figure out their responses to questions about themselves. They reported that these questions about their aspirations and their future plans had never been posed to them earlier. Perhaps in places where there had been experience of ferocious communal violence such as Gujarat or Mumbai, the space and time available in the design of the workshop to elicit self-disclosure was not adequate. We have to recognise the crying and breaking down that occurred during the workshops as articulation of a ravaged personhood. Language fails the purpose of expressing the pain of a hurt self which is told that it is not human and not worth living.

Young Muslim women in Kerala did not hesitate much when faced with questions about what represents them the most. They demonstrated self-conscious articulation and used the most abstract terms to speak about themselves.

> I am myself the most when I am alone. Being alone is significant because a person can think only when he/she is all alone. At that moment one can get peace of mind as well as think creatively.

I think I am quite open for ideas and my attitude towards life is not narrow. I wish to gain more and more knowledge in my life because knowledge never goes waste. My openness is my most defining characteristic.

We are what we are because of our experiences and the people who love us. Life is a journey, what we have got till now is nothing; we still have to go ahead. There are lots of sweet and sour experiences in our life and they are part and parcel of life. All of us get depressed or face a setback in some phase of our life and then we need a person who can listen to us and can support us.

I am yet not sure of who I am. I am still searching. I think if I am too bothered about deciding who I am I might not be open to what I can learn from the journey of life and the obstacles on the way.

I feel that Muslims are seen with disgust in society (*Musalmanon ko log samaj mein hikarat ki nigah se dekhte hein*).

Ek gharib, anpadh insaan ki koi poochh hi nahin hoti... koi uski baat nahin sunta (Nobody asks anything of a poor, illiterate person, neither does anyone listen to such a person).

During a workshop in a Delhi slum since all the participants did not know each other there was a round of introductions in the beginning. The organisation that was hosting the workshop had provided each participant with a thin notepad and a pen each. Knowing that it was a first-of-its-kind experience for most to speak in a group, we gave the participants a minute each to think of what they wanted to say about themselves. A facilitator suggested that they could use the notepad to write and gather their thoughts. The girls seemed nervous and the atmosphere seemed a little tense. A girl gestured that she would share first. She introduced herself and said that she had dropped out of school. The one sitting next to her said that she had dropped out too. Quite a few others said that they too no longer go to school. Barely a few minutes into the introductions and many participants were crying. It was evident that marginalisation was sensed and deeply felt but remained unarticulated with this group of young women. The specifics may be different, even unique, but the condition is shared.

The 'self' also makes an appearance in a subject's perception of the other, not as who she is but as a person who is, in turn, perceiving her as an object. The self-consciousness is motivated by the gaze of the other (Merleau-Ponty 1945) and it is this consciousness that becomes a primary disciplinary force according to Foucault. Thus the phenomenon of self-consciousness is inextricably related to phenomena such as empathy, approval, shame and guilt, etc. (Ghallagher & Zahavi 2013).

Mein ek achchhi larki banna chati hoon. Koi bhi aisa kaam na karoon jis se meri ammi-abba ko sharmindagi ho (I want to be a good girl. I hope never to do anything that would shame my parents).

Bura insaan banna aasaan kaam hai par achchha insaan ban kar rehna bohot mushkil hai (To become a bad person is easy but to remain a good person is very difficult).

The self and its consciousness are both socially situated. This notion of a plural, differentiated 'self' is important because if the 'self' was unified and absolute, its negation would be absolute too. Obviously, it is not so. People think of themselves as rational and objective and yet the structural prejudices are ensconced in their everyday transactions. Women find ways to accept and even perpetuate certain features of patriarchy but also subvert some other when the opportunity arises. These examples point towards the possibility that whenever self is conceptualised in one particular manner it fails to include the self in its entirety. There is always a 'left-over'. It is precisely this filtering process in the self that allows theoretically, the 'self' to have an ability to consciously register the prejudices threatening its negation and to device fragmentary/non-absolute ways to resist these prejudices. This residual self is also a source of perseverance of aspirations of respect and equality despite the intensity of injury to the self.

Aaj tak hamne apne barey mein itna socha nahin… ghuma- ghuma kar poocha… itna baat suna… ke samaaj kya chahta hao, Muslim samajik karyakarta kya chahte hein… Ham sach- mooch kya chahte hein ye soche bina badlav nahin aa payega. (We had never thought about ourselves so much, we were asked in so many circuitous ways… we listened to so many things… what does the society think… what do the Muslim activists want… we will not be able to bring change unless we think about what we really want. (At the debriefing workshop of BMMA field researchers, Delhi.)

Explicit expression of self can become a point of commencement of challenging those conditions that create misrepresentation, or discursive deafness, or point of failure in the field of vision. But, the language of identity is not just vocal, it also has a visuality. Our sense of self is often also articulated through how we dress. Identity is often visually invested in people. My sense of self as a dressed self. It matters everywhere how you dress; it is one of the languages in which the self is articulated, a mode of representation. Seldom is one able to reduce the act of dressing up merely as the need to just cover oneself and go. The layering of *dupattas* and *qameez* over *shalwars* and *burqas* and *chadors* and scarves is also an act of translation of accommodation made by the wearer with the historical notions of covering, modesty, aesthetics on the one hand, and commodification and consumption on the other.

While social control over the dressing of women is a norm, dressing is also often used by women as an act of resistance. Muslim women in different contexts (for example, the Hijab controversy of French schoolgirls) have been known to use their dress to holding the prejudiced mind to the stereotype and then defying the stereotype to force a recognition for the factor that is never acknowledged but always becomes the fulcrum of all prejudice and discrimination against them. Dressing in a particular way is a Muslim woman's way to make the other see her Muslimness, sometimes hybridising the look so as to also dress in a way that she would like to see herself, as a Muslim who is conscious of other cultural ways of being and dressing.

Feminism often ends up being equated with westernisation. To be truly liberated an Indian woman is often expected to also don trousers. A woman who insists on wearing only Indian attire might be accused of being regressive. For instance, an Indian Muslim woman who wishes to assert her identity in her dress by covering her head or wearing an *abaya* or *naqab* cannot be accepted as a woman who feels and demands equality. A young college-going Muslim woman said she consciously decided to wear only *shalwar-qameez* to make a political statement that you did not have to be dressed in trousers to be progressive. She said that wearing *shalwar-qameez* and covering one's head and face with a *dupatta* is a practice that is shared by people of many cultures in India but the reading of Muslim women wearing the same dress is always different.

Assertion of identity through obvious display in dress is seen as visibly antagonistic and many self-avowed feminist find it difficult to accept this also as an act of representation. First-generation African immigrants to USA assert their heritage by wrapping their hair in African turbans or wearing dresses native to their cultures. An academician-poet of Ghanaian origin reports deciding to wear a *namaata* for her academic appearances after experiencing what she calls an 'inarticulate moment of self-awareness' during a poetry reading performance in which she 'realized that cocktail dressing was a violation' of her words (Busia 1993, p. 207).

As discussed earlier, getting dressed is not only an act of adornment and gratification of desire to appear attractive to others but also an act of self-definition. Dressing up is a mode of communication. An act of choosing this or that apparel is an act of articulation; it is saying that I am this or I am not that. The Muslim practice of veiling is no different. Margot Badran (2005) recounts instances of Muslim women in West Asian countries using the practice of donning a veil or giving up wearing it as a political act depending on the contemporary socio-political situation prevailing in the country.

Behavioral and dress codes provide a frame of reference for interpreting the abstract process of social control, representation and signification. Purdah and veil cannot be explained only as having the singular meaning of control over the sexual behaviour of women. Just as women who observe purdah in different forms are diverse, so are meanings they read/inscribe into their practices. Following Geertz (1973), I contend that these meanings are embedded in the social worlds that they inhabit and can be read only with an intimate familiarity of these social worlds. Some wearers may associate piety and religious sentiments with their apparel; for others, it might only be a method to negotiate with their family and community to gain more mobility, more time in school/ university, or permission to work out of home. For some it might be a symbol of who they are, while for others it might be a way to resist the devaluation of their identity. Beleaguered minorities, populations considered superfluous, demeaned and stigmatised individuals in societies across the globe have been known to engage in 'identity work' (Snow & Anderson 1987). It implies the creation of self-concepts that add self-worth, dignity and self-respect. While the conditions that devalue their identity, continually threaten their quest for education, work and indeed life itself, the women display their agency in undertaking this identity work.

It confounds liberal feminists that all women who are free to take decisions regarding their bodies, dress and behaviour would not necessarily choose western liberal feminist ideas. Many women who chose to wear the *naqab* do not feel that it limits them from living a full life as a human being or as an active citizen. If only wearing a form of hijab limited the possibilities for Muslim women in societies where they are otherwise promised equal rights as citizens, then the limit experienced would not be an intrinsic quality of the cloth that covers/adorns the body, rather it would be in the nature of social relations in which the woman is placed with the rest of the society.

In a communitarian or multicultural society it might be possible to recognise that people experience life embedded in a culture and their conception of what constitutes the good life is also embedded within this culture. While it may be argued that not all individuals follow all the customs of their community, it is equally arguable that all individuals do not experience their community as separate from their 'selves' or merely a voluntary association with whom ties may be severed at any time. Why should it be incredulous that modesty and piety might be chosen by a woman, when she has the freedom to choose? A parallel question may be of motherhood experienced as stifling and oppressive by western liberal feminists but on the other hand the protests by Women in Black or Mothers of the Plaza del Mayo are claimed as feminists too. If the values of maternalism must not be essentialised for all women, and piety should not be essentialised for all women, then similarly liberalism cannot be asserted as the only true value governing women's rights and behaviour. Muslim feminists have an equally valid claim to emancipatory potential in their viewpoint and liable to flounder as much in realisation of this potential as any other kind of feminism.

———

In the Jaipur workshop the women were uncomfortable talking. They spoke in such low voices it was difficult to make out what they were saying. They carried embarrassed smiles on their faces. When they spoke of their lives their eyes became moist with tears and they looked frightened. They gave other girls awkward, guilty glances, probably feeling, 'I shouldn't have said that!' They said, 'People disapprove of girls speaking with each other. They say what do you have to discuss? Or that 'girl-talk' is never ending' (*Ladkiyon ki baatein toh kabhi khatam hi nahin hotien*). Some girls shared that when they feel very bad they cry quietly on their own. Some girls have attempted to kill themselves.

At the workshop, the women spent lot of time looking at each other, sometimes giggling, sometimes just scared serious but unable to talk. Then we began by asking everyone to introduce themselves. When the girls started to talk of their lives and problems some of them broke down and cried. Crying together seemed to ease the situation a little. Later, they got talking with each other with less effort than before.... 'Where do you live?' Phone numbers and addresses were exchanged, 'If you know of some work I can do from home let me know... may be then my family will let me meet you.'

In Ahmedabad though, even weeping came with much difficulty; the young women did not allow themselves this 'luxury' for a long time. They visibly forced themselves to be composed and not weep. Never once did the atmosphere ease in the workshop till it ended and they were not expected to talk of themselves any more. Later, they bombarded the researcher with personal questions, probably wanting to know the motivations of her strange quest a little better.

In Delhi, everyone shared that they really enjoyed the meeting. 'We have never spoken our hearts like this ever before. We feel lighter, relieved (*Man halka ho gaya*).' 'No one has ever asked us about our dreams and feelings.' 'I had never thought about myself. Talking and listening to others I feel if I try I may also become something.' Many said, 'More of these should be organised…', 'every month'.

While the women's question must be answered in political and social terms, it has to be emphasised that the interpersonal relationships between women are also extremely important points of beginning of an alternative self-consciousness and formation of self as subject. Reminding ourselves of an earlier discussion in this chapter on the care perspective I emphasise that girl-talk (*ladkiyon ki baatein*) provides an avenue to develop their moral-agentic selves. In sharing their experiences and discovering what is common between them women not only interconnect empathically and provide balm-like feedback to each other but also ascribe wider social meaning to their personal experiences. This self-disclosure is a powerful method of the formation of selfhood which, as mentioned earlier, can be a site for the formation of a selfhood that refuses to be subjugated to the prevailing social and cultural norms.

Oral narratives are formed with the audience in mind. Research studies such as this one could also be a way of weaving and telling stories that we do not dwell upon. How do individuals decide who to tell those stories to that we cannot tell anyone else, such as aspirations that are imagined and savoured for a short while in a workshop? Forbidden aspirations are allowed to blossom if only briefly, possibly imagined only because the space allowed for such an act of imagination.

Girl-talk too allows the young women reprieve from the constant consciousness of being the Other (Friedman 2011). Experiencing solidarity, support and the joy of friendship with other women allows them to take a breath and make sense of their experiences of prejudice, subjugation and violence in everyday life by giving it articulation. Sometimes we are hit by the full import of what we are going through only when we talk about it to our girlfriends and/or hear them vocalise their experiences.

Separation can be discriminatory if essentialised and made permanent. But separatist relationships and spaces could also be experienced as spaces of relief and used strategically to be ameliorative. In these relationships and spaces where they are among those that are equal, women can find a voice to articulate their specific concerns and find resources to surmount their specific problems.

The limitations or restrictions imposed on the Muslim women who want to do something better in their life for their families should be fought against. We are capable of it. It's society that stops women from going out and improving their knowledge.

Sometimes when I am reminded of the situation of girls in Afghanistan and the places in India where riots have taken place I feel awful.

I know so many women who are struggling and putting up with lot of nonsense so that their children can have better lives. They cry and work too hard. I feel that women of our community are experiencing overly harsh situations.

Every woman wants freedom from others' ideas and activities. But in our society women live only at their homes even if they have great dreams to fly high as a bird.

I have seen many girls arguing with their mothers against restrictions. The mothers explain to them the tradition... what can be done... what is impossible... The girls still fight. They say that it is not fair.

The maulanas put so many restrictions on our behavior, Islam never says any of it. We should study the *Hadith* and tell them that they are wrong.

When I see Muslim girls in the meeting I think what could be the way to enthuse them and empower them. Most of them are so weak. They come from very poor families. Their knowledge of hygiene practices is incomplete. They get easily scared and lose confidence. Their body language is so submissive. When they sit it seems that they are shrunk. For the married ones, there is the added responsibility of the children. I think economic independence is the only way out. If they have some skills and are able to make some money then the situation would improve.

I had never thought so deeply about myself. In the meeting everyone had to speak and present, so I had to think about my dreams for the first time. It was so tough.

I really like coming for the sanstha (organisation) meetings. There are so many other girls. We laugh and talk. We also dance... once we begin, we never want to stop dancing. Baji has to scold us and get us back to work. When it is time to go back home, we all get very sad.

I had come for the BMMA meeting so I knew what happened there. Later, I interviewed several girls who could not come to the meeting and I wrote their answers. Another older girl wrote about our localities. We will all make a report of all the discussions and put the report in front of the government. We will tell them what we need to make our dreams a reality.

When we came for this meeting so many questions were asked of us. How was our life earlier, if anything has changed; what do we want from the future and other such questions. I got an opportunity to voice my desires. We got to know about each other. My heart got some solace in the meeting. I would like to come again.

I never talk about things in my heart with anybody. Today, for the first time in my life someone asked me what I wish for. Everyone was given a chance to speak. Girls are usually afraid to speak but today we all tried.

Whether a girl is from a village or from an urban area, the label 'Muslim' carries with it a forced sense that invokes a feeling of 'backwardness'. It is also the sense that is actively felt by the girls. Nowadays whether it is a poor girl or one from a rich family you can discern a visible attempt to dress well and smartly. They may be wearing a *burqa*, or a pinned scarf covering their hair carefully or in a *shalwar qameez* with a *dupatta* covering their head. Even in western attire the attempt is all too evident. At least on a visit outside their home there is an attempt to present a bright and cheerful front.

Those attending such a workshop for the first time showed discernible discomfort with strangers. Many girls removed their *burqas* only in the familiar space of their own homes. For many covering the head and wearing the *burqa* is not a burden, it is a virtue, a symbol of humility. Eye contact is not maintained for a long duration. Even those who do not wear any form of 'purdah' insist that it is the value that is important not the garment itself.

The Lucknow workshop was held with a group of girls who had been active with a women's rights community-based organisation. Since they attend such meetings often, they are also able to alter the agenda of the meetings or the planned training. They find time to chat and sing together. They are more confident in the physical surroundings of the workshop and familiar with its protocols, sitting in a circle, with the expectations of sharing, participation and disclosure. Many of them seem also to have picked up the expectations of the facilitators, reflecting their concerns in the vocabulary they choose for their narratives. Their articulation of aspirations, their identification of who is responsible for the difficulties in their lives, their strategies of defence, all are expressed using the new vocabulary provided by their mentors in the organisations. While some were dissatisfied and angry, others were eager to report the negotiations with their families and take pride in their struggle.

Emancipation or a state of physical and material well-being is the ultimate aim for which discursive projects and practices provide a method. In no way must discursive practices become an end in themselves. Patriarchy, communalism and poverty are not experienced in separate realms of life even though we can loosely demarcate these in separate 'spaces' embodying the various impulses or social relationships in contemporary India. These realms are configured in obviously innumerable permutations and combinations, and it will not be a hyperbole to say that they are also intractably tangled *parts* of a *whole*. Saying that they are interconnected does not mean that they are jumbled meaninglessly or randomly. It merely means that even though cognitively it may be possible to imagine life as consisting of various different 'spaces', in reality all these spaces cannot, for any practical purpose, be separated from each other. I would even say that these spaces might even be at conflict with each other *and* with the space for emancipatory feminist practices. A more prominent role for the marginalised is circumscribed not only by harmonious resonances between these spaces of sisterly existence but also by the contrarian, irreverent and rebellious politics of women of difference. Their criticism can simultaneously be looked at as political strategy and theoretical position.

In NGO gender trainings sex and gender are introduced as irreconcilable poles of a dyad. But how can gender not include the experiences of the body? In fact any individual experience cannot be disembodied for any practical purpose. One does not merely learn to be a woman from society but one learns to be a woman from the society *through the body*.

What this study finally is able to demonstrate then is that the development of a discursive social self that can speak in a manner that she is heard is extraordinary but palpably real. And also that, in this speaking the social self comes into existence. It unifies with the natural self and becomes more human. The process of bringing this unified human self into being is the process which also has the possibility of exposing the structures and processes that prevent the unification by subjugation.

A singular, essentialised category 'woman' does not exist. The women's movement in India has never been able to convene such a congregation in reality. Insisting that it does and that everyone knows what the other may be going through and can represent them is an act of dishonesty. An inclusive feminist movement would be more open to introspection and debate rather than appeal stridently for a unitary sisterhood. It must be said at this point that the polemics presented in this section of the book is not intended to discredit the feminist movement in India but to challenge it into stronger theorisation and practice that acknowledges differences.

Women are not some homogenous angelic category. To imagine women as a 'special' category of human beings who can do no wrong is a part of discourse that fetishises women as nurturers. Let us be fair, in India we have already been witness to women who also kill, maim and destroy those who do not fit into the mainstream definitions of 'us'. Caste atrocities in everyday rural and urban life by women are familiar to us. The elite leaders of the feminist movement preparing the second rung cadre from elite backgrounds are increasingly responding to their bigoted views with an ambivalent and postmodern 'fair enough, this is your view...'. Volunteerism and participation among urban college students is increasingly about self-development and securing a certain lifestyle for people like themselves, more than it is about progress and emancipation of all kinds of women.

The participation of women of difference has been historical and continual in their quest for equality and justice for themselves and their communities in the public sphere in India even though these narratives have been written out of the dominant narratives. The women's movement has also seen such participation but it has aided and abetted the exclusionary writing of history by insisting that women from marginalised communities must leave their other identities behind.

A true impulse for social change originates from experience much more radical than a need for self-exploration and self-development although these will most probably happen along the way in any case. Such a quest for self-development without any vision for the kind of change one is seeking is likely to end up as a single-minded drive for self-indulgence by self-seeking individuals. The form cannot exist only in and for itself. The methodological form of the feminist movement must take shape around a philosophical and ideational core of a vision for a just society in which every single individual and different 'self' has the equal chance to develop, rather than a standardised vision of the few more developed, more evolved, more aware individuals who can lead the rest.

Most women can recall deeply personal experiences when they realise that women are accorded a subordinate status in contrast to men. With more focused interactions with other women and wider exposure to the fact that other women are also normalised by the society in a subordinated role, women may be confronted by a possibility that this scenario need not be accepted as normal. Without any aid from reading or participation in a women's rights group or movement they may question this subordination but without questioning the standards set by the patriarchal norms. As such their analysis would remain limited to the binary of 'man versus woman' and their efforts would be concentrated around competing with men and besting them by becoming more masculine. Muslim women's participation in most women's rights groups and their inclusion in the sisterhood is marked by an insistence that all women must play the gender game according to the said standards. Their efforts are concentrated on all women accepting one view of their position. But imagining all men as being equally powerful is a deep fallacy of liberal feminism (hooks 2004). We have seen in the previous chapter how Muslim women from their position of multiple marginalisations are able to see the way communal violence and discrimination marginalises Muslim men too. This social experience of difference of Muslim women is not recognised in the feminist movement circles. To Muslim women, therefore, the mainstream of the feminist movement seems to act like any other hegemonising force. Muslim women recognise that the powers that are responsible for their subordinated status are complex and multifarious and that all men are not equally powerful. While they might believe that they can strengthen the movement with their deeper insights on these differences, they fear being derided for what is judged as their naive/mistaken/divisive views.

The participation of Muslim women in separate/satellite counter-public spheres may provide them space for a more situated articulation of their interests and their opinions on issues of wider interest, without placing the limiting condition that they give up their 'Muslimness'. In a reminder of girl-talk, a Muslim women's organisation is a strategic separate space where they can get a reprieve from being the other of the dominant Hindu feminist. If non-essentialised and seen as a process in transit to a universalised sisterhood, the separatist spaces of situated feminisms need not be seen as fragmentary disruptive devices. These spaces must not be attacked as backward or divisive but must be seen as spaces of learning for the larger movement. These spaces must be seen as those that can provide additional resources for strengthening the movement, where valid criticism from the margins can arise which must be used to correct the power imbalances between women, and iron out the creases of disagreement.

The acknowledging of Muslim women's situated differences and their points of view within the larger movement is a factor in the acknowledgement of Muslim women's selfhood. Unity despite differences can only be attempted by recognising the manifestations of difference and historicising it, by naming it. It is essential that the differences not be reduced to interpersonal squirms. I can narrate many stories of Hindu feminist friends who I trust with my friendship and can feel the return of their trust in my positioning. I am also sure that there are innumerable Muslim women who have found true friendship and camaraderie with other feminists in the country but the structure of the feminist movement in India does not allow for this kind of solidarity with Muslim women as a group.

Are Muslim women in the country destined to forever circumambulate the feminist movement but never allowed entry inside the sacred precincts by the high-priestesses of the movement unless they shed their Muslimness? Working class women know that they are different from middle-class women. Muslim women and Dalit women know that they are different from Hindu, upper-caste women, respectively. For the women in positions of privilege to assert that they are not different and must not try to be different, can only be read as an act of aggression. To conclude that oppression of all women is similar is in itself an act of oppression. If at all upper-class, upper-caste, privileged Hindu women in the movement are serious about including women from less privileged groups in the movement they must face, and answer honestly, the question of difference between themselves and other Indian women.

Even on those forums where Muslim women discuss issues of gender discrimination they cannot forget that they, along with Muslim men, are targets of communal prejudice as well. If at all we are forced to put in place a hierarchy of discriminations, Muslim women would prioritise the communal discrimination faced by the entire community as a larger and more frightening threat than gender discrimination. In a situation when State agencies like the police and non-State actors like the Sangh and its organs turn predators, Muslim women can read the reality of the oppression of their fathers, brothers, sons and husbands. They cannot be faulted for expressing their solidarity with Muslim men, and for accepting the rag-tag, even limiting solidarity provided by them. The imagery of Muslim men and Islam as faith oppressing Muslim women does not hold well in Muslim women's experiences. The feminist movement wishes Muslim women to define themselves as 'women' based on the shared gender identity but refuse the other identity that they share with Muslim men, their religious identity. Just as Muslim men must come to terms with Muslim women's quest for full humanity, the feminist movement in India must come to terms with it too. For Muslim women in India the quest for equality has been long in progress but barely any progress has been made. Oscillating between the rights organisation dominated by Muslim men on the one hand and Hindu, upper-caste, upper-class women on the other, they have been attempting to create their own fora and spaces where they can articulate their concerns without the limiting demands of both and strengthen their articulations, formulate their perspective and demand the change that they wish for.

> There should be change in the social idea about Muslim women. They alone with their combined efforts and strength can bring some change in their situation.
>
> *Aisa samaj hona chahiye jisma haar insane khulkar bol sake* (we wish for a society where every human being can speak freely).
>
> Muslim women should get educated. Only an educated community is a truly liberated society. People do not respect Muslim women's opinion and it can only take the community further backward.

There is much protestation from the Muslim community against the portrayal of Islam as a faith that discriminates against women. They rightly claim that Islam gave rights to women in areas such as property inheritance much before the progressive West. But much more sustained criticism from within the community is needed of the prevalent sacrifice of Islamic principles of equality of all human beings in favour of the continuity of patriarchal practices. This strange embrace of the legacy of colonialism and orientalism cannot be continued much longer if the followers of Islam wish to let the true spirit of Islam shine. The acknowledgement of equal humanity of Muslim women by Muslim men would be a huge leap in this direction. Western liberal secular feminisms also must face squarely its subversion and deployment by neo-imperialist projects against Muslim societies and, therefore, of Muslim families and women. An acknowledgement of this fact is a condition upon which any solidarity might be built. Western feminisms have to acknowledge that Muslim women cannot be reduced to only unthinking, naive, agency-less victims of Muslim men, and that there are alternative conceptions of a good and meaningful life which are different from the conception of good life in the western liberal tradition.

8
I Did Not Know Myself

Subjectivities are nothing but differences in perspectives and perspectives are not shaped by merely the standpoint of the viewer but also in the way viewers look at the view before them. Thus, what we see in an image is not so much the actual content of the picture but our interpretation of the image, felt at its impact on us. In her book on visual methodologies Gillian Rose (2001) details out some of the aspects of using visual material, especially photographs, by social scientists in research. She deduces that this use is apt because photos 'can carry or evoke three things—information, affect and reflection—particularly well' (ibid., p. 238).

The workshops in this study used participatory exercises which involved self-exploration and self-disclosure. Since it was realised that many young women may feel hesitant in an upfront self-disclosure situation, different techniques were used to help the participants begin to talk about themselves. The contents of this chapter are from the sharing that emanated from a particular exercise called Photolanguage.[1] This exercise is part of a family of projective techniques essentially involving the introduction of an ambiguous stimulus which participants are asked to interpret using their subjective impressions. The principle behind the use of such techniques is that many a times people may not be conscious of deep-rooted feelings/thoughts or that they may be socially conditioned to not articulate some thoughts. Projective techniques are designed to facilitate bringing these expressions to the fore by articulating them through (conscious/subconscious) safe projection on the stimuli. The Rorschach inkblot is an example of a personality test based on a projective technique. Another common example is the psychodynamic interpretation of drawings. While drawing, people frequently project

---

[1] Photolanguage utilises evocative and symbolic pictures for encouraging self-expression, communication and group development. The term was coined in France in the mid-1960s by the religious audio-visual thinkers Will and Claire Belisle, Pierre Babin, and their colleagues at the Centre Recherche et Communication/Audio Visuel Expression de lajoi (CREC-AVEX) in Lyons, France. They developed a method and published several sets of Photo language which, in turn, inspired other collections around the world.

their feelings about their subjects in the way they draw their features and expressions. Young children frequently draw adults as people with disproportionately longer legs compared to torsos because that is how it appears from their perspective. People draw some people larger in size compared to others, projecting their impressions about power imbalances. 'Completing sentences' is another such technique. In gender sensitisation workshops people are often asked to complete the phrases 'if I were a man…' and 'if I were a woman…' to bring to fore their notions of gender roles.

Rose (2001) calls the supportive use of photographs during interviews and discussions to encourage talk on issues that individuals would otherwise not volunteer to discuss, *photo-elicitation*. In photo-elicitation the intrinsic qualities of the pictures are considered important only so far as they elicit important data.

For the present exercise I had put together a fresh set of 40 pictures accessed from news media and other open source websites. At the beginning of the workshop the participants were guided into a meditative reflection exercise in which the animator asked them to think of the major events, associated feelings and experiences of their lives. At the end of the meditation, the pictures were presented to the participants by spreading them out on the floor. They were invited to look at these and were asked to select one or two pictures that they thought most represented them or communicated to them something important about themselves. Once back in the group having chosen a picture, the participants were asked to share with the group what their reasons for selecting the picture were.

The exercise allowed the participants to talk of things important to them while providing them with a safety net as to the extent of disclosure. The exercise generated a lot of curiosity among the participants due to the novelty and distraction factor, helping them focus away from their anxiety and nervousness. It also created in the participants positive anticipation for the training methods. The pictures are not being included in the text because their generic content and aesthetics is not nearly as important as the reflections they conjured in the minds of the participants. As Rose (2001) highlighted, visuals can invoke powerful feelings both from the conscious or unconscious parts of our beings. The visuals that appeal to us contain something that conveys a strong message to our sense of self. This is the reason that different spectators come up with different interpretations of the same image. These reflections found articulation in the workshops and gave all the participants an insight into their own self.

After the sharing was over the participants were asked for their thoughts on the exercise and its experience. Many girls said that they found the exercise very interesting. Someone shared that she had never thought why she liked or disliked a picture because of something inside her and that she would now look at pictures with a new eye. Several participants said that they were taking away from the exercise a method to better understand themselves. The most frequently given feedback about this exercise and even the entire workshop was that the participants got to think about themselves in a manner that they never had. They had never thought about some of the things they expressed here leave alone talked about them.

Of all the exercises and discussion sessions held in the workshop this method was experienced as the most intense and interesting by the participants. The guided meditation helped the participants to focus on their own selves. When they opened their eyes the impact of the images was quite forceful. They were allowed to take their own time to select pictures. Once back in the group with their pictures they were encouraged to speak but were not probed with questions. The levels of sharing were different in different places. As has been shared in Chapters 5 and 7, the women who had experienced more restrictions and had seen not much help coming their way were the least articulate. In Ahmedabad, the girls could barely speak a sentence before they would begin to cry. They had not found much avenue to talk of their experiences and the restriction placed by the patriarchal reactions to communal violence had further repressed them. The effort to keep unwelcome thoughts repressed in the unconscious were also reducing their abilities to engage with their pain.

Even though the participants in the workshop at Sabarkantha, Gujarat had also seen violence, the girls were from poorer backgrounds (many of them domestic workers). They had repressed their traumatic experiences through their work, toil, and through their compulsion to engage themselves in socially accepted and necessary defences. The latter were more amenable to discussing and sharing. But the animators of almost all workshops reported that while many girls could relate to the exercise and share, there were also quite a few who found it overwhelming to articulate whatever it was of their self that was reflected in their chosen picture.

I am here reminded of Freud's assertion that the malaise in the individual is the result of malaise in the society. What we witnessed in these workshops is that women, and especially young women, repress their experiences, desires and dissatisfactions and push them to their unconscious for keeping up the façade of social order. While I have presented my own readings and analyses in earlier chapters, this chapter is meant to be a record of the snippets of sharing during the photo-elicitation exercise highlighting the repetitions, the hesitations, the regrets, the aspirations and the silences as opening a possibility for the participants to get to know the way their unconscious was impacted by their experiences. During the group sessions the participants were not just speakers but they were also active listeners. The girls did not just reflect on the pictures but also what the other participants shared. The echo of other's reflections also had a revelatory impact.

Photo-Elicitation

Doll

- I have selected the photo of a doll as it takes me back to my childhood memories. I want to be like a doll but it seems only like a dream as I have six brothers and three sisters. We do not get to eat three meals every day and as such I don't feel I can ever become a doll. (Raipur, Chhattisgarh)
- I have the picture of a doll. When I was a child, I always wanted to play with a doll, but my grandmother did not give me one. She used to give all the toys to my brother. She also complained to my father about my mother and due to her my father used to beat my mother... (cries)... (Delhi)
- I have a picture of a doll, I chose this as it reminds me of my younger sisters who like to play with dolls. We lost our mother at an early age and so all her responsibilities fell on me. And, then I stopped playing with dolls but I still like them a lot. (Raipur, Chhattisgarh)
- I have a picture of a doll, I like to play with dolls but now I can't play as I am grown up. (Mumbai, Maharashtra)
- I have chosen this picture of a doll... cries... (Ahmedabad, Gujarat)
- I took the picture of a doll because it reminded me of my 7-month-old daughter. But I feel sad because I am not with her always. I

somehow want to complete my course and become a teacher. Just like all mothers I too think about my daughter and her growth. (Calicut, Kerala)

A Lone Bird Flying

- I chose the picture of a bird flying high in the sky. It reminds me that I have a lot of ambitions and I have to achieve them. (Calicut, Kerala)
- I have chosen the picture of a bird. I always want to fly like a bird but I am not free. My freedom has been captured by this society. (Delhi)
- I chose a picture of a small bird flying high in the sky. I don't have freedom in life. But, I wish to have freedom in life so that I can enjoy my life. (Calicut, Kerala)
- I have chosen the picture of a flying bird. I like to go out but my family restricts it as I am a girl. I always want to be happy and stand on my own feet. (Bangalore, Karnataka)
- I have chosen a picture of a flying bird... in our childhood parents don't scold us much but the moment we attain our puberty they place restrictions on us. We also want to fulfil our wishes and want to achieve our dreams. (Raipur, Chhattisgarh)
- I have selected the photo of a bird as I always want to fly high and to touch the sky. I want to be independent and confident so that I can achieve my ambitions all alone as birds do. (Delhi)
- I chose this photograph because this bird is alone and independent. She is flying in the sky to her destiny. All she has is the grace of God. (Cuttack, Odisha)
- I want to fly like this bird beyond all social boundaries and restrictions imposed by culture. When I'll become an advocate I'll fight even with my own family and struggle with society to realise my wishes for sure. (Raipur, Chhattisgarh)
- I have chosen a picture of a flying bird. I feel we as girls are free during our childhood days but as we grow we have lots of work and responsibilities and thus we are under restrictions. (Bhopal, Madhya Pradesh)

- I chose this photo because birds fly independently in the sky. I also want to fly in the sky. I want to become an airhostess. (Cuttack, Odisha)
- I have a picture of a flying bird. If we are confident we can achieve our objectives alone as the big bird is flying alone in the sky to achieve the goal. (Cuttack, Odisha)
- We have to fly in the sky like a bird to achieve the heights of progress. We have to do this on our own just as the bird flies with the help of her own wings. If we have the willpower we can fly as well as proceed against the wind. (Jaipur, Rajasthan)
- A bird is flying in the sky, I wish to be free and independent like this bird, but I know there is no chance of it. (Dindigul, Tamil Nadu)

Bride

- I picked up a picture of a bride whose face was covered with a veil. The picture reminded me of my early marriage but I am determined to build my career. Going to work hard and continue my studies. (Delhi)
- I have a picture of a bride in purdah and it reminds me of my marriage. My marriage was not a success as my husband used to drink a lot and later he committed suicide. Now, I have two children and I am taking care of them. (Dindigul, Tamil Nadu)
- I have a picture of a bride and her expression shows that she is thinking about her future. Every girl has a dream of being a bride. But in reality marriages are decided by parents and not by the bride and groom. (Jaipur, Rajasthan)
- I chose the picture of a bride as I feel my life was destroyed by marriage. I didn't want to get married but I had to and then my husband divorced me. (Raipur, Chhattisgarh)
- This is something which is associated with our lives very closely. I want to get married in a good family and pray that every girl gets such happiness in her lives. (Ahmedabad, Gujarat)
- It is picture of a bride; she is thinking of her future life which is beyond her control. (Jaipur, Rajasthan)

Mother with her Child

- I have a picture where a mother is crying while holding her child; this picture reminds me of my mother's pain. As I lost my father and my mother is working hard in order to secure my future. (Raipur, Chhattisgarh)
- I am from Ahmedabad and got married here. This picture reminded me of my mother. She cared a lot for me; I often remember her.... (cries and stops) (Sabarkantha, Gujarat)
- This picture is from the movie 'Parzania' and it reminds me of the riots that happened in 2002. I always wonder why it happened. (Ahmedabad, Gujarat)
- I chose a picture where a woman is crying while holding her child. I feel that in our community, women experience overly harsh situations and this makes them sad and cry. (Ahmedabad, Gujarat)
- I have a picture where a woman has a baby in her arms and she is crying hard. When I was small, I heard about the Gujarat riots. I saw this picture and thought about the women who faced all the atrocities. I just pray we should not see another riot. (Bhopal, Madhya Pradesh)
- I picked a picture of a crying mother. This picture reminds me of my mother who always cries as my father suspects her and her children. Sometimes he even hits my mother which further deepens my mother's wound. (Sivaganga, Tamil Nadu)
- I chose the picture of woman with a child. She is carrying a child and is very upset and bewildered. It shows the feelings of the riot victims. The mother is crying as she is frightened for the life of her daughter. The majority of Muslims all over India are victims of riots. It pushes them back socially as well as economically. They are not confident about their life or property. These feelings are clear on the face of mother. (Jaipur, Rajasthan)
- I chose this picture as my father left my mother during my childhood. This photo shows my mother's condition. The emotions on the face of my mother express our hard days. Our family was the victim of the atrocities of a man who is my father. The memory of that incident is renewed through this picture. There was only darkness in our life. But the positive efforts of my mother are responsible for my growth and progress. (Jaipur, Rajasthan)

Girl Friends

- I chose the picture of two girls wearing *burqas* and reading a newspaper. It is an image close to my heart. I want to study like these Muslim girls and to do something good for myself. (Delhi)
- I chose pictures of three girls walking together on the street because like these girls I like to be in the company of friends where I can feel free, share, talk, laugh loudly and enjoy myself. (Delhi)
- I have a picture where girls are sitting on swings and it reminds me of my childhood days. At that age, I had no restrictions and I would run away from home to meet my friends and play with them. (Raipur, Chhattisgarh)
- I have a picture of girls sitting and laughing. I chose this picture as I always enjoy the company of my friends and we study together. (Raipur, Chhattisgarh)
- Girls wearing *burqas* huddling together reading newspaper; it reminds me of the school days when I would sit together with my friends to chat in school or walk together to school. I have now dropped out of school and miss such good days and nice moments. (Jaipur, Rajasthan)
- If I would have continued my education, I would have also become something like these girls. I am reminded of my school days by looking at the girls in the picture. They are so like me. (Ahmedabad, Gujarat)
- I am reminded of my school days. We all should study instead of sitting back at home idle. It will help us in our future. (Ahmedabad, Gujarat)
- I like the togetherness in this picture and their love for each other. I don't have a sister. Brothers are different, they just boss you around and there are things which can't be shared with them. (Ahmedabad, Gujarat)
- I chose a picture where girls are sitting and gossiping. It reminded me of my three friends. Like these girls we are also happy and trust each other. There are no differences in friendship. When I become a teacher, I will tell my students that considering we have to leave all our wealth behind in this world then why should we differentiate between the rich and the poor. We should respect each other. (Cuttack, Odisha)
- I have a picture where three girls are laughing and giggling. It appears from the picture that the girls are going to school.

It confirms that purdah is no hindrance to progress. (Jaipur, Rajasthan)
- In this picture three girls are laughing; I want to live happily and enjoy my freedom. I want to travel and see many places. I want to be independent. (Dindigul, Tamil Nadu)
- In this picture, friends are enjoying themselves together, and I like this picture as I always like the company of my friends. We are always together and we are happiest with each other. (Sivaganga, Tamil Nadu)
- In this picture, girls are sitting and studying. I like to study. My parents are sending me to college to study further, as they are well aware of the fact that education is very important for all and especially for girls. (Delhi)
- This photograph reminds me of my friends; we have been together since childhood. Although my friends are not Muslim, there is no discrimination among us. We are always ready to help each other. We want to work with those people who are interested in learning and doing some meaningful work. (Delhi)
- I chose this picture of girls reading a newspaper together on the roadside. I have seen men reading newspapers like this but not women. I feel the women in the picture are independent and confident persons and I want to be like them. (Bangalore, Karnataka)

Single Women

- I picked up the picture of a woman walking in the rain with an umbrella. I like rainfall and used to enjoy the rains a lot when we lived in our village. Cities are different.... (Mumbai, Maharashtra)
- I have a picture of a woman who is alone; I like her as she is my role model. (Sivaganga, Tamil Nadu)
- I picked up the picture of a girl on a swing as it reminds me of my carefree childhood days which I enjoyed a lot. Those days were good, now I have to work at home as well as attend school. There are worries and concerns like getting a job after my schooling. My elder sisters are all educated but they did not get jobs. This makes me feel bad. (Ahmedabad, Gujarat)
- I liked this picture of a girl walking with a guitar; I would have liked to do something similar. (Ahmedabad, Gujarat)

I Did Not Know Myself 131

- I selected the picture of an educated girl standing in front of a tall building. I wanted to become something good in life but couldn't study. I dropped out three years back. Riots affected our schooling badly. Many girls were withdrawn from schools. The school building was stoned and parents did not consider it safe to let their children out, especially girls. (Ahmedabad, Gujarat)
- In this picture a girl is sitting on a swing; I like this picture as I and my friends had played on a swing when we had gone for a picnic. I like to be with my friends where I can feel free, share, talk, laugh loudly and enjoy every moment of my life. (Ahmedabad, Gujarat)
- In this picture a girl is standing alone. This picture is significant because a person can think only when he/she are all alone. At that moment one can get peace of mind as well as think creatively. (Calicut, Kerala)
- I chose a small girl with her head covered. It reminds me of the awful situation of girls in Afghanistan and the places where riots have taken place. (Calicut, Kerala)
- In this photo a girl is passing through a jungle alone without fear or hesitation. It shows that if one is confident she can overcome all obstacles in life. (Jaipur, Rajasthan)
- The girl is going to cross the road in spite of heavy rain with the help of an umbrella. It is an example of conquering one's problems with someone's help. We have to progress in all circumstances. (Jaipur, Rajasthan)
- My photo shows a courageous girl walking along the riverbank with her belongings. She is not frightened about the loneliness and darkness of the path. One should proceed to achieve one's goal in life without any fear. (Jaipur, Rajasthan)
- I have a picture of an educated and modern girl and I wish to be like this girl. In childhood my family allowed me to wear modern dresses but not now. (Dindigul, Tamil Nadu)
- I have a picture of a girl in purdah, I think in our culture, we have to do purdah and thus we can express ourselves as Muslim. (Dindigul, Tamil Nadu)
- I have a picture of a girl in purdah and I wish always to go in purdah as it is safe for us. (Dindigul, Tamil Nadu)
- I have a picture of a girl in purdah. I feel that the purdah system is ok within our society but it differentiates us from others when we go out, for example, in school. I have good friends in school

but when I go to school in purdah, it sends a wrong message to my friends, they look at me differently and this makes me guilty. (Dindigul, Tamil Nadu)
- I liked the picture of a woman walking with a guitar. I want to become a teacher and build a house for myself and bring honour to my family. (Delhi)
- I chose this picture of a sad baby girl. It is a sin to be born as a girl as girls are treated worse than animals and are beaten. My family pressurised me to live a kind of life I have never been happy with. I am working to feed my family... if I leave work they'll be sleeping hungry. I am thankful that this programme is letting girls express themselves and giving a platform to them to come out of home and talk. (Delhi)

Hennaed Hands

- I have a picture of hennaed hands. I chose this as I like the colour and aroma of mehndi. In our school days, we friends put *mehndi* and showed each other. (Raipur, Chhattisgarh)
- I got the picture of a hand with mehndi. Usually we know girls put mehndi during happy occasions. It's always a symbol of happiness. There are several occasions like marriage and Eid where women put mehndi on their hands. (Calicut, Kerala)
- I have a picture of hands with mehndi. When I was small, my mother used to put mehndi on my hand and kiss me. She also said that my hands looked very beautiful with mehndi. She always put mehndi on my hands but now she is no more. (Bhopal, Madhya Pradesh)
- There is a deep relationship between mehndi and a woman. Women of any country like mehndi as we have observed in meeting with tourists. Mehndi is a symbol of colour and happiness. (Jaipur, Rajasthan)

Nature

- I have a picture of a sunset and I chose this as I want to do something in my life so that in the end my parents are proud on me. (Raipur)

- In my picture, the sun is spreading light in darkness. After completing my education, I want to be like the sun and spread light in others' lives. (Delhi)
- I have selected the photo of a rising sun as it reflects the beauty of nature. My parents differentiate between girls and boys. My brothers laugh at me but I shall shine like the Sun. (Delhi)
- I chose this picture with lots of trees in a row. I become afraid when I think of being lost in a place like this which is like a jungle. A place where no one can listen to my pain and I can't share anything with anyone. I hope the world doesn't become like this. (Ahmedabad, Gujarat)
- I like flowers and I never want to pluck a flower. I like being loved by people and I wish that people admire me like they admire a flower. (Ahmedabad, Gujarat)
- I chose the picture of a road having lots of trees. I feel that our lives resemble the road where we have to travel a lot and we should not bother about the obstacles on the way. But a little shade is always welcome. (Ahmedabad, Gujarat)
- I have chosen a picture of a sunset. I chose this photo because I remember the day when my parents were not allowing me to go for a picnic with my friends as I was the only daughter of my parents. I cried a lot and then my uncle allowed me to go. After returning from the picnic I saw a sunset. I will never forget it. (Cuttack, Odisha)

Athlete

- I have a picture of an athlete, I wish to play sports but my family is against it. (Dindigul, Tamil Nadu)
- I have a picture of an athlete. He is the symbol of strength and pace. We need strength and confidence in order to achieve goals in life and one can make his/her own destiny. (Jaipur, Rajasthan)
- I have picked up the photo of an athlete which reminded me of my schooldays where I used to participate in sports. If I get an opportunity I would like to participate in sports and get appreciation from the family and society at large. (Bangalore, Karnataka).

Doors: Open and Closed

- I want to build a big house for my mother. I have chosen the picture of a closed door as I feel society has closed its door completely for girls and wants to confine them within its four walls. I want to open this door and want to clear the IAS entrance examination. (Raipur, Chhattisgarh)
- I chose the picture of an opened gate. I think I am quite open to ideas and my attitude towards life is not narrow. I wish to gain more and more knowledge in my life because knowledge never goes waste. (Calicut, Kerala)
- I chose a picture of closed doors. It shows the limitations or restrictions imposed on Muslim women who want to fly higher and higher. It's society that stops women from going out and improving their knowledge. (Calicut, Kerala)
- I got a picture of a closed door. It resembles my life. My parents found out about my affair at home and then locked me in a room. I was preparing for exams in the same room and only came out to go to write the paper. Somehow I got good marks and now I am studying for my degree course. (Calicut, Kerala)
- I have a picture of broken walls. I lost my father and we live in a *kuccha* house. I love my house and feel it is my lifelong asset. So, I appreciate this picture. (Chanderi, Madhya Pradesh)

Soldiers

- I have the picture of soldiers and I like them as they are fighting against the terrorists and naxalites. (Raipur, Chhattisgarh)
- In this photograph two soldiers are standing and holding guns in their hands. I chose this photo because I want to become an army officer. I joined the NCC in my college. I want to do something for my country. After my teacher's training I will join the army. (Cuttack, Odisha)
- The photo shows the torture of an innocent person by security personnel. It shows the atrocities inflicted by the military on Palestinian people. All over the world Muslims are soft targets of security forces. It may be in Palestine, Iraq, Afghanistan and even

in Kashmir. Security forces are also terrorising Muslims. We have to resist such atrocities and remain united through the democratic process. (Jaipur, Rajasthan)
- I have a picture of soldiers; I like them as they are keeping us safe at the cost of their own lives. They are the protectors of the nation. (Dindigul, Tamil Nadu)

Mosque

- I chose this picture because I really want my parents to go for hajj. (Delhi)
- I have chosen the picture of a mosque whose doors are closed and very beautifully carved. I cherish my memories of going to Ajmer Sharif along with my family and this picture reminded me of the trip. (Lucknow, Uttar Pradesh)

Others

- Two girls jumping, walking over a wooden fence: I wish I had a sister with whom I could play and share things and together we would have been allowed to go to school as well... (cries)... (Ahmedabad, Gujarat)
- I chose the picture of continuous footprints which depict the journey of our life, where we reached till now is nothing, we still have to go ahead. There are lots of sweet and sour experiences in our life and they are part and parcel of life. (Vanimel, Kerala)
- I chose the picture of a hand consoling another. This picture makes me think that we all get depressed in some phase of our life and then we need a person who can listen to us or a helping hand that can support us. (Vanimel, Kerala)
- I chose a picture of a hand calming another person. At the time of any crisis or mental tension every person wishes for a hand that can support him/her. One would feel happiness when someone is there to console them and cheer them up. (Calicut, Kerala)

- I have chosen a picture of a beautiful house and I wish to have this house after my marriage. We are very poor and we live in a small house. (Bhopal, Madhya Pradesh)
- I chose the picture of a ballet dancer as I think the posture suggests freedom and I want to be free and make my own decisions. (Lucknow, Uttar Pradesh)

9

Select Narratives from States

The other sessions in the workshops included a dream mapping exercise where the young women articulated their dream/aspiration juxtaposed on their mothers' dreams, an autobiographical exercise where they were asked to represent their life as a river in terms of social and personal events that have directed and shaped its flow, and finally, a focus group discussion at the end of the workshop where the young women discussed the rhythm of their everyday lives and the issues confronting Muslim women specifically and the Muslim communities at large. Semi-structured in-depth interviews were also conducted with young women who could not come for the workshops for some reasons. The interview guidelines followed, more or less, the trajectory of the workshop in its content, though, of course, not in methodology. Since the full transcripts from the interviews and workshop sessions would be too lengthy to include, what is presented here is a selection of comments that reflect the range in viewpoints shared at the workshops. As before, each paragraph represents a new person or new comment. Some responses on themes like role-models, leisure activities, etc., have been bunched together to avoid repetitious fatigue.

Patna, Bihar

In my childhood I was not able to study. When I saw children going to school I would request my parents to let me go to school. My father was not interested in my studies and he would often say 'what will a girl do with her studies'. I told my mother that I wanted to be like the boys. My father does not have any livelihood. I have four brothers and four sisters and the economic condition of the family is very poor. I stitch clothes to continue with my studies. My mother has got me admitted in a government school.

I come from a very poor family. Since my childhood I have wanted to study. I have six brothers and four sisters. I used to study in the Ayub Urdu Girls High School but my father withdrew me from there. My father feels that a girl has to go to another house and so education is not necessary for her. But, with my continuous effort my mother got me admitted in a government school. I am happy that I got a second opportunity to study. I had to face great difficulties as our neighbours made false accusations against me. My father drinks and gambles also. Sometimes, he beats my mother too. To continue my studies I administer polio drops to children. For this also I have to hear negative comments from others. I have no educated person in my house. I cannot turn to anyone for help, everyone misbehaves. Whenever I am depressed and am overcome with negativity, my mother encourages me.

When I passed standard VIII, my parents were not getting me admitted in any school as they were not permitting me to pursue higher studies. My teachers came to my house and they persuaded my parents as a result of which I got admission in school. Whenever I have been low in spirit or depressed, my teacher has helped me. I love my mother but she doesn't love me. I am very disturbed with the fact that Muslims are accused after every attack on the country. Due to the wrong of one, all are discredited. This country is ours and as such Muslims should not be seen with hatred and branded as terrorists. They should enjoy equal rights. Women in veil should not be called thieves.

Since my childhood I wanted to study but my father was not enthusiastic. My mother wanted that I should study and they used to fight often about this. My father used to beat my mother. One day my father threw all of us out of the house. At this moment my *nani* came to our rescue and gave us shelter. At present we are living at nani's place and my mother has managed to get all the sisters admitted in government school. The Mumbai blasts saddened me. People should change their thought. Muslim women should get more respect in society. We should together take steps and protect the society from fragmentation.

I love painting. I did not get any training but developed this art by self-practice. Due to financial problems I was removed from a good school. I used to face difficulties in studies but there was no one to help. My brother did not help me and my mother used to get angry when I asked questions. They withdrew my name from the school. I want to do something in life and show that there is no difference between a boy and a girl. Girls are considered a burden. They are not permitted to study or talk with anyone. Society should understand that a woman has given birth to me. When people say that Muslims are responsible for the Mumbai blasts they do not know that God has not divided us on the basis of caste and religion. What is wrong is wrong.

I want to be a teacher. I want to send my kids to a good school. I want to go for Hajj. I want to be a good daughter-in-law and want to stay always with my husband and children. My mother wants me to excel in my studies. She also wants me to do Namaaz on time and properly observe Roza.

I want to be a good doctor. I also want to be a responsible citizen of my country. I want to travel all around the world and also go to the Moon.

I want to be a good doctor and want to help society. I also want to make a big hospital in my village and invite other famous doctors here so that people need not go to other places for their treatment.

I want to be a computer engineer. My dream since childhood has been to make my family members happy. I want to spread happiness all over. My mother wants me to be so empowered that I can go anywhere at any time like guys. My mother also wants to do something but we don't have any facility in our village.

I don't like being burdened by household work like cleaning, washing utensils, clothes, cooking. If I got a chance to go back and change something in my life, I would prefer to eradicate the discrimination that is persistent against girls.

I would like to work for the development of our village—construction of hospital, school, and hand pumps.

My role models are Mother Teresa, Sonia Gandhi, Mayawati, Kalpana Chawla, Laxmi Bai, Sania Mirza, Kiran Bedi, Mahatma Gandhi, A.P.J. Abdul Kalam, and Priyanka Gandhi.

I feel my aspirations are tough to achieve; our families face so many socio-economic hurdles. If our family members supported us we would do well. I wish I could have changed the thinking of my parents about girls and tell them about all those Muslim girls who have achieved things for them. Society does affect girls but if parents are supportive society loosens its clutches.

People from Bihar don't enjoy the recognition that people from other states enjoy. While girls from Jharkhand are moving around freely, Bihari girls are not allowed to go out and work.

In the next five years, some of us would be pursuing our education, a few would get married and a few would be in jobs. However, the hurdles while achieving our goals would remain the same. We get no support from our parents to continue our education. I urge society to change its view on several issues so that we can live our lives as we desire.

I strongly feel that there should be some schemes, especially for Muslim girls so that they can grow and come out of their shell and stand on their own feet like other girls. Development of this community is required so that they can actively participate in the growth of the country. The Muslim community is socially, economically, educationally and politically backward. Due to this we have not been able to utilise the opportunities that are available. Leaders should also take keen interest in social development and should show the right path to people instead of playing power games.

The flood has badly affected our lives. Many people lost their lives and I feel very sad about it. Also, the terrorist attack on Taj Hotel disturbed me a lot. Terrorist activities spoil the atmosphere of communal harmony, spread hatred and are a threat to the community.

In India women are just considered good to be kept at home. The families say that girls shouldn't be educated too much otherwise they won't get grooms to marry. Muslim women are exploited in the name of family and religion. Muslim society has always imposed several restrictions on the mobility of women outside their homes and their interaction with the outside world has always been limited. A woman in our country is always caged within the four walls of the home and she is there just to serve her family especially her husband and her in-laws; but things are changing slowly and people's attitude towards women is changing too. Societies do not give much importance to the education of Muslim girls. Parents also support such notions. Almost all of them get married at a very early age and have to share the responsibility of the family. *'Muslim aurato ko apne astitva ko bachane ke liye bohat jhujhna padta hai'* (Muslim women have to struggle a lot for their very existence).

Raipur, Chhattisgarh

I was always in search of family affection and care; unfortunately, I did not get it. I lost my parents at an early age. My brother left me at my uncle's place. I just want a happy married life and I want our own house.

When I was in the 5th Standard, my father got transferred and then he didn't allow me to study further. Somehow, I persuaded my mother to get me admitted in a school. As our financial condition was very bad my mother got a job. She works very hard and now I have passed my 10th standard exams. I am a Muslim girl and society doesn't like me moving about but I know I have the capability to fulfil my dreams. Everyone has a dream but only a few have the capability to accomplish it and it gives pleasure.

I had to struggle a lot in childhood as I lost my father at an early age. My mother sells vegetables and whatever she earns she contributes to my studies. In the 10th standard I worked hard and then completed my 12th standard exams. But, I can't continue my studies further as we don't have the money to pay my fees. I want to get a job and want to keep my mother happy.

At the time of my birth, my father divorced my mother. I was brought up at my grandparents' place. I got married but within a few years my husband got married to some other girl. He hasn't divorced me; I want to stay with my husband and my child forever.

I want to stand on my own feet and want to be a computer engineer. My mother wants that my brother and I should live happily and be successful. I want to study as much as I can and make my family happy. My mother was not educated so she aspires that her children should get a good education and improve the financial condition of our family. I want to be like Julekha Madam.

I want to learn computers and be famous like Sania Mirza. My mother's aspiration is that all her daughters should get good husbands and in-laws.

I want to be an IAS officer and be courageous like Kiran Bedi. I also want that my husband should understand my feelings and emotions. My mother wants that we should have our own house and we should go on Hajj. She also wants us to continue our education so that we can stand on our own feet.

My in-laws tried to burn me alive for dowry but fortunately I survived. My face is all burnt and I cannot face anyone.

The condition of Muslim women is really very miserable. Society has imposed lots of restrictions on women in terms of their education, marriage and happiness. It is even more sad that the government is doing nothing for them; they have become a vulnerable community in such a way that others accuse them for all bad deeds. And, thus their community remains backward.

If the society does not impose any barrier on girls, they would complete their education, and find jobs. However, girls realise that their dreams or aspirations are tough to achieve without the support of their parents, relatives, society and the government. We need the financial as well as moral support from them. There is a need to change the perspective of society with respect to gender and all its conventions.

I can do any work apart from routine housework. I also dislike staying at home. I have a job as a private school teacher and I really love it. After I finish my graduation I want to do a B.Ed. and continue teaching.

I like cooking and studying. I don't like washing clothes but I listen to music while I wash clothes and then it is not such a burden.

I wear a *naqab* before I step out of home and don't go before *ghair mehram*[1] men.

I don't do any kind of purdah. I am an event manager. '*Purda sirf ankhon ka hona chahiye aur mere profession me purdah nahi kar sakti*' (Purdah should be in one's attitude; moreover in my profession I cannot observe purdah).

I wear a scarf and go before everyone.

I don't do any purdah but I also don't step out of my house alone.

In leisure time: namaaz, reading quran, watching television, listening to music, reading newspaper, reading stories, reading magazines, decorating the home, and going to meet friends.

I fear my Abbu so I'll marry according to his wishes but I do dream of having a good husband. He shouldn't have bad habits, and he should be honest.

Society comes after the family, but the restriction on women starts from the family and then it is there at every level. Society keeps an eye on women. We are a part of society and we grow up in society. Societies don't promote education and progress of girls. They impose lots of restrictions on girls. They are not allowed to step out of their homes and do anything. Our society doesn't allow women to keep a mobile. They are not allowed to talk to other males, too much of purdah is part of our Muslim society. They are always instructed about the way they should carry themselves. They say, 'You are a girl, you should walk like this, stand like this, talk less, smile like that, shouldn't stand on the terrace.' They don't send their girls to study with boys.

Our family also says that education spoils girls, they don't obey their parents and marry on their own. They don't respect their elders too.

The condition of Muslim women is the same as other women. They were treated as slaves before and they are treated as slaves even now. They cannot live according to their own will. Society thinks of girls as a burden on families and so believes in marrying them early.

---

[1] Any man whom a woman is not related to directly and is eligible to marry.

I find women are working all the time. They work, eat and sleep... *roz ki bas yahi kahani hai* (that is the story every day). They never take independent decisions and go by what others say.

Women have been suffering for ages irrespective of the distinction of religion. However, a gradual change has begun. Girls are now heading towards schools and colleges.

The lower socio-economic strata are more influenced by caste; not so much the case with the middle class and upper class. They do not bother much about what people would say to them unlike us.

The very fact that you are here to talk about the situation of Muslim women in India says it all. Isn't it their bad condition which caught your attention?

The status of women is just that of a housemaid in the family. They are always taught that they are responsible for maintaining the respect and 'name' of their families. They are groomed to sacrifice their dreams and happiness for men since childhood.

If the girl is beautiful parents think she should get married at the earliest. If the boys are spoiled, the parents think they'll be better after marriage.

I don't know much about the situation in cities, but in villages girls are kept within the four walls of the home, before and after marriage. But a few girls who came from the city and married into the village, work outside: teach, do tailoring or work in the anganvadi.[2] But they have to work within the decent limits imposed on them or else the panchayat[3] can impose a fine on them or give instructions for them to be ostracised. The situation in the city might be different; people might give some independence to women thinking they can bring money and get education. '*Gao me to bus naam aur ijjat dekhte hai aur is kaaran ladkiyon ko puri bandish me rakhte hai*' (In the village the focus is on honour and reputation, and hence the girls live within bounds.)

Delhi

My parents always stopped or restricted me from things in my life. They kept me in so many knots that I never did that I wanted to do in life.

---

[2] Mother and child care centres in rural areas.
[3] Local village governing body.

I was never allowed to study so I couldn't think about what's good for me and what's not. As a result, I am dependent on my family members. Society also didn't treat me well. They did not let me live independently. Whenever I go out from home to any place, I have to bear so many remarks from outsiders. All these things made my thinking limited and my outlook narrow.

I love my parents as they love me a lot. I couldn't continue my education but I am happy that my parents are taking care of my younger siblings as they want them to continue their education. Society believes that I should have tolerance and respect for others and people should be good to each other. I wish that girls should not be forced to stop their education like I did and all of them should study well.

I couldn't complete my education and I regret it but I am learning Urdu and Arabic and still I crave to know more. I wish that no girl should be stopped from attaining education. I am learning stitching so that I can teach this to others free of cost. I wish I could study further.

I wanted to achieve something in my life, so that the world could see me and admire me and be proud of me. But my parents care more about boys than for girls. I wanted to take tuition in 9th standard but I couldn't which troubled me. I also wanted to be a singer but my parents are poor so they can't send me anywhere for training. I want the government to help us so that poor children can also hope, aspire and succeed.

I live in a family where the laws of society are imposed upon us. They do love us but at times it becomes really difficult to take their permission for what I want to do. Although my parents are good and they try to fulfil all my wishes; they are supporting my wish to study. I have a best friend who is an important part of my life. She is my only friend and I love her. I would love to live in a society where everyone tries to understand the problems others are facing. I want to change the attitude of society towards Muslim girls. I want to end the restrictions on us. These restrictions come out of narrow and wrong thinking. All of us dream of becoming something in life but there are some people in society who don't let us progress. Many parents support their children but at times they withdraw support looking at the society outside. Therefore, I want people to think in the right manner and let us go out and study as it's the demand of today's world and we cannot lag behind.

I am born in a family where parents love us and believe in us. My parents want us to study and always bother about it. *Mujhe ghar se niklalne me jijhak si hoti hai* (I feel hesitant to go out of home.) Although we get so many facilities from society but this society consists of people who trouble us and make it difficult for us to go out.

I dream of becoming a police officer and I want that nobody proves me wrong for anything. I want a good home. I want to live my life happily. For now, I want to open my parlour. My mother dreams that I get married soon and I live happily in my husband's home, with his family. My mother also wants me to study and achieve a goal in life. She also wants me to complete my Islamic study.

One of my dreams is to be a doctor; another dream is to go to America and Disneyland. If I cannot become a doctor, I want to study computers and get a good job. My mother wants me to be a doctor and that I study well and achieve something in life. She also wishes that I get married in a nice family.

I want to be a nurse and an actress in serials. I wish I could be any of the two and I don't think I am dreaming of something I shouldn't be dreaming of. My mother dreams of getting me married to a boy from a good family and that my husband should be good to me. She also wishes that I study hard and be good and able. My mother puts in a lot of effort to fulfil my dreams.

I want to be a lawyer and fight for the poor people and counsel them on the oppression that is inflicted on them. I want to spread light like a torch and bring people out of their darkness. I want to visit Darjeeling once in my life.

I want to be famous before the world one day through television and I want that everyone should know my name. I also want my parents to have respect in this world but I know my dreams will not become a reality. I want to get married with a good boy from a good family. I want that my parents get all the happiness in life. I want to travel to Jafarabad, Mumbai and at last to Saudi Arabia (for Hajj). My mother wants that I study till Class 12 and then get married to a boy from a nice family and remain happy. My mother wants me to go to school and thereafter go for tuitions and work at home after that. My mother wants me not to talk to any girl, neither does she want any girl to talk to me.

I love kites but I have never played with them. I have only seen my brother playing with them as flying a kite is a boy's game.

I would like to become a teacher, tailor, doctor, computer operator, or a successful reporter, or study, open a beauty parlour, or learn to apply mehendi.

I would like to be married in five years and live at my in-laws' home.

My role models are Aishwarya Rai, Indira Gandhi, Katrina Kaif, Kiran Bedi, Hazrat Fatima, Sania Mirza and Sonia Gandhi.

I wish to be like my mother, my English teacher, or my friend because I like the way she smiles and talks. I like her eyes too; I want to be like my *Khala* because she stitches good clothes.

I want to be as wise as Sabiha *Baji*.

I want to be like Jhansi Ki Rani as she disliked taking anyone's help for anything. I want to be strong enough to support and protect myself. I dislike people helping me and later on taking credit for what little help they gave.

The bomb blasts in different cities and so many people dying affects me. I feel bad that Muslims are called terrorists. At the same time, it makes me feel frightened.

I fear the violence inflicted on girls in the society in the form of rape and molestation.

I feel bad when Hindus talk about Muslims as bad (people). I also feel bad when I hear about someone's things being stolen as everyone is fighting poverty here. I hate it when there is a fight in the neighbourhood in my community. I regret being born as a girl in this society which discriminates against girls at every step.

Illiteracy among girls is the root cause of many problems and I wish it could be reduced. Families should trust girls and give them more freedom to grow; girls should get education and give good education to their children. There should be a separate madarsa for girls. Muslim women can't grow in India because they have to bear all household responsibilities.

Bharatiya muslim aurato ko prerna dene wale na ke barabar hai aur bediya lagane wale hazar. Aage badhne ki baat hee nahi ki jati. Jisse aurato ko koi rasta nahi milta bus ghar me bachho ki dekh rekh karte raho. (There is no one to inspire Indian Muslim women to grow but a thousand to put them under restrictions. There is no talk of their growth. Women don't find any avenue to grow. They are just expected to be at home and take care of children.)

Sabarkantha and Ahmedabad, Gujarat

My father died when I was small. My three siblings and I couldn't study further after his demise. My elder brother started working as an autorickshaw driver and my younger brother is now studying with the help of an NGO in Delhi. My elder sister got married at a very young age. Another brother dropped out after studying till Class 10. I wanted to study. So many people lost their jobs because of the riots. We also live with the fear of another earthquake and it all makes me feel so helpless that I do not understand what to do.

When I was still a child we had a garage shop. It was sold off later and we became poor. Papa had to begin pulling a rickshaw. My mother helped me to continue my schooling till Class 10. Although my parents agreed to me going out alone to the high school away from this place, others counselled them not to send me out and they agreed. I have no brother. So I want to work and support my parents. The 2002 riots made many women widows; numerous people lost their jobs. Most of the women now do some petty work from home. Now I have started going out alone. I go out to attend computer classes, learn stitching and put henna on women's hands. One shouldn't fear things like riots and rapes, and should not give up studying because of fear. Those who are poor should be guarded by the government.

I wanted to study but because of the lack of money and riots I couldn't study. I studied till Class 7. I had to take care of home so I stopped going out. My father used to drive a lorry.

My mother worked and supported us while our father didn't work. They made me study till Class 7. We had little money at home so I dropped out after that. The 2002 riots were disastrous for us. Our home and basti were all shattered, schools were closed down, shops were burned, women and girls were raped. Men become wage labourers.

We are seven sisters at home. All of us are studying. But two of my elder sisters didn't get jobs when they tried. That made me leave my education after Class 12; our house was destroyed in the 2001 earthquake. It was a financial and emotional loss for us.

I left schooling after Class 10 as I failed in one subject. But I regret it as my other friends are all studying and I know they'll become something unlike me. The 2002 riots affected me a lot. There was curfew. Girls were strictly restricted from going out. So many children were writing their Class 10 board exams then. They would have been badly affected.

I wanted to be a lawyer and a script writer. But because of the environment outside, my parents are afraid to let us go out on our own. There are even some economic problems at home which hinder my way to progress. I did my graduation but I didn't enrol for an LLB because of such problems at home. I like classical music but I couldn't learn it. The

2001 earthquake made many people unemployed and several people became disabled; the rest was done by the 2002 riots. People were building their lives which fell apart again because of the riots. There were economic problems because of which many children had to be withdrawn from school. Girls had to leave because high schools were not located in their neighbourhoods.

I dropped out of school after the riots, as I became sick because of the trauma for a long time. I thereafter requested my parents to let me study but they refused and said that the place has become dirty, *'mahaul kharab ho gaya hai, tum ab nahi padh sakti'*. After the riots, there was fear of *'mahaul'*. This one incident changed our lives so much.

My mother fought with every patriarchal mindset at home to support my education. She worked hard to make us study. Our economic condition was bad but because of her efforts, I am now in my first year of graduation and aim to study further. My dream is to be a lawyer and fight for the rights of the people. I hate the fights and killings in the name of religion and caste.

I couldn't study as my father got me married early. Unfortunately, my husband died. Society posed problems in letting me work outside. I had to struggle to get my three children into school. Now I am teaching stitching to girls and I get paid by the Adarsh Mahila Samiti for this service.

The 2002 riots affected our families badly and I was taken out of school after that. I was told that I will ruin the family prestige if I go out and hence I was made to drop out.

I am studying currently and want to study further but I know very soon I'll be withdrawn as the high school is far from my house and I won't be allowed to go that far to study.

I left school in Class 8. The slums are increasing in the city. While rich children get to study, poor children don't get the opportunity to compete with them.

I wanted to study and contribute something for the social good by becoming a social worker but I couldn't study because there were no good schools in the Muslim locality. My goal, therefore, remains unattained now. Every now and then, some or the other problem can be seen in society. They don't teach Muslim girls. There are issues with our stepping out of home. Therefore, Hindu girls get better jobs and we don't.

After my parents' divorce, my schooling was stopped. There was an economic crisis at home as well. People were of the opinion that studying doesn't even help in getting jobs, so there is no point to it. Moreover, there are no schools for girls in our locality and I wasn't allowed to go too far to study. Although I can share my feelings and speak my mind at home but ultimately I accept what is decided for me.

My parents did not send me to school after the 2002 riots. We had to live in camps for some time. Thereafter I got married. I am teaching tailoring to girls now.

My dream is to work and help my younger siblings to become something. My mother dreams that all her children should get married and live happily.

I want to go out and work, apply *mehndi*.

I wish that all my siblings and I study well. I want to become a teacher. My mother wishes that we all study ahead but we don't have the money to fulfil our dreams.

I want to study and become a teacher, chartered accountant, learn stitching, learn computers and get a job, learn a craft.

Bangalore, Karnataka

My father has undergone a surgery and he is not able to work. And, so my mother works in a garment factory. As our financial condition is not very sound I discontinued my studies. I was aware that this would have an impact on my life and future.

I have nine siblings; my elder brother got separated just after his marriage, this makes us sad. I am studying in Class 10 and my parents are very supportive, but my neighbours are jealous of me and keep making comments about me. I have taken their comments as a challenge and want to do something in my life and thus will show them and will make my parents proud.

I always wanted to study and become a successful woman but my brother prevented me from going to school when I was in Class 8. Another incident which left me and my family in distress was my elder brother's death.

I lost my father and thereafter my mother started working as a washerwoman. My sister and I dropped out of school as our financial condition was poor. At the same time we can't enrol ourselves in schools which provide free education as they are too far from our house and we can't afford the bus fare.

In the next five years, I shall continue my education towards becoming a teacher.

Five years from now I would be married off.

I would talk to my parents and even fight to let me continue my education.

Communal violence has lot of impact on my family. Generally, at home, I hear about socio-cultural norms that I should follow like purdah, that I shouldn't go outside the house as the atmosphere is not good, I should not talk and laugh too much, and I should read the Quran properly.

Family and society force a woman to even stop crying and become completely silent. I cannot travel out on my own. People withdraw girls from college saying the atmosphere is not conducive outside; boys stand outside the college and create trouble for girls. We are checked for everything. If we wear something good, the old women of the families say we have become very fashionable.

Girls do want to study but cannot study because of various limitations and restrictions at home.

Our elders are of the belief that what would girls do even if they were educated, that ultimately they are only required to take care of their children and husbands.

My role models are Aishwarya Rai, Karishma Kapoor, Kiran Bedi, Shabana Azmi, Ragini (a character in the TV serial Bidai), I'll become a role model for others.

My role models are Kiran Bedi, Mother Teresa, Kalpana Chawla, Jhansi Ki Rani, Indira Gandhi, and Sudha Chandran (Actor).

My husband should be handsome like Hrithik Roshan; he should be well-read, a civil engineer or a good auto driver, engineer, computer engineer; he should be caring and loving, simple; must hold a government job, or have a business; he should be smart like John Abraham.

I wanted to get a good husband, but I am in a bad marriage. My husband drinks, beats me, doesn't look after the kids. I have just given up on him.

Five years from now I would be modelling, studying, taking care of my children and bearing household responsibilities, I would be working by then, I would be pursuing an LLB. I'll start my tailoring shop. I would be married by then.

Things in my past that I'd like to change: I would change all the bad school teachers, I would have refused to marry, I disliked studying but now I like it and I wish I could continue, I was bad in Mathematics and hence was always scolded by my teachers; I wish I could have performed well, I had to discontinue my studies. I wish to have married a person of my choice. My past was bad; I would have changed things from the past. I wish I was not born a girl. I was taken aback by the Babri Masjid incident, I was a child then. I wish it never happened. I wish that I could change the mentality of the people.

Calicut, Kerala

I was born as the youngest daughter in my home. And, during my schooldays I developed my interest in becoming a teacher as I was inspired by some of my schoolteachers. I am literally shocked with the emerging number of orphanages and juvenile homes.

Thinking about my personal life reminded me of my hostel days when I cried the most. But at the same time, I learnt many lessons of life then. And as for social events, what influenced me was the death of certain important personalities who held important positions in society.

One of the social events that influenced me the most was the tsunami disaster. How many people were killed and how many more lost their homes and families? I want to help such people by becoming a nurse.

During my lifetime I learnt to be a truthful person and faced everything. Now, I am bold enough to handle all circumstances. I appreciate those great people at the borders who save our country from enemies. I appreciate them as they give their lives for their country.

My life was affected by my friends at all stages of my life and I wanted to get more and more education. I was disturbed by the backwardness of Muslim girls' education and the ill-treatment of girls in many parts of the country.

In my personal life, I learnt to take decisions myself and I was impressed by the great stories of Mahatma Gandhi, Jawaharlal Nehru and other leaders.

My role models are Benazir Bhutto, Sonia Gandhi, Kalpana Chawla, A.P.J. Abdul Kalam, Indira Gandhi, J.K. Rowling and my mother.

My dream is that I should be a good English teacher so that I can teach students in an interesting way.

I want to be a doctor but my mother's dream is that I should be a teacher as she wants me to strictly follow the rules and regulations of Islam. Her wish is much more important for me so I gave up my wish of becoming a doctor. Now I have started my preparation to become a teacher.

I want to be a socialist and a lawyer in a good position. But my mother says girls can't be in high positions so she does not support me.

I want to become a teacher and serve orphans; this is one of my biggest dreams.

My dream is to become a journalist.

I would like to become a teacher, but my parents want me to get married after completing my 12th as in our society they believe that girls should not study much.

I would like to become an IAS officer, a leading woman in politics and internationally connecting Islamic traditions with other countries. And my mother would support me in any career I chose. She always teaches me to be a strong believer in God.

I would like to become an advocate and do social service.

In the next five years, I will be continuing my studies, doing jobs, become an advocate, scientist, doctor, engineer, and get married. I aspire to have a supportive and caring husband.

Girls' dreams can be fulfilled only when they get support from their parents, society and the government. Norms and rituals such as child marriage, gender discrimination are huge limitations, as these hamper their growth and development. Communal riots also create a rift between the two communities. Now, the demand of time is to work hard, challenge power, be open-minded and limit one's dependency on society.

Incidents like the Godhra riots, terrorist activities, and the condition of Muslim countries like Afghanistan make me think about our community. Also, at the local level issues like dowry and domestic violence have an impact on girls' lives.

Chanderi and Bhopal, Madhya Pradesh

When I was studying in the first year of B.Sc., we faced some crisis and I discontinued my education. I want to continue my study but I don't think I will be able to. Now, I want to work to support my family. During Moharram a riot occurred near Chanderi. People were throwing stones at each other and a stone hit an old man. He was injured but people just ignored him and went away. My family member collected some money and treated him. Now, he is well.

I like to play outside and my parents never restrict me. A few times I won prizes and this makes my parents proud of me.

When I was small my father used to beat my mother. My mother was very disturbed and unwell but my father never took her to the hospital. So, we came to our grandparents and got my mother treated. Then my mother, with the support of one of our neighbours, opened a tailoring shop here in Chanderi and began earning. When my mother began her work, society criticised her. Even when my mother sent her daughters to Bhopal for higher studies, society always made fun of her.

My father's work was going well but his partner cheated him. So, we experienced a financial crisis due to which I was not able to continue my studies. When I was 5 years old, I saw my father beating my mother and I can never forget this. My elder sister plays a major role in my life. I love my sister and can do anything for her.

I have attended one counselling session and that changed my life. I met a girl after Class 12. She was involved in some unpleasant incident and with time she became a good friend of mine. I learnt a lot from her experience and now I can live independently in society.

I want to study but my parents want me to get married so I have stopped studying. There are very few who can continue their study even after getting married. My role model is Mother Teresa.

We also aspire to be air hostess, doctor, engineer, and teacher and to help underprivileged people. But, society doesn't allow us to go out of our houses and always puts restrictions on us. I would prefer to study further rather than get married.

We first of all need the blessings of Allah and then the financial and emotional support of our parents and society. Getting educated is the duty of each and every Muslim. I will continue my studies no matter what.

Even for getting education, one needs money. As we are deprived, we are always strangulating our dreams and aspirations.

Muslim women are lagging behind as they don't have access to their rights. Men of the society still consider them servants and if a woman wants to lodge her complaint at the police station, police personnel do not let this happen.

I dislike doing stitching, brooming and dusting, cooking food every day, cooking when I am tired, washing clothes, sitting idle in college, *ghar leepna aatcha nahi lagta* (I don't like to smear the floor of our house with mud paste).

I like sharing all the responsibilities at home. Helping everyone, especially my brother and sister, offering Namaaz, going to coaching class, chatting with family members, going to the parlour, sending messages by mobile phone, going to the madrasa.

I wear *burqa* and cover the lower half of the face.

I do go before everyone but wear *burqa* and also cover my face.

I wear only a scarf or a shawl.

I wear an *abaya*, and do not go in front of *na mehram* men.

I like to read a magazine during my leisure time, Mehekta Aanchal, Femina, or newspapers or novels. I also like to watch cartoon films, news channels, serials and reality shows on television. I like to offer Namaaz and paint.

I want to be a dress designer.

I want to work in a bank, be an office manager, or start some business of my own.

I want to be a teacher, tailor, doctor, beautician or chartered accountant.

I want to work in an MNC and go outside my country for work.

I want to be a software programmer, or fashion designer.

I want to run Mehendi classes.

I love singing and want to be a singer.

I just want to be a common girl.

I want to be a share broker inspired by my teacher who dabbles in shares, but my parents want me to get married soon. I may, therefore, just get married and end up cooking food at my in-laws' place.

My role model is my younger brother who shouldered the responsibility of running the house at 18 years of age.

My role model is Nikki Bawa (beautician), who is doing good work and has done it all by herself.

I look up to my sister who is running her business and at the same time looking after her home and kids very well.

My role model is my cousin who fought against all odds to finish her studies and she is working now.

I am inspired by my teacher who works and is also studying to be a Chartered Accountant now.

My role model is my aunt who is a teacher.

I look up to my father who spent his life with honesty.

My role model is my mother who is illiterate but has made all her children study and all are now standing on their own feet.

I am inspired by my mother, who continued her studies even after her marriage and educated her children with much effort.

My role model is Sonia Gandhi.

My husband should respect my parents and consider them his own mother and father; he should have the wisdom to decide between right and wrong.

My husband should love me and take care of me and not go by people's word. He should make his own decision based on logic. He should be a good human being.

Shakki na ho (My husband shouldn't be suspicious) because I have seen my sister being tortured by her suspicious husband. He should be an accountant to go with my bank job.

Deendaar sauhar chahti hun (I wish for a religious husband).

Older women like my mother-in-law force the young generation to stay in purdah because they have not been given the freedom. She does it because people in the locality say so.

Women are emotional by nature. They can't see others suffering. They can deny their own happiness to see others happy. They are just advisors in the family and nobody takes their advice seriously—it is not given any importance. They have to face so many difficulties.

Society doesn't let a Muslim girl study. They blame that girls want to go out and meet boys so they go out to study. They'll run away with boys so it is better to keep them at home. They even stop her from chatting and laughing with others saying that 'iss tarah haste bolte ek ladki pados ke ladke ke saath bhag gayi thi' (a girl eloped with a neighbourhood boy just chatting like this).

Muslim ladkiyan padhai me piche hai kyoki unke pariwaro ko ijjat jyada pyari lagti hai. Unhe tana diya jata hai jyada oochai par na udde. unhe koi naukari nahi milne wali. (Muslim girls are backward in education because their families are only concerned about their honour. They are taunted and told not to fly too high as they are not going to get any jobs.)

Women are given a low position to men in our society. Women hesitate in speaking their mind because men are not sensitive or considerate enough to listen to them, neither do they treat them with due respect.

The place where we stay and its environment too impacts us a lot. We start adapting to our environment and start thinking like others in the group. We don't try to change ourselves neither do we disagree with them over things.

The Gujarat riots affected me deeply. Women were dragged out of their houses, raped and then killed. The belly of a pregnant women was slit open and her unborn child was hung on the point of sword.

I get affected by riots in general and have been hearing about the riots in Bhopal. Bombay blasts also affected my family a lot.

We cannot forget the Bhopal gas tragedy.

A Muslim girl is not safe outside even if she is allowed to go out. She cannot protect herself, she is not taught confidence. At home, no attention is paid to their health. She is treated like a housemaid and made to stick to regulations imposed by the family on her.

The girls don't object to the suppression they are facing at home. They quietly bear the trauma. They don't raise their voice and oppose it.

Usmanabad, Thane and Mumbai, Maharashtra

I like helping my mother in general housework.

I like reading namaaz, doing household work, filling water, going for tuition, going to college.

My mother is physically disabled, so I help her in doing all the household tasks, and taking care of my brother.

I like studying, stitching, knitting and embroidery work, humming songs while working, reading Arabic, Urdu, Marathi and Maths.

In leisure time I like watching television, listening to songs on the radio, studying, knitting and embroidery, learning Arabic, knowing about Islam, *desh videsh ki khabare dekhna* (seeing news from India and abroad), stitching, and applying *mehendi*.

Wearing *burqa* is in fashion.

Parda to ankhon ka hota hai.

I like doing purdah, we are saved from people's eyes if we observe purdah and society calls us names if we do not wear a *burqa*.

I like doing purdah because Islam instructs us to do purdah.

I only go before other men for some work, I don't like going before unknown men, I cover my face before going to unknown men.

I don't believe in purdah; *Mai ajad khayalo ki ladki hun*. I don't like to remain confined within the four walls of my home.

I want to work and serve marginalised people; I want to teaching, do BA and B.Ed., I want to study further. *Mujhe padhne ka shauq hai* (I am fond of reading).

I want to look like Kareena Kapoor.

I want to study and make my parents proud, I want to become an *aalema*, I like to talk about Islam.

I want to study but my father discontinued my schooling, I wish to become a doctor.

I would become either a lecturer or a collector.

I want to become a nurse.

I want to study and bring some change in the environment at home; I want to help poor people and people who are facing difficulties in life.

The man I marry should be working, he should take me out to places, *wo surat me nahi seerat me aatcha hona chahiye* (He should be a good natured person, it's not important how he looks).

I look like Kajol so my husband should look like Salman Khan, he should be caring, *namaaz ka paband hona chahiye* (he should observe *namaaz* regularly).

I'll have to marry according to the wishes of my parents, I want to marry according to my parents' wishes.

My husband should be wise (*samajhdar*), he should respect women and should be there with me in every trouble, *jo aakhiri waqt tak saath de* (support me till the end).

I want an equally well-read and competent person to be my life partner, *jo mujhse kandhe se kandha milakar chale* (he should walk as a partner with me).

I don't want to get married; *Ammi ki zindagi dekhkar mujhe shaadi se nafrat ho gayi hai* (I hate the idea of getting married when I look at my mother's life).

My role models are Kareena Kapoor, Indira Gandhi and Sonia Gandhi.

I hate all men and so I don't want to get married. My father has tortured me and my mother to such an extent that I hate all men. He had been very cruel to us. I remember an incident when we went to someone's home and it had started raining. When we came back, my father beat her and me. She became unconscious after that beating.

My father has two wives. So fighting is routine in my home every day. I really feel bad about it.

I am a free thinker and an independent person. I don't want to get married. My mother had saved some money for me and my father spent it all. On being confronted by my mother about it he abused her and beat her up. After this incident, I developed an aversion towards marriage.

Five years from now, I'll get more than 85% marks in my BA examinations and do a B.Ed. and become a teacher.

Five years from now, I will have got married.

I will become a teacher first and then get married within five years.

I shall be some officer in five years.

Either I'll be singing on a stage in five years or serving people as a doctor.

I would like to be doing any work.

I would like to help poor people as a doctor, I won't take money from them.

If I could change anything from their past I would change accidents and deaths at home or in the locality (I'll try to forget that incident in which my brother died); my grandfather made my father leave our paternal home, I cannot forget that; I could not get admission in a good school because I couldn't score well in my Class 10 exams.

There is no problem in achieving my dreams, I'll try solving all my problems with utmost courage.

I am not studying hard enough to achieve my dreams.

The monetary problem is an obstacle in achieving my dreams.

It is my father who will not let me fulfil any of my dreams and he also beats up my mother regularly.

I like to study but my brother doesn't let me study,

What can I achieve if I am not even allowed to step out of my home.

I couldn't study because I didn't get the books I needed on time.

I'll fight with all difficulties to achieve my dreams.

To stand on one's own feet seems difficult, monetary support is missing, I don't want to stop achieving something because of constraints, I just want someone to encourage me.

I like flowers and dislike hatred, fighting.

I like helping people and dislike lies.

Poor parents sell their property to get their daughter married and the daughter has to work like a maid in her husband's home.

Even if the girls study they fear not getting employment or not being given permission to work from their homes, they are not allowed to go outside their homes.

Muslim women face many constraints in this society, *bohat saare bandhan hai aur bohat sari rukawate hai* (there are many constraints and impediments.) To live in this society according to our wishes, we must have the guts and willpower to struggle against the suppressing norms that society imposes on girls. It is important to have the courage to change. We must stand against oppression and wrongs.

The reasons for such conditions are many: lack of employment, no one supports the development of women, marriages happen at a very young age, men think that if women start studying they won't be at home and then who will take care of them and who will they dominate. Change needs to come about in the social idea about women.

Women only with their combined efforts and strength can bring some change in their situation, *aisa samaj hona chahiye jisma har insaan khulkar bol sake* (society should be such that each individual is able to speak openly). Only an educated society is a clear and liberated society, people should respect each other's opinions and help each other.

Cuttack, Odisha

I don't like my village because in my village no one likes that girls should go outside. I don't feel any attachment to my society. If my parents allow me to do any kind of work I will do it without caring about society. I want that there should be limits to the purdah system.

I am doing my graduation. After finishing my studies, I want to do a job so that I can make my parents proud. I have two dreams: first, I want to teach those students who have dropped out of school, and second, I want to stop child marriage.

My life is beautiful; I have many dreams, I want to become an airhostess but I don't want to do slavery. My sister is my ideal as she does whatever she wants to. I want to do some good work in my life so that people will remember me for ever.

I want to stand on my own feet but I think I would not be able to fulfil my dream as I belong to a Muslim family. I also want to become a software engineer but due to our financial problem I shall not be able to fulfil my dream.

I wanted to do my post-graduation studies but my parents forced me to take on computer training. I want to shatter the superstitions that are prevalent in my society so that the next generation would be wise enough to make their own decisions. I want to become a good Indian and a good Muslim.

I want to become an army officer as I have always wanted to do something for my country. I joined NCC in +2. I used to go for camp. Muslim society doesn't allow girls to move ahead in life. Though Sania Mirza is

Muslim, without caring about her society she moved ahead. Now, she is famous and has proved that Muslim girls can also do any work.

I want to make a career in ITI. And also receive a scholarship from GNIIT. Our financial condition is not good as my father cannot afford to pay for my studies. I also played basketball for my state but later I was not allowed to go outside. Society never gives any opportunity to girls to move ahead. They always stop us. For this reason, a girl's dream remains a dream only. I want to study science but under pressure from society my father forced me to study humanities. Now I am studying humanities and I want to bust the superstitions which are predominant in our society.

I want to be a singer but I am not able to accomplish my dream. *Ghar aur samaj ke wajah se mera yeh khwab ander hi ander dafan hota nazar aa raha hai* (Due to circumstances at home and in the society my dream is destined to be buried inside me.)

I am the younger daughter of my parents. I want to give all the happiness to my parents so that they don't feel that they don't have any son. I want to show them that girls are no less than boys. I feel that in today's world boys are needed but girls are needed much more than boys as girls make the family sparkle.

Hamare ghar mein burqa pehne ke liye kisi ko majboor kiya nahi jata. Jis ka dil chaiye pahene ya na pahene magar samaj ke logo ke wajaj se majboor ho kar burkha pehena padta hai. (Nobody is forced to wear a *burqa* in our house. Whoever feels like it can wear it or not. But the pressure of society is such that we end up wearing it.)

Hamare mazhab ke logo ki samaj mein kuch izzat hi nahi hai… Gair koam ke log kyun hamare koam ko niche nazar se dekhte hain? (People from our community have no respect in society. Why do people of other communities look down upon us?)

Girls are not given any opportunity to go ahead in life. Even after dowry is given, they are ill-treated by their in-laws. Dowry harassments and deaths are very common in our society.

I have a very small dream. I want a scooty on which I can travel far and complete my studies.

I want to study in the commerce stream but our financial condition is not good. My brother took science and we had to spend a lot on his studies. I want to do a job so that I can support my family and my brothers can avail of a good education.

I want to be a businesswoman but I know this is very difficult to accomplish as our financial condition is not very good. I will try my best to achieve my aim and the day I achieve it, it will be a memorable day for my whole life. My mother's dream is to educate all her children and she always supports us.

I want to be an IAS officer but from our place the tuition centres are very far so I can't afford it. So, I feel I can be a teacher as it is the only profession which is respected by our community. My mother wanted to study but her parents did not allow her. Now, she regrets it and always supports us in achieving our dreams.

I love my friends. On Friendship Day, I was remembering my friends as we are all separated now. I like my teacher as she tells us the real meaning of our life. I have seen that the elders and Maulanas always restrict us, they want us to be at home, do household work, and strictly follow all conventions. So, I am against society and do whatever I feel like doing.

Jaipur, Rajasthan

I had the opinion that the world is beautiful and we can enjoy it. But when I interacted with the realities of life, I saw its ugly face. The way the Muslim community is held responsible for all terrorist activities is highly upsetting. Shahbaz is being tried for the 13 May 2008 incident case that happened in Jaipur. Though, he is innocent, the police is making a strong case against him. The police say that he is the mastermind behind the terrorist activities. Muslims are highly frightened because of communalism and terrorism. This event changed my life and now I am highly religious and want to do welfare work for my community.

When I was a child, the education of my eldest sister was stopped due to old traditions like Purdah and early marriage. This was the saddest incident in my life. I became determined in my heart that I will also not study. But later my father intervened and helped me acquire my education. Now, my father is no more and I am helping my family financially.

My parents are highly religious and orthodox. They are against the education of girls hence I am not continuing with my studies after middle school. They are in a hurry to arrange my wedding as in their opinion I am now of the right age. My life is like a storm in an ocean, not a river. There are no banks.

My dream is that all human beings, particularly Muslims, should be prosperous and well-to-do in India as well as in the world. There should be peace everywhere. Muslims should carefully follow Islam. They should observe the teaching of the Quran in their life in practical terms. The life of Prophet Mohammed (Sunnat) should guide us in our lives.

My dream is that there should be peace in our country. We should not face communal and terrorist activities.

It is very difficult to accomplish one's aim after marriage. Even before I got married though, I had to struggle for my studies.

During my childhood I experienced deep poverty. My parents were not able to bear the expenses of my education. We were eking out a hand-to-mouth existence, so what to say about education. But with courage and hard work, my family's circumstances have improved. Now we are comfortable and I have resumed my education. I have passed the higher secondary examination and will now be going to college for higher studies.

I want to say that when I was studying in school, I saw the attitude of people towards Muslims. They thought that all Muslims are uneducated. They believed that Muslims don't know how to dress and how to communicate with others. Realising this really hurt me. I decided to change their feelings.

My life is miserable as my father has left the family. My mother works hard and earns for the whole family. We are living in distress.

I belong to a poor family. I want to be a doctor. My father drives a *tonga* to make a living. After I passed the secondary examination my father told me that further education for me would not be possible due to the financial condition of the family. This incident changed my whole life. My dream of being a doctor was not fulfilled. Now I am helping my family and working as a teacher. I am disappointed and perturbed that I could not study medicine but I am satisfied that I am at least helping poor children become educated.

We are six brothers and three sisters. Despite being a headmaster, my father discriminated between his son and daughter. All my brothers acquired a good education but the sisters did not get to study beyond the senior secondary level. Fortunately, my husband was very kind and helpful. He understood what was in my heart and helped me appear in the STC examination. I passed the STC examination and now I am working as a teacher as well as an *Anganvadi* worker. The progressive ideas of my husband's family helped me.

I am a good *Mehendi* artist. I want to open a beauty parlour as I have been trained for it.

I want to be a good teacher and teach poor children without taking any fees from them, because many children cannot get education due to poverty. My mother's dream is the same as she wants that my ambitions and dreams should be fulfilled.

My role models are Sania Mirza, Lakshmi Bai, Kiran Bedi, Rahul Gandhi, Sonia Gandhi, Indira Gandhi, P.T. Usha, Kalpana Chawla. Hazrat Khadija and Razia Sultana.

Dindigul and Sivagangai, Tamil Nadu

I dream of becoming an air hostess. Now, we are poor and our financial condition is weak but if I will become an airhostess my family will be happy. My mother wanted to study but she could study only till Class 8. Now, she regrets that she does not work while her classmates are working as teachers. She wants me to continue my study and she is not in a hurry to get me married.

I want to be a teacher but I am Muslim and also poor, so how can I achieve my dream?

I want to be an engineer; I want to travel to foreign countries and build an orphanage for others. These are all my dreams, but they are in my husband's hands; if he will not allow it I can't achieve them.

My daughter is suffering from a heart ailment; I am collecting money for her operation and her successful operation is my only dream.

I live with my family in rented accommodation. I want to have my own house. My husband works in a hotel and our dream is also to have our own hotel.

I wished to marry an educated and financially settled guy. But I got an auto driver and he is only 5th-standard pass. Now, everything is okay.

I have seven siblings and our financial condition is bad. I wanted to be an IAS officer but was able to get education only till Class 12. I got married and my parents had to give a huge sum of money as dowry. I was struggling as my husband was a drunkard. He used to hurt me with lit cigarettes. I ran away from my house and stayed with my mother in rented accommodation. Now, my husband is dead. Society blames me for my husband's death; they accuse me of killing my husband. I am struggling to feed my child. I feel education is not enough but awareness, along with confidence, is very important.

I am a mother of four children. All girl children. So society makes fun of us and pities us.

My family is very caring towards me and I used to learn Arabic from the madrasa. On attaining puberty, my parents fixed my wedding. For a long time, I did not have children and so I was very disturbed. Then, on my mother's request my sister gave me one of her children. I thanked my sister and now I want to fulfil all the desires of my son.

I did my BA and got married. My first husband died and then I married again. Now, I have three children, one from the first marriage and two from the second one. My husband differentiates among the three children and this disturbs me. I work as a nursery teacher. There is no help from society for a woman in trouble.

I was living happily with my family but after my father's death the scenario changed. When I attained puberty my brother forcefully got me married. My husband always treated me badly. I divorced him and then everybody forced me to get married a second time to a much older person. I was against it. I adopted a girl child and I am living only for her. Society told me I am unfortunate. After my divorce, I went to work in a plastics company, but society accused me and levelled allegations against me, they said that it is because of my character that I did not adjust with my husband and got a divorce.

My childhood days were good. I completed my school education and fell in love with a person from a different community. I married him without informing my parents but my parents searched for me and I came back home. I got *taalim* from the madrasa and thereafter my parents fixed my wedding with a relative. Now, I have two children and am leading a normal life. Sometimes however, my husband teases me and even society talks badly about me. So, I am afraid for my daughter's future.

I was the only girl child in my family. My father has a cycle shop and I was enrolled in school. My father was always emotionally wrought. After my puberty, when I was in Class 10 my father's mental condition deteriorated and he committed suicide. Now, I am living with my mother and grandmother. I just want peace for my family. Relatives are advising my mother, 'why are you educating your child in this struggle, search for a groom for her and finish your duty'.

I was the first child of my family. At the time of my birth, my mother's sister came to help us. Without informing my mother, my father got married to my aunt. She also stays with us and has one daughter. We both are enrolled in school. Society always criticises my mother, 'you are the reason for your husband's second marriage. You did not take care of him properly'. Also, relatives keep advising my parents to get me married soon because one more girl is waiting after me. I don't know what will happen.

My family members were happy when I was born, not only my parents, my relatives too. My childhood was happy. My parents cared for me with affection, they never insulted or beat me. Sometimes I did wrong things and my parents advised me. My school and college days were very happy. I enjoyed a lot by dancing in school functions, etc. I am about to complete my PG now and have no intention of getting marrying soon. I am free in my home. My family has confidence in me. I want to be in a good profession, so I am trying to achieve that.

Lucknow, Uttar Pradesh

I want to study and become a teacher. I want to open a hospital for poor people. I also want to provide education to my family members. My mother dreams that I get married happily. She loves my brother more than me. She also wants that my brothers should get married. She wants me to be a doctor.

I want to get higher education and become a pilot. I also want to help poor people. I want to tell my neighbours about women's rights. I also want to empower those girls who haven't come out from their homes, who haven't seen the world outside. I want parents to understand that both boys and girls are the same, that they shouldn't differentiate between them. They should allow both to continue his/her studies. Also, I want girls should not get married at an early age as it has an impact on their mental and physical health. I don't want to follow the traditional and outdated rituals. I want society should progress rather than going back or repeating the same old mistakes.

I want to get education and be famous. I want to visit Kashmir. My mother wants me to get married happily.

Earlier I wanted to get married but now I want to get higher education and I also want to teach others. I want to marry a poor guy and want him to respect my parents.

I want to be *Hadis Rubann*. I want to go to Kashmir and want to get married to a poor guy.

My mother has never beaten me. My mother faced a lot of hardship in bringing me up and my siblings. I tried a lot to get education but my mother did not let me do so as she feels the environment outside is not good. My mother is sick of worrying about my marriage. I don't have a father. My mother is the sole earner for the family and she sells flowers. My mother is easily influenced by whatever others say.

We should not hamper our work because of society as they don't give us anything. I want society should not point a blaming finger at me. My husband can tell me to correct it if I do anything wrong but he cannot be violent with me. It's true that he fulfils our needs but we should raise our voice against violence. I want society to be friendly with girls and not differentiate between genders.

I like to watch television. I don't like it when my parents fight with each other.

There was a time when I joined Naish, I went to Delhi with them and I enjoyed myself a lot. But now, unfortunately I can't go outside my home. I always do stitching work at home. There are some people in society who don't want us to move ahead and walk with them. At the same time, I am trying hard to make them unsuccessful in their mission.

Six years ago, I came in contact with Naish and Tehreek. They made me aware of my rights and showed me a life outside the four walls of my home. Now, I teach Arabic in the Company Bagh School.

My role models are the social workers who are working with us like Naish and Naaz Madam.

I admire my English teacher a lot; I want to be like her.

I do not like to take care of my younger brother and to wait till the night to finish serving food to the elders.

10

A Call for Change

'Aurton ki samasyaein hamarey samaj mein aam baat hein, unko samasya samjha hi nahin jata.' (The problems faced by women are a norm for our society and they are not looked upon as problems.)

I began in this book by laying out the different ways in which Muslim women have been excluded or peripheralised in numerous spheres of life, including the discursive. I also presented glimpses of instances when the young participants of this work afforded us an understanding of their view of the issues and problems they face. It goes without saying that the discourse woven here ultimately aims at gaining equal opportunities and the recognition of full humanity for Muslim women—getting education, economic betterment, and a capacity to dream and create lives in the likeness of their dreams. These demands for equality and recognition have not ignored the experiences of these women within their everyday lives, and the encounters therein with patriarchy and communalism. Being 'Indian Muslim women' is not a homogenised identity. It is also not a hybrid identity but a matrix of differences that is, nevertheless, subaltern and has often proved to be potentially 'lethal' for them.

Who understands a situation better than those who are living it and who would propose better solutions to problems than those who grapple with them in their everyday lives? When we asked the young Muslim women participants of this study what needs to be done in order to bring about a change in this situation, they shared with us numerous ideas regarding the change action that can emanate from various quarters. In my re-reading and analysis I found that their ideas addressed the State, Muslim community, civil society, parents and family members, and the girls themselves, which I have reproduced below largely in their own words. To these I add a few recommendations of my own that the participants of this study have not enumerated but which could help provide a concrete direction to efforts towards realising their expectations and aspirations.

What Would They Like the State to Do?

Government should be willing to help Muslims to progress.

Government's support in general would go a long way.

Education and employment should be provided to the people by the government and government should function towards bettering the condition of Muslim women in villages.

Poverty and lack of education is the main reason for backwardness. Government should spread awareness about various programmes for girls.

We need good government who can take care of our studies and wellbeing.

It is important to treat education of girls as a primary investment.

Muslim girls are going to school now because of the provision of free education. More girls would have got education had it been regulated earlier.

Government should help girls to study even after the 8th standard.

Education should be made compulsory for everyone. There should be a survey in every state, district and muhalla to assess the level of education among Muslim girls.

They should provide scholarship not only to those who fall in the BPL category but to all. Also there should be an increase in the scholarship amount.

Government should open schools at all places for the education of girls, and women and parents should send their girls to those schools.

There should be no admission fees in college. So many girls are not able to join college because they don't have money to pay fees. Even Government colleges asks for money.

We need help like scholarship for children, self-employment or employment at home and education.

The graph of education, skill training and self-confidence has to go up. Education should be made cheaper and of good quality. There should be efforts by the government to reduce poverty. Government should do something for poor Muslim women and their children. There should be programmes for education of both men and women of the Muslim community; they should be given help not empty promises.

Muslims need scholarships from the government so that education is not hampered by their economic conditions.

Quality and cost of education should be brought to a level which would make Muslim girls and their parents more amenable to it.

Muslims feel insecure. At hospitals, schools and police stations they are not treated equally. Government should ensure that they too are treated with respect.

Officials responsible for implementing government policies for people should be checked regularly and taken to task if they do not carry out their responsibilities.

Government should conduct a family survey and promote education of women.

Technical education should be provided to women as it would boost their confidence as well as their chances of getting employment.

While citizens of the State understand its instrumental obligation towards them to consider their interests and provide for them, they also expect it to play an epistemic role. They expect that the State will play the role of the facilitator of communication and knowledge dissemination between the interest and identity groups. They expect that the State would defend the moral ideas guiding decisions regarding the rights of minorities and justify these to other groups. In democracies governance is also about perception. People also wish to see that the State is treating them as equals. Minorities are often left speechless due to lack of opportunity to counter the forces working against their interest. The State could do several specific things for aiding the minorities in their amelioration.

A good place to begin would be to intensify efforts to implement planned provisions for Muslims. Plan documents must use unambiguous language to speak of different minorities such that funds earmarked for Muslims be used specifically for them and not for non-specific development activities for entire 'minority concentrated' districts. Explicit mention must be made of targeted outlays for Muslims within various plan provisions, e.g., within provision for handlooms and handicrafts. Provisions for Muslim girls and their education need to be more concrete and it must be ensured that Muslim girls'/women's access to welfare schemes is not hindered by discrimination. This can be done by appointing Muslim observers in welfare departments and in selection processes for public sector jobs. A sub-plan for the minorities on the lines of the tribal sub-plan and the special component plan for the SCs should be put in place. Social auditing of plan provisions in addition to financial accounting and statistical targeted outlays of programmes meant to facilitate social justice to minorities must be instituted. In this regard, the central government can institute a statutory body for violence mitigation and peace building with a mandate to provide legal aid to victims of violence against minorities, including aiding victims to report violations of human rights and other constitutional safeguards to other statutory bodies like the National Human Rights Commission, National Commission for Minorities, National Commission for Women, etc. This organisation could also make important contributions towards restoring the dignity of victims by aiding in rebuilding livelihoods, assisting in resettlement and rehabilitation of internally displaced victims of communal violence, providing therapy and counselling to individuals, initiating and supporting best practices/innovative community engagement, conducting fact-finding missions and research, supporting research through fellowships and grants to academicians, researchers and NGOs, and conducting monitoring, evaluation and social audit of schemes and programmes for minorities.

How Can the Civil Society Contribute?

Social workers can give guidance to people.
Politicians should take a break from politics and think and do something for people as well.
Activists should talk to the panchayat and family members about issues concerning Muslim women to bring about change.
NGO people should help Muslim community figure out how to improve their conditions. They should tell the people about the benefits of education. They should do something for the education of girls.
Social workers can talk to influential people and try to bring some possible changes. People should be allowed to work for their betterment. Without work and earning nothing is possible.
People should be made more aware of their rights, programmes, provisions and policies. However good a scheme is, if people do not know how to benefit from it, it is just a useless piece of paper.
The government and NGOs should work together to benefit Muslim people.
NGO activists can convince people that given a chance to study, girls can probably outshine boys in performance.

Samaaj me bahu-betiyo ke liye sneh ho. (Girls/women should be treated with affection by society.)

An exclusive women's union is required to look after the development of Muslim women in India.

Civil society could help Muslim women in using media to spread awareness. Newspaper and media should play an active role in awareness generation among people.

With the support of some NGOs, probably the condition of Muslim women can improve. They should reach every woman at their doorstep and make them aware about their rights.

Join hands with people like you who are working in this field and engage in discussion with our elders. If people start understanding it will lead to some change in their behaviour towards girls/women. They will not look down upon us and might start believing in our abilities.

Someone should actually show the society its true and ugly face. We can think of bringing some change if people around realise that it is actually needed.

Society is more conservative and strict for separated and widowed women and their children. Social workers should support single women and their children and bring some change. Their (men's) brain should be washed like we purify water.

...if you want to change something, wake them up from their slumber and start some programme for the improvement of Muslims in India. Associate with people, highlight their problems and find a solution together with them. With education and employment, poverty will reduce and then the situation of Muslim women will surely improve.

Like today, periodically, girls should be given a space to assemble and given a chance to discuss their bad situation and possible solutions for their progress. They should be given the necessary support.

Government is claiming to bring change for many years now but nothing seems to happen. The poor are becoming poorer and rich, richer. They claim to educate and provide employment but nothing is done on the ground. If you (social worker) try to bring about some change in our condition, we will support you.

Men have a major say in women's lives; they should be made more sensitive and supportive towards women.

In Muslim women's reading, the power of the activists, social workers and civil society organisations lies in their specialised knowledge of social change, and state welfare and governance processes. While they express a lot of confidence in the intervention of civil society on their behalf, Muslim women seem to reproach civil society too for not doing enough. Their expectations from civil society are not so much to do with material relief as they are about consciousness-raising, mobilisation and advocacy.

What Should Muslims Do?

Kuch aisa karna chahiye jisse humara pichdapan kam ho. (Something should be done to reduce our backwardness.)

Muslim society is not united; it is divided into different groups. We need to be united in demanding our rights.

Muslims should come together to form a union and take this issue to panchayat and the government.

We should demand our right to equality together. Only this can change the situation.

Apne halaat sudharne ke liye chhote-chhote jhagdon se thoda upar uth kar samadhan sochne honge. Ke kaise apne aas-paas ki chizon ko badlein. (To improve our condition, we would have to rise above the little fights and think about solutions. On how to change things around us.)

It is important to leave conservative thoughts behind, then only can we think of making some progress in our lives.

Girls and women should not be locked inside their homes in the name of purdah; they can be able supporters.

Shariat is used by men to suppress women. With the changing times and hostilities around us we are kept at home with the rhetoric that the environment (*mahaul*) is unsafe for us. This should change.

Everyone is living with fear and domination but men are given extra freedom and a free hand to dominate women. Women are suffering so much and still they struggle for the future of the family. They could do so much more if only the community and men would realise this.

Women should come out in the open and ask for their rights.

How Should Parents/Families Change?

Parents should allow young Muslim women to have a life of their own which is more relaxed.

There should be some action against those parents who do not send their wards to schools.

Parvarish ka tarika badlke himmat paida ki jae, galat ko galaht aur sahi ko sahi bolne ki himmat aae. (People should be encouraged to change their way of parenting; they must inculcate the courage to call out wrong from right.)

The environment at home should be comfortable for girls, not stressful all the time.

Girls should be allowed to decide for themselves. They should not be suppressed and should be allowed to go out.

There should be some change in society. Parents should be willing to cooperate with and support the development of their daughters.

Each Muslim girl should be given education and all parents should be willing to send their girls to school.

I can see the only solution in terms of letting the girl study, learn skills, go out, and achieve things for herself and for the community.

Families shouldn't pay heed to gossiping people and let their daughters go out and achieve their dreams.

Families should make sure that the girls are educated and standing on their own feet before getting married.

The change should start at the level of the family by changing its outlook towards women. There should be no difference in the upbringing of boys and girls. The ambitions of girls should also be taken care of by the family. Girls should be allowed to work and given opportunities to forge ahead.

The way men think about and control women should change.

Parents should not force girls. They shouldn't be guided only by fear. It will keep us backward.

Needless to say Indian young Muslim women have a lot of expectations from their parents, families and their communities. It is the need of the hour for Muslims in India to understand that without the women's condition improving, the community cannot progress. Muslim men especially must come to the realisation that by wielding such crippling control over women's lives and bodies they are not protecting any 'honour' but playing right into the hands of the communal forces and limiting their own agency to transform their life situations. It is only with this realisation that parental control and community surveillance can transform into enabling parenting and supportive community spaces that foster confidence and success motivation in girls.

What Must the Women Do to Improve Their Situation?

> To change the situation, women have to change their own thinking first.
>
> '*Ladkiyan apni baat manwane ki taqat paida kare. Aur aas paas ki bato ko samjhe.*'(Girls should develop the capacity to negotiate their point of view and should understand what is going on around them.).
>
> '*Parde me rehne ka ye matlab nahi ki dar ke raho*'. (Observing purdah does not mean that you should live in fear.)
>
> Muslim women should be educated/self-employed, self-dependent and willing to take decision on their own. They should possess knowledge of *shariat* and governmental provisions meant for them. These are all important to bring about change and development.
>
> They should have the knowledge of *shariat*. They don't know about *shariat* so they believe whatever they are told. *Shariat* clearly says that women should be treated at par with men. Women are here to understand the world and not to fall behind in any respect.
>
> It is important for women to have social and political understanding. They should gain awareness and make others aware too.
>
> Muslim women should stand together to bring change at the level of the family and society.
>
> They (girls) should listen to their hearts and do what it says rather than obeying one and all.
>
> They should come forward and fight for their rights. Be self-confident and self-sufficient. Be free and get education.
>
> My grandma always said we can progress only through education. She said she couldn't study and so remained dependent on others and she wanted us to study.
>
> Girls should try to discuss with seniors in the family the importance of education among Muslim girls.

Muslim women who are educated should obtain positions of power and hold good posts like those of IAS officers and ministers. They will then be able to do a lot for their community and other women.

We shouldn't leave ourselves to fate like we usually do, we should know our potential and make use of it to grow.

To bring change in the situation it is required to bring change in the way we conduct ourselves. We should just think about our own progress and stop interfering in other's business and hampering their progress in life.

There are just a few girls who make an effort to make themselves aware by reading newspapers or asking someone who knows things regarding education and training.

I think we girls are also responsible for our miserable conditions. *Agar hum ye thhaan le ki humme kuch ban kar dikhana hai to shayad kuch naya badlav aa sakta hai* (If we brace ourselves and decide that we shall show everyone by becoming something, then probably there will be a change).

In the end it is hoped that this book may become a point of commencement of challenging those conditions that create misrepresentation and discursive deafness. I should count my efforts and the efforts of other participants of this study across India, as successful, if the book manages to provide some ideational and methodological resources to prepare the ground for action, enabling Muslim Women in India to participate as equal citizens who can speak for themselves and are not always already spoken for.

Bibliography

Abbas, T. (2007). *Islamic Political Radicalism*. Edinburgh: Edinburgh University Press.
Abels, P. & Abels, S. L. (2001). *Understanding Narrative Therapy: A Guidebook for the Social Worker*. New York: Springer Publishing Company.
Abu-Lughod, L. (ed.). (1998). *Remaking Women: Feminism and Modernity in the Middle East*. Princeton NJ: Princeton University Press.
Agnes, F. (1992). Protecting women against violence? Review of a decade of legislation. *Economic and Political Weekly*, 27(17), 25 April.
Agnes, F. (1995). Hindu men, monogamy and uniform civil code. *Economic and Political Weekly*, 30(50), 3238–3244.
Agnes, F. (1996). The hidden agenda beneath the rhetoric of women's rights. In Dutta, Agnes & Adarkar (eds), *The Nation, the State and the Indian Identity* (pp. 68–94). Calcutta: Samya.
Agnes, F. (1999). *Law and Gender Inequality: Politics of Women's Rights in India*. Delhi: Oxford University Press.
Agnes, F. (2009). Interview by Yoginder Sikand. *Pakistan Christian Post*. Retrieved from http://www.pakistanchristianpost.com/detail.php?interviewid=70
Ahmad, I. (2003). A different Jihad: Dalit Muslims' challenge to Ashraf hegemony. *Economic and Political Weekly*, 38(46), 4886–4891.
Ahmad, I. (2009). *Islamism and Democracy in India: The Transformation of Jamaat-e-Islami*. Princeton, NJ: Princeton University Press.
Ahmed, A. (1993–1996). *Muslims in India (Volume I–IV)*. New Delhi: Inter-India Publications.
Ahmed, A. (2002). *Discovering Islam: Making Sense of Muslim History and Society*. London: Routledge.
Ahmed, I. (1983). *Modernization and Social Change among Muslims in India*. New Delhi: Manohar.
Ahmed, I. (ed.). (1978). *Caste and Social Stratification among the Muslims*. Delhi: Manohar.
Ahmed, L. (1992). *Women and Gender in Islam*. New Haven: Yale University Press.
Akbar, M. J. (1988). *Nehru: The Making of India*. Viking Adult.
Akbar, M.J. (1991). *Riot after Riot*. Delhi: Penguin Books India.
Alam, A. (2003). Democratisation of Indian Muslims: Some reflections. *Economic and Political Weekly*, 38(46), 4881–4885.
Alam, A. (2009). Challenging the Ashrafs: The politics of Pasmanda Muslim mahaz. *Journal of Muslim Minority Affairs*, 29(2), 171–181.
Alam, J. (1999). Is caste appeal casteism? Oppressed castes in politics. *Economic and Political Weekly*, 34(13), 757–761.
Al-Hibri, A. Y. (1999). Is western patriarchal feminism good for third world/minority women? In Susan Okin (ed.), *Is Multiculturalism Bad for Women?* (pp. 41–46). Princeton, NJ: Princeton University Press.

Bibliography 177

Al-Hindi, K. F. & Kawabata, H. (2002). Toward a more fully reflexive feminist geography. In P. Moss, K. F. Al-Hindi & H. Kawabata (eds), *Feminist Geography in Practice: Research and Methods* (pp. 103–116). Hoboken, NJ: Wiley-Blackwell.

Ali, A. (2001). Evolution of public sphere in India. *Economic and Political Weekly*, 36(26), 2419–2425.

Ali, A. H. (2006). *Infidel*. New York: Free Press. (Translation published in 2007).

Ali, S. (2002, December). Collective and elective ethnicity: Caste among urban Muslims in India. *Sociological Forum*, 17(4), 593–620.

Allen, C. (2010). *Islamophobia*. Farnham: Ashgate Publishing.

Anand, D. (2005). The violence of security: Hindu nationalism and the politics of representing 'the Muslim' as a danger. *The Round Table*, 94(379), 203–215.

Anderson, B. (2006). *Imagined Communities: Reflections on the Origin and Spread of Nationalism*. London: Verso.

Anwar, A. (2001). *Maswat ki Jung (in Urdu)*. New Delhi: Vani Prakashan.

Appadurai, A. (2004). The capacity to aspire. *Culture and Public Action*, 59–84.

Arendt, H. (1958). *The Human Condition*. Chicago: University of Chicago Press.

Asghar Ali, A. (2000). *The Emergence of Feminism among Indian Muslim Women: 1920–1947*. New York: Oxford University Press.

Asselin, M. E. (2003). Insider research: Issues to consider when doing qualitative research in your own setting. *Journal for Nurses in Professional Development*, 19(2), 99–103.

Badran, M. (2002). Islamic Feminism: what's in a name? *Al-Ahram Weekly Online*, 569, 17–23.

Badran, M. (2005). Between secular and Islamic feminism/s. *Journal of Middle East Women's Studies*, 1(1), 6–28.

Badran, M. (2008a). *Feminism in Islam: Secular and Religious Convergences*. London: Oneworld Publications.

Badran, M. (2008b). Engaging Islamic feminism. *Islamic Feminism*, 25.

Badran, M. (2009). *Feminism in Islam*. London: Oneworld Publications.

Bandura, A. (2001). Social cognitive theory: An agentic perspective. *Annual Review of Psychology*, 52(1), 1–26.

Bandura, A. (Sept. 1989). Human agency in social cognitive theory. *American Psychologist*, 44(9): 1175–1184.

Barlas, A. (2002). *Believing Women' in Islam: Un-reading Patriarchal Interpretations of the Qur'an*. Austin, TX: University of Texas Press.

Barlas, A. (2006). *Four Stages of Denial, or, my On-again, Off-again Affair with Feminism: Response to Margot Badran*. Discussion Series, 'Global Fury/Global Fear: Engaging Muslims'. Ithaca College, 23 October 2006.

Barnier, A. J. & Sutton, J. (2008). From individual to collective memory: Theoretical and empirical perspectives. *Memory*, 16(3), 177.

Barthes, R. [(1968) 1988]. The death of the author. In N. Wood & D. Lodge (eds), *Modern Criticism and Theory: A Reader* (pp. 167–172). London and New York: Longman.

Bayoumi, M. (2010). The God that failed: The neo-orientalism of today's Muslim commentators. In A. Shryock (ed.), *Islamophobia/Islamophilia: Beyond the Politics of Enemy and Friend* (pp. 79–93). Bloomington, IN: Indiana University Press.

Bell, GD. (1963). Process in formation of adolescents' aspirations. *Social Forces*, 42, 179–185.

Bennett, W. L. & Entman, R. M. (eds). (2001). *Mediated Politics: Communication in the Future of Democracy*. Cambridge: Cambridge University Press.

Berger, P. L. & Luckmann, T. (1966). *The Social Construction of Reality: A Treatise in the Sociology of Knowledge*. New York: Doubleday.

Bhambri, C. P. (2005). Reservations and casteism. *Economic and Political Weekly*, 40(9), 806–808.

Bharucha, R. (2003). Muslims and others: Anecdotes, fragments and uncertainties of evidence. *Economic and Political Weekly*, 38(40), 4238–4250.

Bhaskar, I. & Allen, R. (2009). *Islamicate Cultures of Bombay Cinema*. New Delhi: Tulika Books.

Bhatty, Z. (1996). Social stratification among Muslims in India. In M. N. Srinivas (ed.), *Caste: Its Twentieth Century Avatar*. New Delhi: Penguin.

Blumer, H. (1967). *Symbolic Interactionism*. Englewood Cliffs, NJ: Prentice-Hall.

Brass, P. R. (1997). *Theft of an Idol: Text and Context in the Representation of Collective Violence*. Princeton, N.J.: Princeton University Press.

Brass, P. R. (2005). *The Production of Hindu-Muslim Violence in Contemporary India*. Seattle, WA: University of Washington Press.

Brass, P. R. (1996). *Riots and Pogroms*. New York: New York University Press.

Buijs, F. J. & Rath, J. (2002). *Muslims in Europe: The State of Research*. New York: Russell SAGE Foundation.

Burke, A. (2003). Private griefs, public places. *Political Geography*, 22, 317–333.

Busia, A. P. A. (1993). Performance, transcription and the languages of the self: Interrogating identity as a 'post-colonial' poet. In S. M. James & A. P. A. Busia (eds), *Theorizing Black Feminisms: The Visionary Pragmatism of Black Women* (pp. 203–213). London: Routledge.

Chandra, B. (1979). *Nationalism and Colonialism in Modern India*. New Delhi: Orient Longman.

Chatterjee, P. (1993). *The Nation and its Fragments: Colonial and Postcolonial Histories*. Princeton, N.J.: Princeton University Press.

Chaudhary, N. (2003). Speaking the self into becoming. *Culture and Psychology*, 9(4): 471–486.

Chodorow, N. (1978). *The Reproduction of Mothering: Psychoanalysis and the Sociology of Gender*. Berkeley: University of California Press

Cooley, C. H. [1964 (1902)]. *Human Nature and Social Order*. New York: Schocken Books.

Dabashi, H. (2009). *Post-orientalism: Knowledge and Power in Time of Terror*. New Brunswick, NJ: Transaction Publishers.

Das, S. K. & Samaddar, R. (2009). Ways of power, minorities, and knowledge of minorities: An assessment of research policies and practices. Mahanirban Calcutta Research Group. Retrieved from http://www.mcrg.ac.in/

Davis, D. E. (2012). Urban resilience in situations of chronic violence. Center for International Studies (May).

De Certeau, M. (1984). *The Practice of Everyday Life*, trans. Steven Rendall. Berkeley: University of California Press.

Denzin, N. & Lincoln, Y. (eds). (2008). *Collecting and Interpreting Qualitative Materials*. Los Angeles: SAGE Publications.

Dodds, K. (2007). *Geopolitics: A Very Short Introduction*. New York: Oxford University Press.

Douglas, M. (1966). *Purity and Danger: An Analysis of the Concepts of Pollution and Taboo*. London and New York: Routledge.

Dworkin, A. (2006). *Intercourse*. NY: Basic Books.

Dwyer, S. C. & Buckle, J. L. (2009). The space between: On being an insider-outsider in qualitative research. *International Journal of Qualitative Methods*, 8(1).

Eagleton, T. (1996, 2008). *Literary Theory: An Introduction.* London: John Wiley & Sons; Minneapolis: University of Minnesota Press.
Engineer, A. A. (1985). Communal fire engulfs Ahmedabad once again. *Economic and Political Weekly,* 20 (27), 1116–1120.
Engineer, A. A. (1988). *Delhi-Meerut Riots: Analysis, Compilation, and Documentation.* New Delhi: Ajanta Publications.
Engineer, A. A. (1989). *Communalism and Communal Violence in India: An Analytical Approach to Hindu-Muslim Conflict.* New Delhi: Ajanta Publications.
Engineer, A. A. (1991a). Socio-economic backwardness of Muslims in India. *Occasional Paper,* 5(7), May, Institute of Islamic Studies.
Engineer, A. A. (1991b). *Communal Riots in Post-independence India.* Delhi: Universities Press.
Engineer, A. A. (1991c). The bloody trail: Ramjanmabhoomi and communal violence in UP. *Economic and Political Weekly,* 26(4), 155–159.
Engineer, A. A. (1995). *Lifting the Veil: Communal Violence and Communal Harmony in Contemporary India.* Hyderabad: Sangam.
Engineer, A. A. (2002). *Islam in India: The Impact of Civilizations.* New Delhi: Shipra Publications.
Fachandi, P. G. (2010). Ahimsa, identification and sacrifice in the Gujarat pogrom. *Social Anthropology,* 18(2), 155–175.
Fachandi, P. G. (2012). *Pogrom in Gujarat: Hindu Nationalism and Anti-Muslim Violence in India.* Princeton University Press.
Farber, N. B. (1989). The significance of aspirations among unmarried adolescent mothers. *The Social Service Review,* 63(4), 518–532.
Faridi, II. et al (eds). (1992). *The Social Structure of Indian Muslims.* New Delhi: Institute of Objective Studies.
Fazalbhoy, N. (1997). Sociology of Muslims in India: A review. *Economic and Political Weekly,* 32(26), 1547–1551.
Flynn, T. (2006). *Existentialism: A Very Short Introduction.* Oxford: Oxford University Press.
Fraser, H. (2004). Doing narrative research. *Qualitative Social Work,* 3(2): 179–201.
Fraser, N. (1990). Rethinking the public sphere: A contribution to the critique of actually existing democracy. *Social Text,* 26(25), 56–80.
Fraser, N. (1997). *Justice Interruptus: Critical Reflections on the 'Postsocialist' Condition.* New York: Routledge.
Freire, P. (1993). *Pedagogy of the Oppressed.* London: Penguin Books.
Friedman, A. (2011). Girl talk: Feminism and domestic architecture at Frank Lloyd Wright's Oak Park Studio. In D. Van Zanten (ed.), *Marion Mahony Reconsidered* (pp. 23–51). Chicago, IL: University of Chicago Press.
Fukuyama, F. (1989). The end of history. In P. O'Meara, H. D. Mehlinger, M. Krain (eds), *Globalization and the Challenges of a New Century: A Reader* (pp. 161–180). Indiana University Press.
Fukuyama, F. (1992). *The End of History and the Last Man.* New York: Free Press.
Gallagher, S. & Zahavi, D. (2013). *The Phenomenological Mind.* New York: Routledge.
Galtung, J. (1981). *The True Worlds: A Transnational Experience.* New York: Free Press.
Galtung, J. (1990). Cultural violence. *Journal of Peace Research,* 27(3): 291–305.
Gandhi, R. (1999). *Understanding the Muslim Mind.* New Delhi: Penguin Books India.
Gans, H. (1997). Toward a Reconciliation of 'Assimilation' and 'Pluralism': The Interplay of Acculturation and Ethnic Retention. *International Migration Review,* 31(4), 875–892.
Geertz, C. (1973). *The Interpretation of Cultures.* New York: Basic Books.

Geertz, C. (1983). *Local Knowledge*. New York: Basic Books.
Giddens, A. (1984). *The Constitution of Society*. Oxford: Polity.
Giddens, A. (1991). *Modernity and Self Identity*. Stanford: Stanford University Press.
Gilbert, N. (ed). (2001). *Researching Social Life*. London: SAGE Publications.
Gilligan, C. (1982). *In a Different Voice: Psychological Theory and Women's Development*. Cambridge: Harvard University Press.
Gilligan, C. (1987). Moral orientation and moral development. In E. F. Kittay & D. T. Meyers (eds). *Women and Moral Theory* (pp. 19–33). Savage, Maryland: Rowman & Littlefield Publishers.
Gitlin, T. (1998). Public spheres or public sphericules. In T. Liebes & J. Curran (eds), *Media, Ritual and Identity* (pp. 168–174). London: Routledge.
Goffman, E. (1959). *The Presentation of Self in Everyday Life*. Oxford: Doubleday.
Goffman, E. (1961). *Asylums*. New York: Anchor.
Goffman, E. (1971). *Relations in Public*. New York: Basic Books.
Goffman, E. (1974). *Frame Analysis*. New York: Harper and Row.
Goffman, E. (1981). *Forms of Talk*. Philadelphia: University of Pennsylvania Press.
Goffman, E. (1983). The interaction order. *American Sociological Review*, 48, 1–7.
Göle, N. (1996). *The Forbidden Modern. Civilization and Veiling*. Ann Arbor: The University of Michigan Press.
Griffin, C. (1996). See whose face it wears: Difference, otherness and power. *Feminism & Psychology*, 6(2), 185–191.
Guru, G. (2012). *The Cracked Mirror: An Indian Debate on Experience and Theory*. Oxford University Press.
Habermas, J. [1990 (1983)]. *Moral Consciousness and Communicative Action*. Massachusetts: MIT Press.
Habermas, J. [1989 (1962)]. *The Structural Transformation of the Public Sphere: An Inquiry into a Category of Bourgeois Society*. Cambridge: MIT Press.
Halbwachs, M. (1992). *On Collective Memory*. University of Chicago Press.
Haraway, D. (1988). Situated knowledges: The science question in feminism and the privilege of partial perspective. *Feminist Studies*, 575–599.
Haraway, D. (1991). *Simians, Cyborgs, and Women: The Reinvention of Women*. London and New York: Routledge.
Harding, S. (ed.). (2004). *The Feminist Standpoint Theory Reader*. New York and London: Routledge.
Harding, S. G. (ed.). (1987). *Feminism and Methodology: Social Science Issues*. Bloomington, Indiana: Indiana University Press.
Harrison, F. (1969). Aspirations as related to school performance and socioeconomic status. *Sociometry*, 32(1), 70–79.
Hasan, M. (1990). Adjustment and accommodation: Indian Muslims after partition. *Social Scientist*, 18(8/9): 48–65.
Hasan, M. (1995). *India Partitioned: The Other Face of Freedom* (2 Volumes). Delhi: Roli.
Hasan, M. (1997). *Legacy of a Divided Nation: India's Muslims since Independence*. New Delhi: Cambridge University Press.
Hasan, M. (1998). *Memories of a Fragmented Nation: Rewriting the Histories of India's Partition*. Edinburgh Papers in South Asian Studies # 8.
Hasan, M. (2004). Resistance and acquiescence in North India: Muslim responses to the west. In M. Hasan & N. Gupta (ed.), *India's Colonial Encounter*. New Delhi: Manohar.

Hasan, M. (2008). *Moderate or Militant: Images of India's Muslims.* New Delhi: Oxford University Press.
Hasan, M. (ed.). (2001). *Introduction in India's Partition: Process, Strategy and Mobilization.* New Delhi: Oxford University Press.
Hasan, M. & Roy, A. (eds). (2005). *Living Together Separately: Cultural India in History and Politics.* Oxford University Press.
Hasan, Z. & Menon, R. (2004). *Unequal Citizens: A Study of Muslim Women in India.* New Delhi: Oxford University Press.
Hasan, Z. & Menon, R. (2005). *Educating Muslim Girls: A Comparison of Five Indian Cities.* New Delhi: Women Unlimited.
Hasan, Z. (2000). Uniform civil code and gender justice in India. In P. R. DeSouza (ed.), *Contemporary India: Transitions.* Delhi: SAGE Publications.
Hasan, Z. (ed.). (1994). *Forging Identities: Gender, Communities, and the State.* Boulder, CO: Westview Press.
Hasan, Z. & Menon, R. (2006). *In a Minority: Essays on Muslim Women in India.* Delhi: Oxford University Press.
Haslam, S. A., Oakes, P. J., Reynolds, K. J. & Turner, J. C. (1999). Social identity salience and the emergence of stereotype consensus. *Personality and Social Psychology Bulletin,* 25(7), 809–818.
Heidegger, M. (1962). *Being and Time.* New York: Harper & Row.
Hill, T. (1989). The Kantian conception of autonomy. In John Christman (ed.), *The Inner Citadel: Essays on Individual Autonomy* (pp. 91–105). Oxford: Oxford University Press.
Hobsbawm, E. (1983). Introduction: Inventing traditions. In E. Hobsbawm & T. Ranger (eds), *The Invention of Tradition* (pp. 1–14). Cambridge: Cambridge University Press.
hooks, b. (2004): *The Will to Change: Men, Masculinity, and Love.* New York: Washington Square Press.
Horkheimer, M. (1931). The present situation of social philosophy and the tasks of an institute for social research. In G. Hunter, M. Kramer & J. Torpey (trans.) (1993). *Between Philosophy and Social Science: Selected Early Writings* (pp. 1–14). Cambridge, MA: MIT Press.
Hunter, W. W. (2002). *The Indian Musalmans.* New Delhi: Rupa & Company (First published in 1871).
Huntington, S. P. (1993). The clash of civilizations? *Foreign Affairs,* 72(3), 22–49.
Huntington, S. P. (1996). *The Clash of Civilizations and the Remaking of World Order.* London: Simon & Schuster.
Husain, M. G. (2004). *Muslim Youth and Madrasa Education in Purnea District of Bihar.* New Delhi: Institute of Objective Studies.
Hussain, S. (2008). *Exposing the Myth of Muslim Fertility: Gender and Religion in a Resettlement Colony of Delhi.* New Delhi: Promilla & Co Publishers.
Hyman, D. A. (2000). Do good stories make for good policy? *Journal of Health Politics,* 25(6), 1149–1155.
Hyman, H. (1953). The values systems of the different classes: A social-psychological contribution to the analysis of stratification. In R. Bendix & S.M.Lipset (eds), *Class, Status and Power* (pp. 488–499). Glencoe, Ill: Free Press.
Jaffrelot, C. (1999). *Hindu Nationalist Movement and Indian Politics, 1925 to the 1920s: Strategies of Identity Building, Implantation and Mobilization.* London: Christopher Hurst.
Jaffrelot, C. (ed.). (2005). *The Sangh Parivar: A Reader.* Delhi: Oxford University Press.

Jalal, A. (1996). Secularists, subalterns, and the stigma of 'communalism': Partition historiography revisited. *Indian Economic and Social History Review*, 33(1), January–March.

Jalal, A. (1998). Exploding communalism: The politics of Muslim identity in South Asia. In S. Bose & A. Jalal (eds), *Nationalism, Democracy and Development: State and Politics in India*. Delhi: Oxford University Press.

Jalal, Ayesha. (1999). Exploding communalism: The politics of Muslim identity in South Asia. In Sugata Bose & Ayesha Jalal (eds), *Nationalism, Democracy and Development: State and Politics in India*. Delhi: Oxford University Press.

Jameson, F. (1981). *The Political Unconscious: Narrative as a Socially Symbolic Act*. Ithaca, NY: Cornell University Press.

Jameson, F. (1981). *The Political Unconscious: Narrative as a Socially Symbolic Act*. UK: Methuen.

Jameson, F. (1991). *Postmodernism, or, the Cultural Logic of Late Capitalism*. Durham: Duke University Press Books.

Jameson, F. (2000). Globalization and political strategy. *New Left Review*, 4(Jul–Aug), 49–68.

Jamil, G. (2014). The capitalist logic of spatial segregation. *Economic & Political Weekly*, 49(3), 52–58.

Jeffery, P., Roger, J. & Jeffery, C. (2004). Islamisation, gentrification, domestication: A girls' Islamic course and rural Muslims in western Uttar Pradesh. *Modern Asian Studies*, 38(1): 1–53.

Jenkins, L. D. (1999). Competing inequalities: The struggle over reserved legislative seats for women in India. *International Review of Social History*, 44(S7), 53–75.

Jenkins, L. D. (2001). Becoming backward: Preferential policies and religious minorities in India. *Commonwealth and Comparative Politics*, 39(2), 32–50.

Jha, Manoj K. & Shajahan, P. K. (2009). Social topography of delineated others: Muslims in contemporary India. In Abdul Waheed (ed.), *Minority Education in India: Issues of Access, Equity and Inclusion*. Centre for Promotion of Education and Cultural Advancement of Muslims of India, Aligarh Muslim University and Serials Publication.

Jha, Manoj K. & Sharma, Shalini. (2009). Representing Muslims as intimidating others. In Seema Sharma & Manoj K. Jha (eds), *Opposition to Silence*. New Delhi: AlterNotes Press.

Jha, Manoj K. (2009). *Riots as Rituals*. New Delhi: Manak Publications.

Kazi, S. (1999). *Muslim Women in India*. London: Minority Rights Group International.

Kazi, S. (1999). *Muslim Women in India: A Report*. London, UK: Minority Rights Group.

Khalidi, O. (2006). *Muslims in Indian Economy*. New Delhi: Three Essays Collective.

Khalidi, O. (2009). Muslim experience of Indian Democracy. *Islam and Democratization in Asia*, 163–188.

Khan, N. A. (2009). *Islam, Women and Violence in Kashmir: Between India and Pakistan*. New Delhi: Tulika Books.

Kidwai, S. (2003). *Images of Muslim Women: A Study on the Representation of Muslim Women in the Media, 1985–2001*. New Delhi: WISCOMP.

Kirmani, N. (2009). Claiming their space: Muslim women-led networks and the women's movement in India. *Journal of International Women's Studies*, 11(1), 72–85.

Kishwar, M. (1998). Pro-women or anti-Muslim? The Shah Bano controversy. In Madhu Kishwar (ed.), *Religion at the Service of Nationalism*. Delhi: Oxford University Press.

Kynsilehto, A. (2008). *Islamic Feminism: Current Perspectives*. Occasional Paper No. 96, 2008. Tampere Peace Research Institute.

Laidlaw, J. (2010). Agency and responsibility: Perhaps you can have too much of a good thing. In M. Lambek (ed.), *Ordinary Ethics: Anthropology, Language, and Action* (pp. 143–164). New York: Fordham University Press.

Lefebvre, H. (2002). *Critique of Everyday Life: Foundations for a Sociology of the Everyday*, Vol. 2. Trans. John Moore. London: Verso.

Lewis, B. (1990, September). The roots of Muslim rage. *The Atlantic*. Retrieved from http://www.theatlantic.com/magazine/archive/1990/09/the-roots-of-muslim-rage/304643/

Little, D. (1986). *The Scientific Marx*. Minneapolis: University of Minnesota Press.

Maher, F. A. & Tetreault, M. K. T. (1993). Frames of positionality: Constructing meaningful dialogues about gender and race. In *Constructing Meaningful Dialogue on Difference: Feminism and Postmodernism in Anthropology and the Academy*. The George Washington University Institute for Ethnographic Research Anthropological Quarterly, 66(3), 118–126.

Mahmood, S. (2005). *The Politics of Piety. The Islamic Revival and the Feminist Subject*. Princeton and Oxford: Princeton University Press.

Mainuddin, M. (2010). Understanding reality: Population growth, distribution and educational status of Indian Muslims. *Asia Pacific Journal of Social Sciences*, 2(2), 82–104.

Majid, A. (2002). Politics of feminism in Islam. In Saliba et al. (eds), *Gender, Politics and Islam*. New Delhi: Orient Longman.

Malpas, S. (2002). *Jean Francois Lyotard*. London: Routledge.

Mamdani, M. (2005). *Good Muslim, Bad Muslim: Islam, the USA, and the Global War against Terror*. Delhi: Permanent Black.

Marx, K. & Engels, F. (1976). *Collected Works, Volume 5*. New York: International Publishers.

May, T. (ed.). (2002). *Qualitative Research in Action*. London: SAGE Publications.

McIntosh, P. (2008). White privilege and male privilege. In Bailey, A. & Cuomo, C. (eds), *The Feminist Philosophy Reader*. New York: McGraw Hill.

Mead, G. H. (1934). *Mind, Self and Society*. Chicago: University of Chicago Press.

Menon, N. (2001). Embodying the self: Feminism, sexual violence and the law. *Subaltern Studies*, 11, 66–105.

Merleau-Ponty, M. (1962). *Phenomenology of Perception*. Routledge.

Mernissi, F. (1991). *Women and Islam: An Historical and Theological Inquiry*. Oxford: Blackwell.

Merrifield, A. (2002). *Metromarxism: A Marxist Tale of the City*. London and New York: Routledge.

Metcalf, B. D. (1995). Presidential address: Too little and too much: Reflections on Muslims in the history of India. *The Journal of Asian Studies*, 54(4).

Mistry, M. B. (2005). Muslims in India: A demographic and socio-economic profile. *Journal of Muslim Minority Affairs*, 25(3), 399–422.

Moghadam, V. (2002). Islamic feminism and its discontents: Toward a resolution of the debate. *Signs: Journal of Women in Culture and Society*, 27(4), 1135–1171.

Moghadam, V. (2005). *Globalizing Women: Transnational Feminist Networks*. Baltimore and New York: The Johns Hopkins University Press.

Moghadam, V. (ed.). (1994a). *Gender and National Identity: Women and Politics in Muslim Societies*. London: Zed Books.

Moghadam, V. (ed.). (1994b). *Identity Politics and Women: Cultural Reassertions and Feminisms in International Perspective*. Boulder, CO: Westview Press.

Mondal, S. R. (1992). Muslims in India: An enquiry into their minority status, backwardness, special rights and development problems. *Journal of the Indian Anthropological Society*, 7(2), 149–160.

Mondal, S. R. (1997). *Educational Status of Muslims: Problems, Prospects and Priorities*. Inter-India Publications.
Mondal, S. R. (2003). Social structure, OBCs and Muslims. *Economic and Political Weekly*, 38(46), 4892–4897.
Nainar, V. (2000). *Muslim Women's Views on Personal Laws: The Influence of Socio-economic Factors*. Bombay: WRAG.
Nora, P. (1996). General introduction: Between memory and history. *Realms of Memory: Rethinking the French Past*, 1, 1–20.
Nurmi, J. E., Salmela-Aro, K. & Koivisto, P. (2002). Goal importance and related achievement beliefs and emotions during the transition from vocational school to work: Antecedents and consequences. *Journal of Vocational Behavior*, 60(2), 241–261.
Nussbaum, M. C. (2001). *Women and Human Development: The Capabilities Approach* (Vol. 3). Cambridge: Cambridge University Press.
Nussbaum, M. C. (2007). *The Clash Within: Democracy, Religious Violence, and India's Future*. Cambridge: Belknap Press.
Offenhauer, P. (2005). *Women in Islamic Societies: A Selected Review of Social Scientific Literature*. Federal Research Division, Library of Congress, Washington D.C.
Olesen, V. (2003). Feminisms and models of qualitative research. In Denzin and Lincoln (eds), *The Landscape of Qualitative Research*. London: SAGE Publications.
O'Reilly, A. (ed.). (2004). *From Motherhood to Mothering: The Legacy of Adrienne Rich's of Woman Born*. Chicago: SUNY Press.
Pandey, G. (1990). *The Colonial Construction of Communalism in North India*. Delhi: Oxford University Press.
Pandey, G. (1992). In defense of the fragment: Writing about Hindu-Muslim riots in India today. In *Representations 37, Special Issue: Imperial Fantasies and Postcolonial Histories*, Winter, 27–55. University of California Press.
Pandey, G. (2001). *Remembering Partition: Violence, Nationalism, and History in India*. Cambridge: Cambridge University Press.
Pandey, G. (2006). *The Construction of Communalism in Colonial North India*. New Delhi: Oxford University Press. (original work published 1991).
Panikkar, K. N. (ed.). (1999). *The Concerned Indian's Guide to Communalism*. New Delhi: Viking Penguin India.
Pargeter, A. (2006). North African immigrants in Europe and political violence. *Studies in Conflict & Terrorism*, 29(8), 731–747.
Patel, S. & Deb, K. (2009). *Urban Studies Reader*. New Delhi: Oxford University Press.
Polkinghorne, D. (1983). *Methodology for the Human Science*. Albany: SUNY Press.
Ralph, D. (1988). Researching from the Bottom: Lesson of participatory research for feminists. In Dawn Currie (ed.), *From the Margins to the Centre: Selected Essays in Women's Studies Research* (pp. 134–141). Saskatchewan: The Women's Studies Research Unit, University of Saskatchewan.
Rangnath Mishra Commission. (2007). Report of the National Commission for Religious and Linguistic Minorities, Ministry of Minority Affairs. Retrieved from http://www.minorityaffairs.gov.in/reports/national-commission-religious-and-linguistic-minoritie
Rege, S. (1998). Dalit women talk differently: A critique of 'difference' and towards a Dalit feminist standpoint position. *Economic and Political Weekly*, 33(44), WS39–WS46.
Resch, R. P. (1992). *Althusser and the Renewal of Marxist Social Theory*. Berkeley: University of California Press.

Rich, A. (1977). *Of Woman Born: Motherhood as Experience and Institution.* London: Virago.
Ritchie, C., Buchanan, A. & Flouri, E. (2005). *Aspirations and Expectations.* Briefing paper for National Family & Parenting Institute. Retrieved from http://www.nfpi.org/data/research/docs/aspirations.pdf
Roberts, D. (2006). *The Totalitarian Experiment in Twentieth Century Europe: Understanding the Poverty of Great Politics.* London and New York: Routledge.
Rose, G. (1997). Situating knowledges: positionality, reflexivities and other tactics. *Progress in Human Geography,* 21, 305–320.
Rose, G. (2001). *Visual Methodologies: An Introduction to the Interpretation of Visual Materials.* London: SAGE Publications.
Runnymede Trust. (1997). *Islamophobia: A Challenge for Us All.* London: Runnymede Trust.
Sachar Committee Report (Prime Minister's High Level Committee). (2006). *Social, economic and educational status of the Muslim community of India: A report.* Cabinet Secretariat: Government of India. Retrieved from http://www.minorityaffairs.gov.in
Saggar, S. (2009). *Pariah Politics: Understanding Western Radical Islamism and What Should Be Done.* Delhi: Oxford University Press.
Said, E. W. (2001). The clash of ignorance. *The Nation,* 22 October. Retrieved from https://www.thenation.com/article/clash-ignorance/
Said, E. W. (1997). *Covering Islam: How the Media and the Experts Determine How We See the Rest of the World.* New York: Random House.
Said, E. W. (1978). *Orientalism: Western Conceptions of the Orient.* Abingdon-on-Thames: Routledge & Kegan Paul Limited.
Said, E. W. (2001). The Clash of Ignorance. *The Nation.* Retrieved from http://www.thenation.com
Said, E. W. (2004). *From Oslo to Iraq and the Road Map.* New York: Pantheon.
Saliba, T., Allen, C. & Howard, J. A. (eds). (2002). *Gender, Politics and Islam.* New Delhi: Orient Longman.
Sarkar, M. (2008). *Visible Histories, Disappearing Women: Producing Muslim Womanhood in Late Colonial Bengal.* New Delhi: Zubaan Books.
Sarkar, T. & Butalia, U. (eds). (1995). *Women and the Hindu Right: A Collection of Essays.* New Delhi: Kali for Women.
Sarkar, T. (2002). Semiotics of terror: Muslim children and women in Hindu Rashtra. *Economic and Political Weekly,* 37(28).
Schbley, A. & McCauley, C. (2005). Political, religious, and psychological characteristics of Muslim protest marchers in eight European cities: Jerusalem Day 2002. *Terrorism and Political Violence,* 17(4), 551–572.
Schneider, B. & Stevenson, D. (1999). The ambitious generation. *Educational Leadership,* 57(4), 22–25.
Schneider, N. C. (2009). Islamic feminism and Muslim women's rights activism in India: From transnational discourse to local movement—or vice versa? *Journal of International Women's Studies,* 11(1), 56–71.
Scott, J. C. (1998). *Seeing Like a State: How Certain Schemes to Improve the Human Condition Have Failed.* Yale University Press.
Scott, J. C. (2008). *Weapons of the Weak: Everyday Forms of Peasant Resistance.* New Haven: Yale University Press.
Sen, A. (2007). *Identity and Violence: The Illusion of Destiny.* London: Penguin Books.

Shahabuddin, S. (2002). Comments on Yoginder Sikand's article on Dalit Muslims. *Journal of Muslim Minority Affairs*, 22(2), 479–481.
Sharoni, S. (1995). *Gender and the Israeli-Palestinian Conflict: The Politics of Women's Resistance*. New York: Syracuse University Press.
Shehabuddin, E. (2011). Gender and the figure of the 'Moderate Muslim': Feminism in the twenty-first century. In Judith Butler and Elizabeth Weed (eds), *The Question of Gender: Joan W. Scott's Critical Feminism*. Indiana University Press.
Sikand, Y. (2001). A new Indian Muslim agenda: The Dalit Muslims and the All-India Backward Muslim Morcha. *Journal of Muslim Minority Affairs*, 21(2), 287–296.
Sikand, Y. (2005). *Bastions of the Believers: Madrasas and Islamic Education in India*. New Delhi: Penguin.
Sikand, Y. (2008). *Issues in Madrasa Education in India*. Hope India Publications.
Snow, D. A. & Anderson, L. (1987). Identity work among the homeless: The verbal construction and avowal of personal identities. *American Journal of Sociology*, 1336–1371.
Spivak, G. (1993). *Outside in the Teaching Machine*. London: Routledge.
Spivak, G. C. (1988). Can the Subaltern Speak? In C. Nelson & L. Grossberg (eds), *Marxism and the Interpretation of Culture* (pp. 271–313). Urbana: University of Illinois Press.
Stanley, L. & Wise, S. (1983). *Breaking Out: Feminist Consciousness and Feminist Research*. London: Routledge & Kegan Paul Books.
Talbot, C. (1995). Inscribing the other, inscribing the self: Hindu-Muslim identities in precolonial India. *Comparative Studies in Society and History*, 37(4), 692–722.
Tilley, C. (1991). *Material Culture and Text: The Art of Ambiguity*. London: Routledge.
Tilley, C. (1994). *A Phenomenology of Landscape*. London: Berg.
Valentine, G. (2002). People like us: Negotiating sameness and difference in the research process. In P. Moss (ed.), *Feminist Geography in Practice: Research and Methods* (pp. 116–126). New Jersey: Wiley-Blackwell.
Van der Veer, P. (1994). *Religious Nationalism: Hindus and Muslims in India*. Berkeley, CA: University of California Press.
Varshney, A. (2002). *Ethnic Conflict and Civic Life: Hindus and Muslims in India*. New Haven: Yale University Press.
Varshney, A. (2003). *Ethnic Conflict and Civic Life: Hindus and Muslims in India*. Yale University Press.
Vasudevan, R. S. (1995). Film studies, new cultural history and experience of modernity. *Economic and Political Weekly*, 30(44), 2809–2814.
Vatuk, S. (2008). Islamic feminism in India: Indian Muslim women activists and the reform of Muslim personal law. *Modern Asian Studies*, 42(2/3).
Wadud, A. (1999). *Qur'an and Women: Rereading the Sacred Text from a Woman's Perspective*. Oxford: New York.
Wadud, A. (2006). *Inside the Gender Jihad: Women's Reform in Islam*. National Book Network.
Watson-Franke, M. B. (2004). We have mama but no papa. In A. O'Reilley (ed.), *From Motherhood to Mothering: The Legacy of Adrienne Rich's of Woman Born* (pp. 75–87). New York: SUNY Press.
Wearing, B. (1998). *Leisure and Feminist Theory*. London: SAGE Publications.
Weber, M. (1993). *Basic Concepts in Sociology*. Citadel Press.
Winkelmann, M. J. (2007). *Reaching the Minds of Young Muslim Women: Girls' Madrasas in India*. Gurgaon: Hope India Publication.

Wright, T. P. (1997). A new demand for Muslim reservations in India. *Asian Survey*, 37(9), 852–858.
Zainuddin, S. (2003). Islam, social stratification and empowerment of Muslim OBCs. *Economic and Political Weekly*, 4898–4901.
Zakaria, R. (2013). *Malala, the Muslim Feminist*. Retrieved from http://america.aljazeera.com/articles/2013/10/14/malala-yousafzaiislamfeminism.html

Index

alienation, 52
aspirations and dreams
   adjustment against, 76–77
   definition, 70–71
   fashion, young Muslim women in India, 71–75
   labour, 69
   researching, 71

discursive colonisation
   communal violence, 3–4
   creation of Pakistan, 2–3
   distribution of geopolitical awareness, 12
   equality between genders, 14
   Fukuyama, phobic positioning of Islam, 18
   lack of theorisation, 4
   mainstream cinema, role of, 3
   Margot Badran, views of, 17
   Moghadam, views of, 17
   Muslim women, 1, 6–7
   Muslim women's organisations in India, 15
   Muslims in India, 1–2
   Nilufer Gole, report, 16
   Orientalism, 12
   researches and Muslims, 5–6
   Shahbano case, 8–9
   sociological studies on Indian Muslims, 7–8
   Understanding the Muslim Mind, 10
   vote bank, Muslims, 11

emancipation, 116

feminism, 110

labour
   aspirations and dreams, 69
   capacity to aspire, 79
   mother as aspiration, 80–87
   Muslim women, 77–79
   social position, 69–70

Madrasas, 10
marginalisation
   everyday of inhabiting, 52–58
   Lefebvre's views, 52
Muslim vote bank, 11
Muslim women
   agency, 58–62
   Ahmedabad workshop, 113–115
   behavioral and dress codes, 111–112
   civil society contribution, 170–172
   counterpublic spheres, participation of, 118–119
   government's support, 168–170
   Jaipur workshop, 112
   Lucknow workshop, 115–116
   parents and families, change in, 173–174
   portrait of researcher, 41–51
   representation and listening, 22–25
   women role in improvement, 174–175

narratives from states
   Bangalore, Karnataka, 149–151
   Calicut, Kerala, 151–152
   Chanderi and Bhopal, Madhya Pradesh, 152–156
   Cuttack, Odisha, 159–161
   Delhi, 143–146
   Dindigul and Sivagangai, Tamil Nadu, 163–165
   Jaipur, Rajasthan, 161–163
   Lucknow, Uttar Pradesh, 165–166

Patna, Bihar, 137–140
Raipur, Chhattisgarh, 140–143
Sabarkantha and Ahmedabad, Gujarat, 146–149
Usmanabad, Thane and Mumbai, Maharashtra, 156–159
Noorjahan, 22

oppressed communities
   representation, 26
Orientalism, 12

photo-elicitation
   athlete, 133
   bride, 127
   doll, 125–126
   doors, open and closed, 134
   girl friends, 129–130
   hennaed hands, 132
   lone bird flying, 126–127
   mosque, 135
   mother with her child, 128
   nature, 132–133
   single women, 130–132
   soldiers, 134–135

representation and listening
   Ahmedabad workshop, 31
   Friere's views, 30
   Jaipur, Rajasthan, workshop in, 29
   Mumbai's Mumbra, workshop in, 28–29

Muslim women, 22–25
narrative methods, 27
Noorjahan, 22
oppressed communities, 26
personal narratives, 26–27
speaking as, 33–40

self, 105
   explicit expression of, 109–110
   Muslim women in Kerala, 107–108
   philosophical literature, defined as, 106
   plurality as, 106–107
   self-consciousness, 108–109
structural violence
   Muslim populations, 62–68
subjectivities, 122
   photographs, supportive use of, 123

Understanding the Muslim Mind, 10

violence
   after-effects of, 105
   cultural, 89
   Cuttack city workshop, 91–94
   direct collective, 95–99
   memory, 99–104
   memory and experience of, 88
   needs and negation, 89–90
   sisters of Ishrat Jahan, 94
   young women and, 90–91

About the Author

Ghazala Jamil is Assistant Professor at the Centre for the Study of Law and Governance, Jawaharlal Nehru University. She has earlier taught at Department of Social Work, University of Delhi; and Departments of Regional Planning and Urban Planning at the School of Planning and Architecture (SPA), New Delhi. She has also worked full-time and as consultant with various development organisations in the past.